FRANCESCO'S
KITCHEN

FRANCESCO'S KITCHEN

AN INTIMATE GUIDE TO THE AUTHENTIC FLAVOURS OF VENICE

FRANCESCO DA MOSTO

PHOTOGRAPHY BY PIA TRYDE

EBURY
PRESS

1 3 5 7 9 10 8 6 4 2

Published in 2007 by Ebury Press, an imprint of Ebury Publishing
Ebury Publishing is a division of the Random House Group

Text © Francesco da Mosto 2007

Photography © Pia Tryde 2007,
except photography on pages 18, 96, 108, 149, 167, 169, 181, 253, 254, 288 (right), 301, 312 © Francesco da Mosto 2007

Francesco da Mosto has asserted his right under the Copyright, Designs and Patents Act 1988 to be identified as the author of this work

The Random House Group Limited Reg. No. 954009
Addresses for companies within the Random House Group can be found at **www.randomhouse.co.uk**
A CIP catalogue record for this book is available from the British Library

The Random House Group makes every effort to ensure that the papers used in our books are made from trees that have been legally
sourced from well-managed and credibly certified forests. Our paper procurement policy can be found on **www.randomhouse.co.uk**

Editor: Deborah Savage · Translator: Jeremy Scott · Design: Strathmore Publishing Services, London EC1
Map: Rodney Paull · Marbled paper designs courtesy of Legatoria Polliero Venezia

Printed and bound by
Butler & Tanner, Frome, England

ISBN: 9780091922283

To buy books by your favourite authors and register for offers
visit **www.rbooks.co.uk**

Contents

a mio padre

Introduction

A source of wonderful aromas and colours, the kitchen at home was where I, as a boy with a healthy appetite, first became intrigued by Venetian cuisine, the many secrets and the long traditions behind it. I cannot call myself a cook, let alone a professional expert but, eating two or three times a day, one notices how small changes in ingredients and combinations can make a perhaps insipid or dull dish become a real delicacy.

This book is partly an exploration of an often unnoticed result of the mercantile spirit that used to be such a feature of Venice, looking at how the city's openness to outside influences meant that its cuisine absorbed ingredients and flavours from the *terra firma* (mainland Italy) and further afield. It discusses not only how, why and whence certain produce arrived in Venice, but also the very individual way in which, historically, Venetian cuisine developed upon these raw materials. Obviously, personal taste comes into play, too, as it has throughout history: Casanova, Goethe, Byron and all the doges had their particular favourites. The playwright Goldoni, for example, was particularly fond of *sarde in saòr* (fried sardines in a sweet and sour mix): he gives us a version of the recipe, almost identical to the version we make today, in one of the many plays in which he so vividly depicts eighteenth-century life, *Le donne de casa soà* (*Ladies and their homes*).

Essentials of Venetian cuisine

My father was always game for trying out new recipes, lovingly creating new combinations of ingredients and flavours. I, of course, was always willing to test the results. This is how he introduced a collection of recipes exploring traditional Venetian cuisine; it demonstrates his inimitable style:

> The tastes and flavours of Venetian cooking originated long ago, on the islands of the lagoon. As time went on, ingredients and flavours from the mainland would be added, with experience of the food of the East also playing its part in stimulating the culinary imagination. However, the basic characteristics were still true to the flavour of the fish, game and garden vegetables that had been at the origin of Venetian cuisine. The ancient recipe for *broeto* (fish soup) bears witness to this continuing sense of tradition, as do the various soups made with molluscs, the different recipes for baked, grilled and fried fish, and the local delicacies of *umido di seppie* (squid in its

ink) and wonderful *sardine in saòr*. Nor should one forget local cooks' skill in exploiting the full taste of beef, game and liver, with finely judged combinations of ingredients that, in some cases, achieve results worthy of the best international cuisine.

Focus on flavour

The Venetian diet is made up of a few fundamental ingredients: polenta, rice, beans, garden vegetables, fish, especially sardines and stockfish, and parsley. 'Crops up everywhere, like parsley', is an Italian expression that seems custom-made for the extensive use of the herb in Venetian cooking. These foundations, combined with intelligent, meticulous and careful methods, have given rise to a whole range of dishes and flavours that bring out the true flavours of the produce used. For example, fish should taste of fish and not be doused in lemon juice (when the fish is fresh, this addition radically changes its flavour).

Just a few simple condiments distract us from the original taste of the ingredients. Oil and butter are used to sauté the finely chopped onion that forms the basis for these condiments, and sauces. A common addition to this base is cured pork fat, *pancetta* (a type of bacon). Garlic is generally used as a whole clove for flavouring the frying oils and removed when it has turned golden brown; it is also occasionally finely chopped – for example, when cooking molluscs or making fish soups – and might even be left whole throughout cooking (when roasting meats). Lard is almost never used these days, except in a few special cases such as frying *fritelle* or some other traditional desserts.

The foods that are now the main staples of Venetian cuisine were actually imports to the region. Maize, for example, arrived here in the sixteenth century and had to be imposed upon diffident farmers by the Venetian state; in Lombardy, too, there was reluctance to grow the crop until people were driven by desperation by famine resulting from the plague of 1630. Beans, of course, came from the Americas around the same time as maize, and rice came to Venice thanks to trade links with the Arab world; specially laid rice fields in the Verona area were created in the first half of the sixteenth century.

A brief geography of the Veneto

The Veneto is a place of water, of lagoons, lakes, rivers and canals. Bound on one side by the Adriatic and crossed by the mighty Po river, the region extends right up to the feet of the soaring red rocks of the Dolomites. The landscape combines mountains, foothills, plateaus and coastline, so a journey of a couple of hours can bring you from the salty air of the sea to the bare peaks

of the mountains. This is a place of small cities and towns, where families still gather around hearths to eat soups, where food is still served with authentic simplicity.

The warm sparkling light on the waters of the Venice lagoon greets not only the planes coming in to land at Venice airport, but also the flocks of migratory birds that pass through here on their journey north. This vast expanse of water is also a perfect resting place when, at the next change of season, they take to the wing once more to search out the sun, heading south. Landing here is like sliding to a halt at a ready-laid table, richly provided with fish, salt, plants and the essence of life itself that is so carefully nourished by the tides that silently breathe between the lagoon and the Adriatic every six hours or so.

For the people of the lagoon, too, fish represents living wealth and is a keystone of Venetian food. The abundance of stocks and the ease with which fish could be – and still is – caught played a part in the fleeing Veneti's decision to settle here around the fourth century, following their escape from the advancing hordes of invading barbarians. Attila the Hun himself passed this way in AD 451. The enigmatic waters of the lagoon provided an impassable barrier as the Huns' horses shied away from the apparently treacherous mud around its banks. The oscillating tides and obscure shallows and channels also made it nearly impossible for subsequent enemies to navigate their way into Venice by ship. Meanwhile, the marshy refuge of the lagoon provided a wealth of food: delicious vegetables flourished on the islands and fish and other marine delicacies could be caught with ease. On the first settlements in the Rialto area, cooking must have started with freshly caught fish being grilled over an open fire. Later, of course, refinements arrived from the East. Through-out its existence, the Venetian Republic exercised severe control over food markets to make sure that all the city's inhabitants – even the poorest – could eat.

Among the Veneti who came from the mainland, were some goatherds who brought their flocks with them; the coastal city of Caorle actually takes its name from the word for goat ('*capra*'). Having found refuge and food on the islands of the lagoon, the settlers gradually learned to look to the sea as their main (almost exclusive) source of food. An echo of these early times still survives on the island of Burano, where a traditional Christmas Eve dish of rice and beans is made using the fat from large grey mullet. The diet of the early settlers would later extend to include the feathered or four-legged game caught in the hinterland and the islands of the estuary supplied plentiful vegetables. Salt was produced in the lagoon and trade links introduced numerous spices. The result, here as elsewhere in Europe, was the development of a diet and way of life that made it possible to move beyond the grimness of the early Middle Ages.

Towards a new gastronomic style

Natural simplicity, innate mildness and serenity and the appreciation of freedom offered by their position modelled the character of the Venetians. And as their force of character won out against adversity, they began to develop a gastronomic style that befitted the spontaneity of the way they lived – so closely and harmoniously interconnected with vital resources at the boundary between air, land and water, between the sea and the continent, between Venice and the growing world beyond. Food was prepared simply but with flair, exalting the flavour of the ingredients, liberally incorporating innovations gleaned via exploration, and also avoiding any complicated combinations of sauces, spices and herbs.

In this way, Venetian cuisine has always been 'modern', its naturalness based on a serious view of life whereby you have to make sacrifices in order to obtain anything, have to earn before you can spend. True, there were moments when Venetian food fell short of this simplicity. Through its links to the East, and the Byzantine Empire especially, the city was introduced to a vast range of spices, acquired from people whose expression of *joie de vivre* was somewhat more tumultuous. Having established itself since ancient times in the production of and trade in salt, Venice sought a monopoly position over the European trade in spices, which were used to preserve food and to cover the flavours of ingredients that were not at their best. As a result, eastern customs found their way into both Venetian and Italian cuisine.

Ginger, cinnamon, nutmeg, turmeric, cloves, saffron, galingale, varieties of cane sugar, cassia, camphor and, of course, pepper, were all mainstays of Venetian trade. Today, little of this kaleidoscope of spices remains in the cuisine of Venice and the Veneto; even pepper is now used conservatively, though once – because it was relatively expensive – it was a status symbol, a prized ingredient for soups, pasta recipes, fish and meat dishes, sauces and stuffings. It was even put in wine, added to desserts and used in cheese. Apothecaries, too, used to prescribe pepper: as a cure for stomach ache, toothache, insect bites or to improve sexual potency.

At the table, the people of the Veneto have always preferred to be able to see what they are eating. Boiled meats, for example, may have been served with sauces – perhaps just oil, garlic, parsley and a pinch of pepper or the more elaborate *salsa pevarada, salsa verde*, horseradish sauce or even a mix of crusted bread, herbs, hard-boiled eggs and anchovies – but in each and every case, these were and are still served separately, never covering the meat.

As for popular cuisine in Venice, this was largely to be found in the streets where hawkers and stall holders offered soups, rice dishes, polenta with butter or cheese, desserts prepared using beef blood, cheap fried fish, *fritelle* (sweet dumplings), *bovoleti* (snails),

female cuttlefish with eggs (known as '*da riso*' because they were used in risotto) or male cuttlefish ('*da cocia*', referring to the fact they were caught in nets). And like hawkers and street traders everywhere, each had their own cry: '*Co tenari! Folpi da riso! Tenari da cocia*' ('Tender risotto cuttlefish! Tender netted cuttlefish'); '*Che tondi e grossi! I go caldi!*' ('Plump and tender! Warm goby fish!').

It might seem strange, but pizza, a dish that is considered typically Neapolitan, also features in the history of Venetian cuisine, even if it was prepared in a different way here. One could say that the history of pizza goes back to the very earliest days of human civilization, when men first mixed water with crushed millet or wheat to make a dough to be cooked between stones and glowing embers. And whilst there is no denying that it was the Neapolitans who popularized pizza all over the world, Venice too had its version: sixteenth century records refer to *picca*, introduced at the time of the Roman conquests. The arrival of maize changed things, following the development of polenta as a carbohydrate staple. Recently, pizza has once more become popular here, following an inexorable global trend.

Fish and seasonality

Venetian cuisine really comes into its own with grilled and fried fish, and its very special fish soup. However, the range of flavours runs through a wide variety of antipasti (shrimps, mussels, clams, mantis prawns, cuttlefish, etc.) to grilled scampi, turbot, monkfish, sole or mullet, and fried calamari, eel, scampi, shrimp, soft-shelled crabs, sardines, sliced cuttlefish and pectin clams. Other contributions to this symphony of fish include scallops, baked in the oven with butter and parsley; razor-shell clams, pan-tossed with garlic; coral-coloured spider crabs, boiled and dressed with a little oil, lemon and parsley; *sarde in saòr*, fried sardines marinated with pine nuts and raisins; cuttlefish in their ink; and an endless variety of seafood risottos. Recipes also took advantage of the availability of fresh vegetables – which figured in a number of risottos and in that rural classic *pasta e fagioli* (pasta and beans) – as well as many different salad greens and chicory varieties grown in the estuary areas.

Salumieri were important food stores in old Venice. The word '*salumen*' comes from the medieval Latin term that refers to salted or dried foods so, along with the ham, bacon and salami you find in modern-day *salumieri*, there was smoked and dried herring, smoked or barrel-preserved salmon, stockfish, and dried mullet or mackerel. By the beginning of the sixteenth century other varieties of meat were being eaten in substantial quantities by the patrician classes in Venice and the other cities of the mainland; great favourites were game birds such as pheasants and even splendidly plumed peacocks.

Venice is not the only part of the Veneto where fish plays a predominant role in local cuisine. Vicenza, for example, is famous for its *baccalà* (stockfish or dried codfish), which is soaked and then cooked in the oven with oil, butter and milk, together with anchovies, white flour, salt, pepper and parsley. The end result is a gastronomic masterpiece. Vicenza is also remembered for the graceful architectural masterpieces created by Andrea Palladio. Also in the area, towards the foothills, where you find places like the small town of Marostica (where human chess games date back to the middle of the fifteenth century, when 'living' chess was chosen as an alternative to a bloody duel) which have produced recipes such as *paeta con la melagrana* (turkey with pomegranate sauce), the famed *torresani* (pigeons) of Breganze and *bigoli con l'anara* (fat spaghetti with duck). Also reflecting the interconnectedness of man and nature is the fact that many dishes are associated with a particular period of the year, measured out with the seasonal accompaniment of local vegetables (asparagus, sweet garden peas, artichokes, mushroom varieties and rich-smelling truffles). Cheeses, too, have their seasons, as do the various local wines: Gambellara, Montebello, Breganze, Montegalda and Barbarano. There is an almost religious reverence for wines in this area, and for the several varieties of Bassano grappa, a distilled spirit still associated with the memory of the alpine troops who, during the First World War, defended these peaks with great courage, fortitude and self-sacrifice, reinforced by swigs of grappa.

Natural works of art

Farther west stands Verona, at a great crossroads between the rocky heights of the mountains, the expanse of Lake Garda and the plains that stretch towards Mantua in one direction and Brescia in the other. Its location has naturally meant that this area was exposed to all the cultural influences at work in the history of the western Veneto. No Carnival here is complete without the colourful parades from the district of San Zeno to the magnificent Piazza dei Signori – or without the traditional gnocchi that are served on these occasions. Another princely culinary tradition is the famous *pastizzada de caval* (horse stew), probably inherited from the Goth or Lombard invaders who passed this way so many centuries ago. Verona is also home to a number of fine risottos, which tend to be more liquid than elsewhere, and *paparele*. Lake Garda provides large and tasty fish, one of the boasts of local cuisine: carp, trout, tench and perch. These are accompanied by famous wines such as Bardolino, Valpolicella, Soave and Recioto, whose bouquet evokes images of the warm sun beating down on the sloping hills that run either side of the river valleys. No mention of food

in Verona can omit reference to the city's famous desserts and cakes, especially *pandoro*, as light and golden as one imagines the tresses of the local romantic heroine, Juliet, immortalized by Shakespeare.

The Eugeanean Hills form a sort of balcony from which to view the mountains one side and the sea to the other. This is the type of infinite landscape seen in paintings by Leonardo da Vinci, suggesting to the imagination that which the eye cannot perceive, in the peace of vegetable plots, gardens and the sound of timid, distant church bells. Set amid this idyll (now hard to appreciate among the factories and congested highways of the prosperous north-east Italy), Padua, too, has a worthy cuisine crowned by the resources offered by its hills: tender grilled capons; golden egg pasta lasagne, fat roasted guinea-fowl and highly prized toresani (a type of pigeon). The farms of this area are animated by strutting chickens and waddling geese – which make a magnificent meal, perhaps followed by desserts made with polenta such as *pinza* and *zaleti*.

Moving east

Travelling towards Treviso, one comes to another convergence, between the Alps and the Adriatic. Known to Venetians as the '*Marca Gioiosa*', the view is towards the sea in one direction and the ring of the Asolo Hills in the other. These were the inspiration for the fifteenth-century painter Giorgione, who transformed them into muted landscapes where trees, rocks and houses are illuminated with dazzling touches of light. The countryside here still evokes thoughts of the past, of such events as the great thirteenth-century feast held at Treviso. For the occasion, a 'Castle of Love' was erected and draped with rich fabrics. The defenders of this fort were women and girls, whilst those besieging it were divided into three teams made up of men from Treviso, Padua and Venice. The first team tried to get the ladies to surrender by beseeching their prayers: 'Madame Beatrice, Madame Fiordilice, *ora pro nobis*.' The youths of Padua tried to take the citadel by pelting it with food: capons, ravioli, tarts, pies and chickens. The Venetians opted for more refined missiles: walnuts, ginger, cinnamon, other spices and coins and ducats. Such gentility was appreciated by the ladies and the castle was surrendered to the Venetians, who then raised the Standard of St Mark above its walls. The indignant Paduans felt insulted and broke the pole bearing the banner. This not only put an end to the party, but also led to such bitter discord between Venice on the one side and Padua and Treviso on the other, that an actual war broke out the following year and was only resolved by the direct intervention of the Pope and the patriarch of Aquileia, a powerful ecclesiastical dignitary.

Still, the Treviso marches are a calm and tranquil place, and the local gastronomic delights are clear evidence of the pleasure that the people here take in preparing varied and unusual dishes. The risottos are made with *luganega* (sausages), with the *chiodini* or *porcini* mushrooms from Montello, plump quails and estuary eel caught in the river Sile. Beans, too, are widely used, with a range of recipes, including a pasta and bean dish (with non-egg pasta) and a very tasty bean and tripe soup. And, of course, one should not ignore the local *baccalà* (stockfish or salted codfish), which is similar to the Vicenza version. Other local dishes that are worth trying include *zuppa coada*, with pigeons, tripe and chicken, and the renowned purple *radicchio* of Treviso and Castelfranco, which adds a brilliant note of colour to any meal. One almost gets the feeling of flavours that bring together the warmth of the local sun with traditions that the Longobards of Friuli brought with them from the Baltic, along with their Nordic sagas.

Wild food

The source of the river Piave is near Belluno. As it trickles over rock after rock, it swells until it becomes home to sea trout and small *marsoni* – fried and served with polenta – are a staple dish of the towns and villages along its banks. Here, in the deep valleys that nestle within the peaks of the Dolomites, food must be robust and substantial for local people to withstand the intense cold in winter and the spring and autumn rains. Hence, such specialities as risottos and pasta dishes made with the famed red beans of Lamon, barley soup and the rich creamy milk produced by the cows that graze on the mountain pastures.

This cooking has developed around large, open kitchen fires where demijohns of full-bodied red wine are warmed, on grates stirred by mighty fire irons, while gleaming copper pots bubble with the daily supply of polenta and roasts turn on a spit. All this against a background of the characteristic long silences of mountain folk, staring in anticipation at smoking irons on which food is being prepared and feeling the warmth of the fire melt the pungent cold in their bones. This is reassuring, unadulterated family food. Here, hunting is inevitably a significant source of ingredients such as pheasant, venison, roe deer, wood grouse, hare and black partridge – all of which can be served in stews, in *salmì* or *alla cacciatora*. Then there are spit-roasted goat and chops and ribs roasted on an open fire of aromatic wood. Simple and healthy milk, butter and ricotta are also essential to alpine cooking, with meals ending in rich desserts such as walnut tarts and *consegi* (biscuits for dunking in sweet wine). All to be followed, inevitably, by a selection of grappas – made with myriad infusions like plums or juniper berries – as well as other

distilled spirits made from camomile, passion-flower or bitter gentian. Kept in flasks on the kitchen wall, these turn shivers of cold into shivers of pleasure.

As the large Adige and Po rivers reach out towards the Adriatic, they form a wide delta whose fingers are lined with dense banks of canes and reeds. These are the fish-farm areas, known locally as '*valli da pesca*', which are also great hunting territory. In this area of wild, untamed nature, the gourmet is well served – especially in winter, when hunters pick off mallards and other wild ducks from inside their hides; the male duck can weigh up to 6 kg (13 lb) and has a 'harem' of up to eight females, each producing as many as 16 ducklings. Birdlife is rich among the waterways and marshes of the Veneto, where crustaceans, molluscs, fish, insects and aquatic plants are in rich supply. One variety of duck found here is the *anatra muta* – the so-called 'mute duck' and subscriber to the saying 'silence is golden', which too many humans ignore. Originally from South America, these ducks are found skewered above open fires in hunting lodges and *trattorie* dotted along the waterways, canals and avenues of the Veneto. Cooking in this part of the Veneto skilfully exploits the various flavours of tender young eels, small dark-fleshed guinea-fowl, and – the absolute monarch of these waters – sea bass. The Po is also home to the sharp-nosed sturgeon, which patient anglers can hook in early spring, when the intrepid fish tries to swim back upstream against the current.

Venetian food and religion

For the people of the Veneto, gathering at the table is not just about eating; it is an opportunity to talk and exchange views on life. Like a religious ceremony, a meal brings people together in celebration of brotherhood and affection; it is an expression of an ability to endure through time – and of a willingness to help others to do so. From the earliest days of its history, the Republic of St Mark rendered homage to religious authorities. Venice, in fact, considered itself heir to the Roman Empire, continuing a tradition established by the Edict of Thessalonica of AD 380, in which the Emperor Theodosius proclaimed Christianity the State religion. However, respect for Rome did not mean total submission; the Venetian Republic retained the right to choose candidates for the major ecclesiastical offices within its territory. Much to the chagrin of the Pope, the Church could decide the appointment of almost none of the patriarchs (cardinals) and bishops in Venetian dioceses; the Republic supplied Rome with about three names, from which the appointee had to be chosen.

It was for this reason, therefore, that the Republic attached so much importance to the honour that the doge paid religious authority when he made official visits to churches and convents. Generally, these famous *andate* were in thanksgiving for victory against the enemies of the state or for relief from natural calamities and plagues. One such visit took place before the year 1000 and was in thanksgiving for the defeat of the Naretan pirates who had raided Venetian territory and carried off women and jewels. Setting off in hot pursuit, the Venetians managed to recover the ladies and the gold and thenceforward 2 February – the religious feast of the Purification of the Virgin Mary – became known as '*la Festa delle Marie*'. On this occasion, marriages were blessed and the doge made his *andata* to the church of San Pietro in Castello, built at the far end of the city in the Castello district, formerly known as Olivolo. There are various theories for that name: the island is shaped like an olive or that olive trees grew here.

Another famous celebration occurred on the feast day of Venice's patron saint, St Mark the Evangelist (25 April). The doge invited all the major government officials to a banquet where it was traditional to serve *risi e bisi*, a sort of pea risotto in which the quantity of peas outweighed that of rice. Given that the uncertainties of the weather might mean that ripe garden peas were not yet available locally, these were sometimes ordered from the sunnier side of the peninsula, Liguria – not pods but entire plants, which were kept watered throughout the journey so that the doge and his guests could enjoy the full flavour of freshly picked peas.

Food and taxation were also linked during the times of the *Serenissima*. Inhabitants of Poveglia, formerly one of the most prosperous centres in the lagoon whose fortune has suffered many alterations (including use as a hospital department and the totally abandoned state it is in today), were required to pay the doge an annual tribute of fish and fruit. The 'gifts' were presented in a special ceremony by 17 representatives chosen to visit the doge on the third day of Easter. 'May God give the Lord Doge all that is good. We have come to dine with you,' they would say. The doge responded: 'You are welcome.'

'Will you receive our tribute?'

'Most certainly. In what manner?'

'We wish to kiss you.'

The ritual required that one of the representatives kiss the doge 'on the lips'. Then the master of ceremonies seated everyone, and at the end of the meal the representatives withdrew, having paid a tribute of 29 lire.

In 1786 the German writer Wolfgang Goethe witnessed the *andata* that the doge made every 7 October to the Church of Santa Giustina to commemorate the victory of the Christian fleet over the Turks at Lepanto in 1571. However, this was one of the last occasions on which this ritual would be celebrated, given that Napoleon dealt the *coup de grace* to the Venetian Republic just a few years later, in 1797.

Opposite: Picnicking in the 1930s: this is my great uncle who was well known for extracting the secrets of the finest chefs in Europe, especially of those who worked in restaurants near casinos!

Festivities, fashion and food

At the height of its prosperity and power, in the fifteenth and sixteenth centuries, Venice was home to many confraternities of clerics and laymen, to innumerable craft guilds and the so-called *Compagnie di Calza*. These latter brought together young noblemen from Venice and beyond, who met to express their mutual friendship and esteem in musical and theatrical entertainments, games, regattas and competitions. If they were related by marriage or blood to the *compagni*, women too might take part in these events; but it was very rare indeed for non-patricians of either sex to be admitted.

At the end of the fifteenth century companies of this kind, which had amusing names, included *Belli* (handsome), *Soprani* (sopranos), *Signorili* (gentlemen), *Fraterni* (brotherly), *Perpetui* (everlasting) and *Ortolani* (vegetable growers), one of whose members was Francesco Maria della Rovere, Duke of Urbino and Captain General of the Venetian Militia. During his stay in Venice, Alfonso d'Este, Duke of Ferrara, was invited to join *I Potenti* (powerful), a *compagnia* which was responsible for organizing a feast in honour of the Duchessa di Bari and the Duchessa di Ferrara (Alfonso's wife, Eleonora d'Aragona). The celebrations took place in May 1493 and started with a banquet, followed by a regatta, a ball and a beauty contest. Not to be outdone, *Gli Immortali*, a few years later ordered a sort of *bucintoro* (ceremonial ducal galley) to be built for the festivities in honour of the bishop of Asti and various ambassadors. On a subsequent occasion, each member of this *Compagnia degli Immortali* paid 100 ducats towards the cost of the celebrations held in honour of Federico Gonzaga; the money was spent on specially adorned boats, balls, parades and a supper for 300 guests, followed by a play.

By the eighteenth century, the world had changed markedly. The Enlightenment in England and France was generating new ideas, and that same spirit of renewal was felt in Venice as well. The Republic had behind it 1000 years of history, greatness and tradition but now it, too, was developing a new philosophy of life. Though slow, this process of change was also reflected in the way people ate. Venice had long been a meeting point between East and West and now it would become a meeting point between the old and the new. The quantity and quality of food changed, as did meal times. The new fashions required that Venice fall in line with the cities of the mainland and call upon the services of French chefs (these *monsù* had already made their appearance in Naples, for example).

If one wants to get a better idea of the eating habits of all classes of Venetian society in the eighteenth century, one should look at life in the city's inns and hostelries, which at the

time totalled 48. Here, tourists were served by staff of both sexes, who might also keep them company until late into the night; a local by-law laid down that waitresses had to be over 30 years of age. In his *Osterie Veneziane*, Elio Zorzi writes:

> Once upon a time Venetians usually had two meals a day. *Merenda*, served between 11 and midday, was generally a light meal of one course; *pranzo*, served at the 'ducal hour' of five in the afternoon, was made up of much more substantial fare, with soup, risotto or pasta and two or three other courses. Five o'clock was referred to as the 'ducal hour' because it was when the doge ended public audiences, when the State Chancellery closed and when the various magistrates and councils suspended work so that all could go for pranzo. In addition, a small supper (*cena*) was eaten in the wee small hours of the morning usually after leaving the theatre.

My great great grandfather, Andrea, still kept alive this habit of eating at five in the afternoon, the time which – as an official at the Venice Custom's Office – he finished work; the old working timetable had been maintained even though Venice was by then governed by the Austrians. And what was the typical menu for a five o'clock *pranzo*? Broth and boiled meat.

As time went by, the times of *merenda* and *pranzo* began to reflect differences in social class. The populace kept local traditions alive, whilst the patrician classes began to ape the French nobility – and not only in the time of their meals: the grandiose Villa Pisani at Strà, near Padua, seems intended to rival the grandeur of Versailles itself (fittingly, Napoleon insisted on staying there). The historian Pompeo Molmenti describes how, throughout the eighteenth century, the Venetian patricians' delight in the good life continued:

> They spent, took outings and squandered wealth; they concerned themselves only with enjoyment and had no thought for tomorrow. Their days were full of idle tasks, their most important commitments being gaming and eating. The chairs around the card tables were almost always occupied; the sideboards were almost always laid out with food for guests who might arrive unexpectedly. Banquets were enlivened by the numerous gangs of friends and hangers-on who passed from dining room to dining room. Sometimes, the patricians would compete to see who could offer the most succulent and sumptuous meals, with the result that druggists and physicians prospered. Sometimes, tables were laid out in three different rooms: in one, soups and boiled meats were served, from whence the guests passed into a second room for roast and cooked meats, and finally into a third, where there was an abundant spread of desserts, fruit and ice cream.

The magnificence of Venetian hospitality was, naturally enough, put on full display when illustrious foreigners visited the city. On those occasions, celebrations and entertainments might end with bull-baiting in some of the city's *campi*; this popular 'sport' was banned in the early nineteenth century – soon after the fall of the Republic – when overcrowding lead to the collpase of a podium. In reference to popular cooking, which remained rooted in ancient traditions that have been maintained in present-day Venetian cuisine, Molmenti observes: '… only very few days of the year were celebrated with rich meals and special dishes; in general, the populace had simple tastes and were so restrained in their drinking that one rarely saw them drunk in the streets.'

Both populace and patricians had their 'gastronomic calendar', which followed the seasons and was punctuated by a few festivities that were associated with particular dishes. For example, Christmas Eve dinner traditionally comprised *botarga* (dried fish eggs), followed by *bisato* (eel), clam risotto, salmon, savoy cabbage and sweet mustard – with a type of nougat for dessert. Carnival meant ravioli, turkey, a mozzarella-like cheese and of course, *frittele* and *galani*, whilst on the first day of Lent one was supposed to eat chick-peas. Throughout Lent, roasted almonds were all you could expect for dessert. Easter was for lamb and *focaccia*; a cake made into the shape of a chicken or dove. The Feast of *La Salute* (still celebrated every 21 November), which marks the end of one of the worst plagues in Venice's history is still celebrated with *castradina* (dried, smoked mutton); the Feast of *Il Redentore* (third weekend in July) is welcomed with stuffed duck; and on the eve of the Feast of Santa Marta (which overlaps with *Redentore* but is now virtually obsolete) it was fried sole. On the other days of the year, one ate whatever there was.

Spices – and so much more

 THROUGHOUT most of its history, the Venetian Republic worked to increase its military and economic might not simply by the sword but also by establishing close trading links and political alliances with nations far and near. The result was a prosperous and opulent state, whose artistic and cultural wealth was the envy of Europe; and a key factor in all this was the trade in rare merchandise that the city acquired from distant lands.

There is a story of seven Venetian witches who at midnight every day went to the Fondamente Nuove, where they boarded a ship and set out around the world on their mission of sorcery. One day the owner of the vessel in question realized, from knots that he had not tied, that someone else was using his boat. He hid in the stern and waited. At midnight the witches arrived and cast off. The head witch then stood up to count the other members of the gang, each of whom rose in her turn: 'Up one, up two, up three, up four, up five, up six, up seven'. But still the boat did not move. They looked around them for the explanation, and while the owner of the boat trembled with fear that they might find him, the head witch herself hit upon the reason for the delay: 'One of you must be pregnant… Up eight! At which point the boat set off, sailing over the waves. When they docked, the witches disembarked. Shortly afterwards, so did the owner, curious to find out where he was. It was so dark that he could not see anything. He bumped into a tree but was so startled he merely snatched at a branch, pulled it off, and hurried back to his hiding place. The happy band of witches finally returned, and set off with an 'Up eight, because one of you is pregnant.' In the wink of an eye they were back at Venice's Fondamente Nuove and they hurried off to their homes before the cock's crow. The boat-owner himself then came ashore and, when he looked at the branch in his hand, he saw it was laden with dates, a fruit that grew only in Alexandria. Later that day he met up with some friends, to whom he showed the branch with fresh leaves, recounting the story of his night visit to Alexandria. Naturally, they believed him: it is well known that almost every night witches get up to all sorts of sorcery and magic.

Venice's imports from distant lands included much more than dates. Asia Minor, for example, supplied *damaschine* plums, peanuts, walnuts, almonds, hazelnuts and the raisins that have been used in Mediterranean cooking since the days of Noah. Before being laid out to dry (in the sun or in an oven) the bunches of grapes were left to soak in an alkaline solution or in a light lye of boiling-hot potash. The most famous varieties of dried grape were the *sultanina* and those that came from Corinth, Asia Minor and Spain; there was also the prized *zibibbo* raisin, which was entirely without pips. Other fruits, such as figs, were laid out to dry on straw mats. The fig is a very sweet fruit that has long been a part of local culinary traditions. Given their abundance and the fact that they ripened all together, figs were very cheap when dried and thus became synonymous with poverty: the derogatory expression 'a wedding with dried figs' is used when someone does something on the cheap. Figs could also have dangers rather more significant than social stigma: the Treviso-born pope Benedict XI died eight days after eating from a basket of poisoned figs, which had been presented to him as a gift.

In the past, salt and sugar were costly and almost impossible to get hold of. The rarity of these commodities would become the basis for Venice's vast trading empire. The hub of trade with the Orient, the city imported not only spices, but also the cane sugar that so intrigued people who were used to having no other sweetener than honey (easily separated from the beeswax but very difficult to break down into natural sugars).

As with everything from the Orient, cane sugar was wrapped in mystery, associated with the weird and wonderful tales that all sailors brought with them back from the East. We do know that it must have arrived in Venice some time after the year 1000, as a result of the Crusades. Having established a sizeable trade in the cane sugar

imported from the Orient, from Cyprus and from the Greek Islands (Crete, in particular), Venice would by 1150 have become Europe's main 'sugar exchange'. In that very year precise laws were passed to regulate the trade in this rare and costly commodity, which was sold wholesale at the Rialto and retail by the city's apothecaries and druggists. This central position in the sugar trade led to the foundation of refineries and to the creation of plants for extracting sugar from beets grown in the Veneto itself.

Sugar-cane had already been known for thousands of years to the Chinese and the Indians, who used it to make a sweet syrup – perhaps they even made crystallized sugar. The Persians – and hence Alexander the Great – were aware of its existence, with the result that sugar-cane plants were smuggled into Africa and the Mediterranean basin to start plantations. So industrial (or, in this case, agricultural) espionage has always existed.

From the early centuries of the second millennium onwards contacts with Byzantium and the Arab world had a marked influence on Venetian cuisine, leading to the introduction of various spices. Famous products of the day were the so-called *Sacchettis Venetis,* which were stuffed with costly delicacies and aromatic herbs, such as pepper, saffron, coriander, ginger, cassia bark, indigo, amber, cinnamon, nutmeg, cumin, cloves and the resin of the Siamese benzoe tree – all of them so valuable that in some wills they are even specified by name as part of a legacy.

The markets and streets of Venice bustled with foreigners. At the Rialto, the centre of Venetian trade, one could encounter Jewish, Dutch, Tuscan, French, Genoese and German merchants. These latter were the first group to set up a *Fondaco* (trading station) in which to store their merchandise ready for dispatch. Nutmeg, ginger, cinnamon, red galingale from China, cloves, star anise (for digestive liqueurs), saffron (first introduced into Spain in the ninth century by the Arabs), curry, pepper (particularly that from Madagascar, which was used in marinating fish) – each of these could become the equivalent of currency, traded for such merchandise as Murano glass. In the wholesale spice market, reserved more for bankers than for druggists and apothecaries, there was an auction system, characterized by the peculiarity that offers were secret and whispered from ear to ear; the *messeri del pepe* who acted as 'brokers' here were State appointees. There are those who say that pepper was in such high demand because it was used to conserve meat; its aroma could cover the strong odour of victuals which were past their prime. However, others have pointed out that, given its extremely high price, those who could afford pepper could also afford fresh meat and fish.

The medical treatises and pharmacopoeias of the day identified the specific properties of each of these valuable spices: pepper was 'a good antidote against poisons', nutmeg was 'good against freckles', cinnamon 'calmed intestinal disturbances' and cloves 'warmed the heart'. Most of these pharmaceutical wonders were grown in the Indies, in the Malay archipelago and in Southern China – all places where the only westerners were missionaries and the odd intrepid merchant.

Thus it was usually Malay or Arab traders whose ships transported goods to Europe: not only sugar-cane but also spices, scented lacquers, shellac, silk, pearls and precious stones. These vessels unloaded their cargoes in the ports of the Persian Gulf or the Red Sea, with the merchandise then being transported farther westwards in caravans. A rich trading centre for these goods was Byzantium, which attracted the costly trade from Trebizond on the Black Sea and from Antioch and Alexandria in the Muslim Mediterranean. Venice pushed its way into this market with ever greater insistence. Eventually, these commodities played such a role in its trade that the city printed daily lists giving the average cost at the Rialto of various spices, which were often used in place of hard cash.

When in 1498 the Portuguese rounded the Cape of Tempests – since known as the Cape of Good Hope – everything changed. Now there was a trade route around Africa. In 1504 Vasco de Gama, whose expedition was financed by Florentine bankers, sailed some 27,000 miles to India and beyond, into the very heart of the 'spice lands'. He brought back to Lisbon a cargo of thousands of tons of pepper and other spices, yielding a 400 per cent return on initial investment. The centre of the spice trade had now shifted to the Atlantic seaboard. Venice went through a time of economic crisis and a number of banks in the city failed.

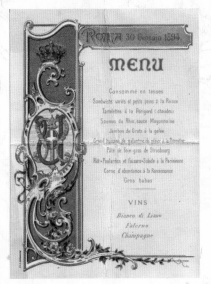

A dinner given by the Savoy royal family in Rome in 1884 shows how international menus had become.

Antipasti

Antipasti

The following pages include a selection of classic Venetian antipasti, inspired by the city's restaurants and taverns, which lay out fish, shellfish and crustaceans in displays that not only whet the appetite but also please the eye. Bright red prawns, pale pink shrimp, *schie* (local grey shrimp), *canocie* (mantis shrimp), small octopus, cuttlefish eggs, *peoci* (mussels), *garusoli* (murex snails, also used for purple dye in antiquity) and other types of shellfish are all best served with a simple dressing of olive oil and abundant lemon juice. This brings out their flavour and means that they effectively perform their function of stimulating the appetite. If you go in for heavier dressings, then you risk ruining the balance between the various courses, with the result that you just cannot finish the meal or end up regretting it next time you get on the bathroom scales. Fortunately, I have no bathroom scales; my appetite for these tasty treats is as voracious as that of the Chioggia fisherman whose last will and testament was nothing less than a hymn to seafood, addressed to his sweetheart: '*Bella, cu moor, vestime de sepe, soterime su un monte de concie, in cusinèelo de barboni fritti e un cavatale de anzoeti rosti*', (Dearest, if I should die, dress me in cuttlefish, bury me under a mound of *canocie*, with a little pillow of fried mullet and a bolster of roast red mullet).

Chioggia is a fishing town in the extreme south of the Venetian lagoon and legend has it that the local population are descended from the Phoenicians. It has a very distinctive sing-song dialect – perhaps those long vowels developed over centuries by making it easier to understand what is being shouted from one boat to the next.

Most of the types of boat used by Chioggia fishermen are flat-bottomed, or almost flat, because they are designed for fishing in the often shallow waters of the lagoon itself. Boats around here are often named after the type of fish they are used to catch. The fishermen were usually poor folk, obliged to sell the best of their haul, however much they may have wanted to eat it themselves. Sometimes, to improve their catch, the men ventured out into the Adriatic to fish the large shoals that were driven towards the coast by storms further offshore. However, this was a risky business because their flat boats were not designed for the deep and rough waters of the open sea and survivors lost little time in displaying their thanks to God, in the form of silver offerings to St Andrew, their patron saint.

Amongst the crustaceans, those which figure most successfully in menus are lobster, scampi, prawns, *schie* and various kinds of crab, including *moeche* (soft-shell crabs). They can be the basis for an entire seafood meal, from antipasto, through risotto, pasta, soups and main course. For me, though, the lobster is the crustacean *par excellence*. True warriors of the sea, they remind me of some sort of beast of heraldry, with those enormous claws that are as terrifying for other marine fauna as they are for us. There are, in fact, two types of lobster served in Venice: the *astice*, whose blackish shell only turns red when it is cooked, and the more noble and mild-mannered *aragosta*. The plump, red meat of both is one of our most prized seafood delicacies. Both types of lobster prefer the deep, clear waters on the other side of the Adriatic, which provide the perfect habitat for all those crustaceans that prefer clear and limpid waters.

No less tasty is the orange-red shelled spider crab. Greatly appreciated as an antipasto, the meat is served in the shell itself and dressed simply with oil, lemon juice and parsley. Another type of local crab that provides meat of a more full-bodied flavour is the *granzo poro*.

As for scampi, they too have their own nobility of lineage. This variety of prawn was originally a native of the waters of Norway; it only arrived in the Adriatic after progressive migrations brought it some five thousand miles along the coasts of Europe. A sort of miniature lobster, with large pinkish pincers and delicately flavoured flesh, scampi is the boast of any menu and can be prepared in a variety of ways: fried, boiled (and served with yellow or pink mayonnaise), grilled or *alla busara* (in a tomato, chilli and garlic sauce). Even larger in size, the *mazzancolla* (imperial prawn) cuts a proud figure as antipasto, first course or main dish.

A tolela *(small* tavola *or painting on wood) is a votive offering left by the fishermen of Chioggia in thanks for being spared a terrible fate at sea. In this example, the fisherman had to anchor himself just beyond the lagoon until a storm passed and it was safe enough to navigate through the sea mouth back into the lagoon.*

Of the various types of crab available, mention should be made of *mazanete* (female crabs still containing their eggs, which used to be sold ready-boiled in the streets of Venice) and *moeche* (harvested in the short season when they shed their carapace, and therefore soft-shelled). These latter are kept in large wooden tubs, and the fishermen painstakingly spend hours everyday selecting the soft crabs at the time their shells are changing from the rest of the group and then take them to market. I call them the 'caviar of the lagoon' because at high season *moeche* can fetch upwards of €50 per kilo.

The delicate lagoon environment is very special, with the shallow waters changing in depth, temperature and saltiness from winter to summer, and day to day depending on the currents and tides. Among the 50 or so species of fish and crustaceans that are best adapted to this particular environment there is the small *schie*, which is so at home in the Venetian lagoon that it is to be found only here and has developed as a species with characteristics that distinguish it from other pink or red shrimps. Grey in colour – though purple-reddish when cooked – *schie* are a great delicacy in Venice. Another, more recent, arrival in the lagoon is a larger, blue-grey shrimp that was originally a native of the waters of Japan; this, too, seems to be flourishing here.

Fishing in the lagoon has historically provided livelihoods for entire families and indeed communities, and this is still the case, to an extent. But it hasn't always been an easy way to earn a living. There is a story of a local fisherman driven to despair by the fact that he could not even catch enough fish to feed his pregnant wife. A bargain was struck with a mysterious stranger: in return for a lifetime of wealth and comfort, the fisherman would have to hand over the child that was about to be born. This exchange was to take place at night after one year, one month and one day from the baby's birthday; however, if on that night the fisherman could tell the stranger the 'Twelve Words of Truth', he would be allowed to keep his child.

After he had made the deal, the fisherman's business flourished, though he found it difficult to enjoy his new success because he was haunted by the thought that he would have to surrender his son. Finally, he told his wife of the tragic pact, and she reassured him that she knew the 'Twelve Words of Truth' and, when the time came, would tell him them. However, the formula that the woman recited – 'The four legs of the table, the four legs of the chair and the four legs of the grate' – sounded so disastrously wrong that the fisherman was sure he'd have to surrender both wife and child. It was a stormy night, and the first person to knock on the cottage door on that fateful evening was an old man, soaking wet and numb with cold. He asked for shelter and the fisherman let him come in and gave him a chair by the fire so that he could dry out. Still sitting there when the stranger arrived to demand 'payment', the old man – to everyone's surprise – spontaneously recited the correct answer to the riddle, the 'Twelve Words of Truth':

One. That there is none above God.
Two. Two Fools asleep at Table.
Three. Three Patriarchs: James, Jacob, Abraham.
Four. The Four Evangelists that Sustain the World.
Five. The Five Books that Christ Condemned.
Six. The Six Valleys of Vallonea.
Seven. The Seven Lamps that Burnt Jerusalem.
Eight. The Eight Souls in Noah's Ark.
Nine. The Nine Gilders who Gilded the Sun.
Ten. The Ten Virgins of Our Lord.
Eleven. The Eleven Disciples of Our Lord.
Twelve. The Twelve Apostles of Our Lord.

The shivering old man was St Martin and the stranger was the Devil, who, as he fled, shouted back the rhyme:

Martin Martello, if it weren't for you
Cow and Calf would have been my due.

Opposite: Emilio is giving me some moeche (soft-shell crabs), collected from the vieri *(wooden tubs) where the crabs are kept during their moulting season.*

Sardelle salate
Marinated sardines

Serves 4
400 g / 14 oz salted sardines
1 white onion, finely chopped
50 g / 2 oz olive oil
75 ml / 3½ fl oz strong
wine vinegar
pepper

Sardines used to be the main catch of fishing boats that sailed out from Burano, the picturesque island in the northern part of Venice lagoon, and the towns at the sea-ward extremities of the lagoon – Chioggia in the south to Caorle in the north. The Chioggia fleets also ventured further south during the glory days of the Serenissima, down as far as the coast of the Papal States, to catch sprat (*Clupea stratus*), which are known in Venetian as *papaline*. This liberty with papal resources perhaps gave rise to the local saying 'First Venetians, then Catholics', a creed reflected in many aspects of city life: in 1353 a certain Renier da Mosto was excommunicated by the Pope for having sentenced a priest who was considered to be working against the interests of the Republic.

The salting of fish was very common, given that in the whole region there was no other way to preserve the abundant catches made in the Adriatic between April and October or to prepare durable stores to be kept in ships' galleys over long voyages, and Venice was rich in salt, which lay at the foundation of its trading empire.

———&&&———

Clean and bone the sardines, wash them thoroughly in cold water and cut into fillets. Then place in a covered dish, together with the onion. Pour on the oil and the vinegar and sprinkle with pepper. Cover with a tight-fitting lid and leave to marinate in the fridge or some other cool place for at least a day. A perfect antipasto, these salted sardines really tickle the tastebuds and stimulate the appetite.

Sardine sott'olio
Sardines in oil

Serves 4
400 g / 14 oz canned
sardines in oil
1 garlic clove
a few fresh sage leaves, chopped
100 g / 3½ oz tomatoes, skinned,
de-seeded and chopped
40 g / 1½ oz butter
2 large grilled peppers, sliced
100 g / 3½ oz pickles
2 hard-boiled eggs, sliced

The origin of this typically Venetian antipasto is not clear, though the existence of a church known as San Pietro delle Sardelle leaves one in no doubt about the long-standing importance of this fish in local culture. The church is on the island of Pellestrina, which forms part of the narrow southern seaboard of the lagoon. Fishing – and sardine fishing in particular – yielded the wealth that financed the rebuilding of the church here in 1646, hence the name. Another version of the story, however, alleges that the fisherman were rather tight-fisted when it came to donating to the church fund and so were punished with poor catches until they placated St Peter by offering a solid-gold sardine.

———⟨⟩———

Buy good-quality sardines preserved in olive oil. Bone and skin before laying out on a dish. Crush the garlic and mix it with the chopped sage and tomatoes; then fry for a few minutes in the melted butter, to make a sauce. Leave to cool before pouring the sauce over the sardines and, just before serving, arrange the sliced grilled peppers, pickles and hard-boiled eggs attractively on top.

Schie
Deep-fried grey shrimps

Serves 4
500 g / 1 lb small schie
or small raw shrimps
oil, for deep-frying
salt

When I go to my friend Nino, a fishmonger at the Rialto, to buy shrimps or *schie* (the local variety of small grey shrimp), he encourages me to enjoy them alive. 'Just snap off the head and they're ready to eat… Shrimps are like men, a bit tough and not so good. But *schie*! They're like women. They make your mouth water… and the flavour lingers.'

The classic way of preparing schie is to fry them in hot oil, so that they become crunchy on the outside. You eat the whole thing, serving them with soft polenta. *Schie* can also be prepared '*in saòr*' or boiled; but this requires more attention as it can only be done with the larger *schie*, which need to be shelled first, and this calls for too much patience.

———⟨⟩———

It's like preparing french fries. Drop the schie into hot oil and, when they are between a golden and a reddish colour, remove them (about 2 to 3 minutes); if cooked for longer they become like cardboard. Place on kitchen towel to absorb excess oil.

Serve sprinkled with salt, with soft polenta to accompany.

Fortagia de gamberetti
Shrimp omelette

Serves 4
6 fresh eggs
generous 50 g / 2 oz butter
200 g / 7 oz shelled shrimps
salt and pepper

In Asiago, in the highlands of the Veneto, eggs are associated with a quaint springtime custom: when young people were out walking in the woods and meadows, a girl who took a fancy to one of the boys would offer him an egg, the symbol of fertility, tied in her handkerchief. If the feelings were mutual, the young man would reciprocate with a doughnut, a gesture that amounted to a formal promise of marriage within the year.

While eggs, especially chocolate ones, are also the Easter symbol *par excellence*, I more readily associate them with pink shrimps, which make a marvellous shrimp omelette.

Beat the eggs in a bowl with salt, pepper and a little water. Pour the mixture into a large pan in which you have melted the butter. When the mix begins to set, add the shrimps and cook on a moderately high heat for a couple of minutes. Then turn the heat to low and continue cooking until the egg is firm and dense. Serve in slices or, once cooled, chop into cubes and serve on a plate, with toothpicks so people can help themselves.

Folpetti
Octopus salad

Serves 4
12 small folpetti, *cleaned*
30 ml / 2 tbsp extra virgin olive oil
juice of 2 lemons
fresh parsley sprigs
1–2 celery sticks, chopped,
or 4 whole radishes
salt and pepper

The favourite riddle of my six-year-old son, Pierangelo, goes like this: 'What animal has its head in its belly and its belly inside its head?'. As round as a door handle and the same violet-red colour as beetroot, *folpetti* (the local octopus) are much smaller than their more frightening cousins found in the markets of Palermo or along the Tyrrhenian and Ligurian coasts.

Enjoyed for its firm, solid flesh, the Venetian *folpetto* is a typical snack, eaten dressed with just a little oil, salt and pepper. Until a few decades ago, large copper kettles of *folpetti* stood at the door of nearly every *osteria*, or were wheeled about by vendors hawking their wares. While the *osterie* are traditionally taverns offering simple food and wine, today they are virtually indistinguishable from *trattorie* and restaurants; indeed inverse snobbery has made one of the finest restaurants in Venice call itself *osteria*!

Choose small *folpetti*, preferably of uniform size. Cook them in boiling water, then remove and cut lengthways and lay out on an oval dish. After dressing with extra virgin olive oil, salt, pepper and a lot of lemon juice, garnish the dish with sprigs of parsley, chopped celery or whole radishes.

Cape sante
Scallops

Serves 4
16 very large cape sante (scallops)
fine dried breadcrumbs
30 ml / 2 tbsp oil
and 30 g / generous 1 oz butter
1 garlic clove
chopped fresh parsley
half a glass of dry white wine
juice of 1 lemon
salt

These are better known as *coquilles Saint-Jacques*; but in the rest of Italy they are called *ventagli* (fan clams), an obvious reference to their appearance, while the Venetian name – 'holy clams' – comes from the fact that scallop shells were a symbol of medieval pilgrims.

⎯⎯⎯⎯ ✺ ⎯⎯⎯⎯

After removing the scallops from their shells, roll them in the breadcrumbs. Select the eight largest shells and clean them well with a metal brush.

In a frying-pan, melt the butter with the oil and then add the whole garlic clove for a few minutes to flavour the mix. Remove the garlic and add the parsley and scallops. Cook these for 15 minutes, turning regularly, so that the scallops become a rich, old gold colour. Towards the end of the cooking, add the wine and the lemon juice. When cooked, place the scallops in pairs in the cleaned shells, then sprinkle with a little more parsley and some of the juice in which they were prepared.

Scallops can also be cooked in the oven, after being carefully cleaned, inside their shells. Pour over a mixture of wine, chopped garlic, parsley and butter. They take 10 to 15 minutes, depending on the oven and are ready when most of the liquid has evaporated from the shell and the scallops become more white and opaque-looking.

Once empty, larger scallop shells make charming side-plates for dishes such as potato salad.

Bòvoli rosti
Fried snails

Serves 4
400 g / 14 oz large snails,
purged and ready to cook
plain white flour for dusting
100 ml / 3½ fl oz extra virgin
olive oil
chopped fresh parsley
½ garlic clove, finely chopped
salt

The discovery of snail shells by archaeologists at the site of some of the oldest prehistoric settlements in the Veneto, and elsewhere, reveals that these molluscs have long been part of the human diet; they are known to have been popular in Ancient Rome. After all, snails were easy to gather – even for children – and certainly posed none of the threats of the wild animals which men were beginning to learn to hunt. And as *corgnoi* became a part of the basic diet, every home had its *corgnolera*, a wicker cage used both in gathering and keeping snails. The mollusc also gave rise to a number of local expressions: *dormir come un bovolo* ('to sleep like a snail' – that is, a lot); *fare in 't un bovolo* ('curl up like a snail', when sleeping); *aver la casa in testa come i bovoli* ('carry your home with you like a snail' – that is, be responsible for everything), *bovolo de condanti* ('convict's snail' – the chains that linked together the group of men rowing a single oar in a Venetian war galley); *bovolo de l'aqua* (a vortex or whirlpool) and, of course, *a scala a bovolo* (a spiral staircase).

Found throughout Europe, snails are most common in hilly areas (up to 1500 metres above sea-level), though they don't mind the humid plains. For cooking, the best snails come from fields where salad greens are grown. Rather than finding your own, buy them at the market, where you can find those raised specifically for the pot.

Although the taste may be excellent, the slimy texture can be off-putting and it is imperative that the preparation eliminates all traces of slime from snails' bodies and includes a stage for purging because they would otherwise be indigestible. Purging can be done by keeping the snails in semolina, bran, sand or sawdust. Mucous layers are removed by soaking in cold water for a number of hours. If they are large, a tasty way of preparing snails is to fry them; this is particularly popular in Padua, where the snails are known as '*càpari*'.

Wash the snails well and drop into boiling water, the initial stage of their cooking process. Then shell them. Dust lightly with flour and then fry them in olive oil. Before serving, sprinkle with salt and chopped parsley mixed with a little garlic, taking care not to overwhelm the delicate flavour of the snails themselves.

Snail sellers from a series of engravings called Le Arti che vanno per via nella città di Venezia *by Gabriele Zompini, an artist of the late eighteenth century.*

Le Moeche di San Marco
St Mark's soft-shell crabs

Serves 4
600 g / 1¼ lb live moeche
3 eggs, beaten
200 g / 7 oz olive oil
plain white flour, for coating
salt

The fishermen of Chioggia are particularly skilled in harvesting *moeche* (soft-shell crabs) from the mudflats of the lagoon. These are male crabs that cast their shells in spring and autumn and thus, for a brief period, are to be found in this vulnerable soft-shelled state. The name *moeche* is also given to anyone without willpower or strength of character (or vice versa, the crabs may have been named after spineless people!). For example, when the Venetian Republic, already sinking into political decline in the latter eighteenth century, issued a coin in which the head of the Lion of St Mark appeared within a border that vaguely resembled a crab motif, irreverent residents of Chioggia did not hesitate to nickname it '*la mo'eca*', mocking the growing impotence of the Venetian State.

During the moulting season, the harvested crabs are kept in large wooden tubs along the canals in the lagoon, immersed in water, and they have a tendency to eat each other under the crowded conditions of their cage. Twice a day, the fishermen painstakingly sort through the tubs to find those that have just shed their shells, and they are whisked off to market – 'saved' from a similar fate at the hands of their cannibalistic brothers.

I prefer to eat them the simple way fishermen do, without stuffing and just coated in flour and deep-fried in oil.

———— ✸ ————

Leave the live *moeche* to purge themselves for some time in a bucket, changing the water frequently. Then place the live crabs in a bowl containing the beaten eggs and some salt for at least a couple of hours. While gorging on the batter, the crabs fill their bodies with it and, ultimately, drown themselves.

Heat the oil to a very high deep-frying temperature.

Break off the crab claws, coat the bodies with flour and deep fry in hot oil. The crabs are ready when they are between an old gold and reddish brown colour, after 7 to 10 minutes; if you fry them too long they dry out. Drain them of excess oil, liberally sprinkle with coarse salt and serve with freshly prepared soft polenta.

For a *frittata* or *fortagia de moeche*, add the fried crabs to an omelette made in the usual way with 6 eggs, adding 50 g / 2 oz of grated Parmesan to the egg before cooking and a good handful of finely chopped fresh parsley to serve. This variation is a noted speciality of Treviso and typically served around Lent when eggs are available in abundance.

Baccalà mantecato
Creamed stockfish (or codfish)

Serves 4

650 g / 1¼ lb stockfish (or codfish),
soaked in cold water overnight
very good olive oil
25 g / 1 oz fresh parsley,
finely chopped
1 garlic clove, finely chopped
salt and pepper

This Venetian recipe for stockfish produces a dish that is so light and creamy it is a sure hit with everyone, young and old; particularly the young, who like soft food and fish without any bones! Properly prepared, it definitely merits greater international renown. Furthermore, it is a very convenient recipe because the dish is served cold and thus can be prepared in advance, saving you last-minute worries about how it is going to turn out.

———— ⤬ ————

Rinse the fish in plenty of cold water before it is pre-soaked. Place a piece of pre-soaked stockfish in a lot of cold water, bring to the boil and then leave to sit in the water for 20 minutes or so. Drain the fish, then carefully skin and bone, breaking the flesh into small pieces. Now comes the difficult part, which will turn the stockfish into a light and fluffy cream. Use a wooden spoon to vigorously beat together the pieces of fish with plenty of olive oil; pouring it into the mix very gradually until you have a white paste. Now continue pouring in a little more olive oil at a time until the creamy mixture can't absorb any more. Add the parsley and garlic and salt and pepper to taste.

Baccalà mantecato should be served on brightly coloured plates to make the most of the vivid colour contrast. It is usually accompanied by slices of grilled yellow polenta or it can be spread on toast.

Cape Longhe in padella
Pan-tossed razor clams

Serves 4
1.5 kg / 3½ lb cape longhe
60 ml / 2 fl oz olive oil
25 g / 1 oz fresh parsley, chopped
3 garlic cloves
salt

These razor-shell clams are better known in Italy by the Neapolitian term *cannolicchi*. Reaching up to over 10 cm (4 inches) in length, the clams burrow vertically into the sand on the shoreline of the Venice Lido, where people go early in the morning to collect them. The trick is to look for two small holes about 3 cm (1¾ in) apart – these are the air holes through which the clams breathe. Slide your thumb, index and middle fingers deep into the sand on either side of those holes and simply pull the shell out. I love razor clams and eat them raw with a bit of lemon juice immediately after catching them.

If you are short-sighted, lazy or suffer from a bad back, there's always the Rialto fish market, where you can find fresh, good-sized *cape longhe*.

———— ✸ ————

Cook the clams in a deep pan with the oil, parsley and garlic cloves, removing the garlic when it turns reddish gold in colour. Cook the clams for about 10 minutes on a high heat; more liquids are released by the clams. Serve, shelled or unshelled, in a bowl with the cooking juices, seasoned with a little salt if necessary and accompanied by slices of toasted bread.

Granseola alla veneziana
Dressed spider crab

Serves 4
6 large granseole
aromatic herbs, such as rosemary,
sage and/or bay leaf (optional)
100 g / 3½ oz olive oil
6 lemons
chopped fresh parsley
salt and pepper

The expression *'prendere un granchio'* ('catch a crab') means 'to get a dud'; it derives from the disappointment of fishermen who find nothing but scrambling little crabs when they pull in their nets, instead of valuable fish. However, the insinuated animosity towards crabs could also be that of cooks who, when faced with this 'armoured vehicle', are intimidated by the task of prising it open. But the tastiness of the meat should make the effort more than worthwhile. Although Italian men – perhaps still in the grip of a medieval mindset – tend to think of themselves as the undisputed captains of the domestic ship, women know that their menfolk, lovers of good food, can be induced to surrender their command within the walls of the home in exchange for rewards from the stove.

Whatever the truth, crabs have always been something of a delicacy in Venice – particularly the four main varieties, which have truly unmistakable flavours. Generally, the local crabs are quite small and never reach the size of the giant Japanese *Macrocheira*, nor even that of the crabs caught off the coast of Britain. The largest local variety is called *'granseola'*, the feminine form of the Venetian word for *'granchio'* (crab). A member of the spider crab family (*Maja squinado*), it is hardly an elegant creature: the humped, knobbly shell with its nervous antennae or eyes looks rather comical, when alive, balanced on long spindly legs. However, when prepared for the table, the *granseola* becomes a very elegant dish indeed, with the bright red shell now bursting with tasty crab meat. As with all crustaceans, the preparation is not complicated but requires a great deal of patience to get all the meat out of the shell and claws.

Boil the *granseole* for 30 minutes, with or without the aromatic herbs, as you wish. When a greyish froth begins to form on the surface of the water, remove the pot from the stove and leave to cool. Remove the crab meat from the shell, setting aside the tasty meat from the body and claws; discard the eggs and the blackish and 'furry' parts. Thoroughly wash the shell in order to bring out its bright red colour.

Season the meat with oil, lemon juice, a little chopped parsley and salt and pepper and then return to fill the shell. Serve cold, or heat quickly under a grill and garnish with parsley leaves.

A more elaborate version of *granseola* is served with mayonnaise and garnished with capers, anchovies and sliced boiled egg.

Eighteenth-century life in the palazzi of Venice

ENICE was at the peak of its splendour in the eighteenth century, when the city became synonymous with sophisticated elegance, pleasure and luxury; a place that combined art, salon culture and conspicuous consumption. With regard to the latter, it is said that, during the eighteenth century, a member of the wealthy Labia family – which had been raised to the aristocracy as a result of the financial support it had supplied during the War of Candia – one day gave a 'banquet for forty gentlemen' at which all the tableware was solid gold. When the meal was over, Labia flaunted his wealth by tossing every single piece of the service into the canal beneath the window, punning upon his family name: '*L'abbia o non l'abbia, sarò sempre Labia*' ('Whether I have these or not, I will always be a Labia'). It is, however, also said that a net had been prepared beneath the window so that the tableware could be recovered as soon as the guests had left.

Eighteenth-century Venice was renowned for its good-time atmosphere. Pleasure and self-gratification ruled; and this state of affairs naturally attracted a number of foreigners from Europe and beyond. By then, Carnival celebrations lasted for six months of the year and continued unperturbed by political instability or social problems; even the funeral of the penultimate Doge was held 'on the quiet' so as not to cast a pall over the merry-making. While Venetian patricians sought the pleasures of the spirit or the body in luxurious palaces and the city's theatres and gaming-rooms, the populace, too, had their amusements. Venice's *osterie* were crowded; wandering troupes of players performed *Commedia dell'Arte*; and the various popular festivities in St Mark's Square were full of masked figures, mountebanks and those enjoying the thrill of bull-baiting.

Sometimes, the humbler folk were even invited to solemn state occasions. For example, 100 *arsenalotti* (workers at the Venice shipyards) were invited to the state banquet held on Ascension Day, the feast when the Doge cast a wedding ring into the sea; the presence of the workmen was intended to commemorate the decisive contribution they had made to Doge Pietro Orseolo II's defeat of the Narentan pirates.

The menu for one such official banquet begins with a total of 10 antipasti – including fine plump oranges, salted tongue, Florentine salami, pastries and tarts, large savoyard biscuits, *millefeuille*, curds, large citrons and sponge. The more illustrious state figures, who – together, with the foreign ambassadors – ate in a separate room from the *arsenalotti*, were served 12 *ardover* (a distorted version of the French term *hors d'oeuvre*). They then went on to the main dishes, which totalled 13 (the workmen had slightly fewer). Such courses included a large number of different meats – for example, a pigeon sauce lasagne and roast and boiled chicken – plus the most highly prized types of fish. Then came such vegetables as artichokes and fennel.

Venetian palaces of the fourteenth century, built when the city's architecture was still influenced by Byzantium, were intended to be not only homes, but also offices, warehouses and public expressions of wealth and power. As time went on, this display of wealth became perhaps the most important function, with *palazzi* providing a rich setting for balls, receptions, gambling and banquets.

As an example of these later *palazzi*, one might cite Palazzo Grimani near Santa Maria Formosa, which was built in the middle of the sixteenth century by Cardinal Grimani, a great collector of Greek and Roman antiquities. One of the guests here was Henri III, King of France, who enjoyed a triumphant reception when he visited Venice in 1574. Like all important visitors, the French king was shown around the Arsenale, where he was served sumptuous refreshments with exquisite confections of candied fruit and, most amazingly of all (something that had never been seen before), knives, forks, plates and even a tablecloth all made of sugar. Even then, Venetian society aimed to bedazzle and astonish – a characteristic that became further confirmed as the years passed.

Another form of conspicuous consumption was gambling, something to which the Venetian aristocracy became

Opposite: *Giacomo da Mosto, Governor of the Peleponnese (Greece), 1698.*

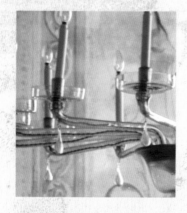

devoted. Casanova himself is credited with having introduced lotteries in the eighteenth century – but this was hardly an arduous task in a city where gaming was all the rage. By then, a number of the aristocratic *palazzi* had their own *ridotti*. Located on the floor below the splendid halls that were used for the official receptions, balls and banquets that added lustre to the family name, these more private spaces were elegant salons given over to the pleasures of conversation and the prevailing mania for gambling. The low-ceilinged interiors reflected the Venetian taste for intimacy and opulence, with elegant furniture, polychrome stucco work in pastel shades of green, pink and blue, gilding and wall mirrors to reflect the light of candles. The *ridotti* also had spy holes so that is was possible to check on callers and enable gamblers to make a timely (and secret) retreat if these should prove to be unwelcome.

One of the most fashionable *ridotti* was located in the San Moisè *palazzo* of the ancient Dandolo family, whose ancestors included the famous Doge Enrico Dandolo, who had attacked Constantinople during the Fourth Crusade in the mid-thirteenth century. This palace had, in 1542, been the residence of the Bishop of Rhodes, French ambassador to Venice, who having gained knowledge of some of the Republic's secret deliberations passed on the information to the Ottoman court. When the traitors were exposed by certain public functionaries, the bishop gave them refuge in the palace but two of the *Procuratori di San Marco* breached a wall of the building and entered with a body of armed men. Intimidated, the ambassador handed over the traitors, who were then sentenced to be hanged.

It was a later Dandolo who, in 1638, had the *ridotto* created within the *palazzo*; during Carnival, gambling in such places was authorized, with the state delegating certain patricians to act as 'bank'. At the beginning of the eighteenth century, one of the visitors to this *ridotto* was King Frederick IV of Denmark, disguised with the traditional Venetian *bauta* mask. The king was particularly lucky that night and won a lot of gold from one specific Venetian gentleman. However, when the time came to settle debts, the monarch demonstrated all of his regal magnificence by deliberately knocking the table so that the money fell on the floor and could be recovered by the unfortunate gentleman.

As time passed, the Venetian government realized that games such as *faraone* and *bassetta* were swallowing up entire fortunes and ruining families. Thus, on 27 November 1771, a law was passed that stated 'the house situated in the district of San Moisè and known under the name of *ridotto* is from this day forth and for all time and years to come closed forever to the grave abuse of gambling'. Gaming came to an end at San Moisè, but the ever-inventive devil simply moved his temptations elsewhere. Just two years later, a Captain of the *Eccellentissimi Esecutori contro la Biastemia* (Most Excellent Guardians against Blasphemy) donned a *bauta* mask and, together with other police agents, carried out a raid on a room in an *osteria* in the district of St Mark's. There, he surprised numerous people who had for some time, night and day, been engaged in the playing of *bassetta* and *faraone*. A total of about 100 lire was confiscated from the 'bank'; the tables and chairs were seized; the hosteller was fined six silver ducats; and all of the gamblers, including a few priests, were ordered to appear before the magistrate the following day.

During the latter years of the Republic – and in the period of French rule which followed – *ridotti* flourished once more as gambling-houses. However, with the advent of the Austrians they were again banned.

Towards the end of the eighteenth century some *palazzi* became hotels. One of these, at Santi Apostoli, was owned by my family and became the Leon Bianco hotel, soon recognized as one of the 20 best hotels for the wealthier visitors to Venice. One guest, in summer 1769, was the young Austrian emperor Joseph II. Though he was travelling incognito, he was recognized and so a number of extravagant entertainments were organized in his honour. The emperor himself, however, considered one proposal by the Venetian government to be just too excessive: this would have involved the creation of a 'Garden of the Hesperides' in St Mark's Basin, stretching some 150 metres from the island of San Giorgio Maggiore to the Guidecca Canal and complete with a lake containing real fish, and glass trees and flowers. The whole thing was merely intended as a preliminary amusement to a banquet to be held on the island of San Giorgio! Though the plan, drawn up in full detail, was never actually implemented, it did provoke a wave of ill-feeling, particularly amongst young intellectuals who were influenced by the revolutionary ideas arriving from France. These were, after all, difficult days for the Venetian exchequer – in spite of some 50 years of relative peace, the Republic had massive debts – and for the system of Venetian government: the number of those who had the right to attend the Great Council had shrunk to less than 1000 and sometimes meetings did not even achieve the necessary quorum.

Some years later another visitor to the city was the future Tsar of all the Russias, Grand Duke Paul Pietrovich, with his wife Maria Fyodorovna. Travelling under the names of 'Comte and Comtesse du Nord', they too stayed at the Leon Bianco. Soon, the city was abuzz with the news that 'we are about to see the son of Catherine the Great'. Everyone wanted to welcome the Grand Duke and Duchess in a manner befitting their station, but the fact that they were travelling incognito made things rather awkward. How was one to combine respect for their privacy with respect for their rank? Consummate politicians, the Venetians showed themselves perfectly able to reconcile their own desire for splendid entertainments with the royal couple's desire to remain unrecognized. For example, one of the celebrations envisaged a giant model of a dove flying around St Mark's Square to light a number of torches and then come to rest on a 40-metre high model of the Arch of Titus in Rome – the whole thing being triggered by just a slight gesture of the Grand Duchess's hand.

As for Grand Duke Paul Pietrovich, he was amazed by the discipline and restraint of the crowds of spectators: instead of ranks of soldiers, the well-wishers were kept in line by a mere five ushers from the Council of Ten. '*Voilà*!' he is said to have exclaimed. 'The effect of the wise government of the Republic. These people form one family.' He might have been enthusiastic about all things Venetian, but the Venetians themselves had one or two criticisms about all things grand-ducal: the royal couple failed to leave a tip when they attended a banquet at the Arsenale, they did not make the customary offering to the local orphanage and – most serious of all – they left part of their bill at the Leon Bianco unpaid.

Rice dishes & risottos

A radiator installed in the early 1900s doubles as a plate warmer in the dining room.

Rice dishes & risottos

The term 'spaghetti-eater' may not be intended as a compliment, but I believe the rest of the world envies Italy as the home of pasta dishes. The one injustice in this almost automatic association of Italian cuisine with pasta is that it overlooks a dish that has been a tradition here for even more centuries, particularly in the Po-valley area: risotto, a smooth and delicate first course that is second to none.

One of the finest things for which the countries of the Mediterranean are in the East's debt is rice. Since it was brought back by those who had served in Alexander the Great's campaigns in Persia and beyond, rice has been one of this area's staples. Brought into Italy by the Arabs, the crop was already being grown in Sicily before the year AD 1000 and then spread northwards thanks to the House of Aragon.

As everyone knows, rice originated in China (the techniques being used in the paddy fields of some 5000 years ago were very similar to today's). From there, its cultivation spread along large rivers to other areas of Asia and rice established itself as the staple that it remains today, being served with small quantities of animal proteins or simple sauces.

In Italy, rice was a particular hit in the Po valley because the presence of large, non-seasonal rivers meant that there were constant supplies of water for the rice fields. But the Italians were not content to leave rice as a humble foodstuff of the poor. By grafting together different varieties of plant, they gradually developed a rice that was rich and substantial, transforming the short-grained cereal of Asia into the elegant rice of today with its characteristic vitreous sheen.

Husking the rice was a very delicate matter, because the outer husks had to be removed without damaging the inner grain, which not only served for food but also supplied the seeds for the following year's crop. One of the earliest solutions adopted was to employ unshod ponies to 'dance' in circles around the threshing floor, crushing the husks but leaving the grains undamaged. With the advent of mechanization, of course, things changed. One of the few still-functional remnants of that initial period of industrial archaeology can be seen in the Old Ferron Rice Works at Isola della Scala, outside Verona. Built around the middle of the seventeenth century, this mechanical husker still bears the lion-and-eagle crest of the Venetian Zenobio family, for whom it was constructed. Powered by the waters of the Fossa Zenobia, the machine consists of an enormous waterwheel (more than

7 metres in diameter) that drives wooden 'pestles' that husk the rice in seven 'mortars' of red Verona marble. At the time, the husking process was carried out night and day, so workers always had to be on hand to 'remove the white' – the husked rice – which then had to be sifted to get rid of other impurities. The rice produced in this area is almost always dwarf *Vialone Veronese*, which is high in starch and readily absorbs liquid, hence is perfect for making Venetian-style risottos.

Up until about a century ago, the Venetian, Lombardy and Piedmont regions ate *minestre,* which contained small quantities of rice (cooked softer than nowadays) mixed with meat or vegetables in rather liquid dishes – for example, *risi e bisi* and *risi e luganega.* These days, however, risottos characteristically contain more rice than other ingredients and are much denser, so take more time to digest. Though risotto dishes can be found throughout the Po Valley and indeed the rest of Italy, it is the Veneto that has the greatest number and variety of recipes. In fact, the range of ingredients is such that one sometimes wonders what is not used here to make risottos.

But why did risottos become so popular in the Veneto? it is partly to do with the climate. In the north, dishes had to be both filling and warming, but in the sun-drenched south there was no such need for hearty soups and so spaghetti made a perfect first course instead. Another advantage of rice was that it is easy to store. Thus in the depths of winter, when fresh vegetables were in short supply, rice could be used to stretch out a meal and was affordable even for the less wealthy.

The Feast day of Venice's patron saint, St Mark, was celebrated by an official banquet to which the Doge invited all members of the Great Council. One of the main dishes on that occasion was the humble *risi e bisi* (rice and peas), which – as befitted the rank of the guests – was then followed by the best fish the Adriatic and local rivers had to offer, the choicest fruits and vegetables of the season, pastries and preserves, and the finest malmsey, Greek wines and *vin di Cipro* (a wine liqueur from Cyprus).

Rice even figured in Venetian plays, with Carlo Goldoni's miserly Sior Todaro Brontolon advising that 'Rice should be put on early, so that it swells up and increases in quantity… It should be boiled three hours…', a line that was sure to raise a laugh with an audience that appreciated its rice *al dente*. However, even if you are not deliberately trying to get it to expand to maximum volume, rice is not always the easiest thing to cook correctly. It is imperative to take great care when preparing rice, recognizing that it is ready when it becomes a uniform alabaster colour and the grains no longer have a cornea-white core.

A useful indicator of quantity is four cups of rice to serve four people and so on. Risottos must still be smooth (runny) enough to be described as *all'onda* (on the wave). There used to be few

types of rice available locally but developments in agriculture have yielded a number of varieties that are employed according to the grain size and cooking properties: *carnaroli, vialone, vialone nano, vialone gigante, arborio, maratello, rizzotto, balilla*. For *minestre* (soups), it is best to use a short-grain rice because it blends best with the texture of the dish. *Canaroli, arborio* and *vialone nano* varieties are best for risottos.

Before cooking, rinse the rice well under running cold water. This removes some of the starch, which would otherwise make it too sticky. Never soak the rice in water, however, as that would make the end result soggy. When cooking risottos, after frying initial aromatic ingredients such as garlic and onion and adding the rice, stir for a minute or so to coat the grains in the cooking juices, but make sure the rice doesn't start to toast. Then add the wine, if using, and cook, stirring frequently, until the rice has absorbed it. Then add stock (which you should have ready to hand, boiling hot), a ladleful or so at a time, pausing for it to be absorbed before adding more, and stirring nearly all the time. If the stock runs out before the risotto has finished cooking, use boiling water instead.

While the Chinese cook rice in lots of (cold) water with a little vinegar and salt, then drain it before adding any sort of sauce or other ingredients, the Venetian method is to blend the rice with meat or vegetables and cook them together. As you will see, this works to the advantage of all the ingredients, forming a smooth and creamy dish.

A limited number of recipes are given in this section but there are dozens of local risottos that I have not been able to include. Among Venice's specialities are *risoto a la bechèra* (with chicken giblets and pieces of veal), *risoto ae masanete* (small crabs) and *risoto a la bosega* (large tender grey mullet), as well as various other seafood ones. Padua has risotto with frogs and Verona has risotto with goose livers. And, of course, new recipes are being developed all the time. For example, the Venetian mainland was recently represented at an interregional cooking competition by *risoto al imbriago* ('drunk risotto', using red wine), and there are recipes for risottos made using fennel, celery, nettles, courgettes, pumpkin, radicchio, juniper berries and even potatoes. Whichever version you choose to make, don't forget an important guiding principle for rice in the Veneto: it is mixed first with water, then with wine.

Risi e spezzati
Rice and split peas

Serves 4
200 g / 7 oz split peas
45 ml / 3 tbsp olive oil
50 g / 2 oz butter
½ onion
500 ml / 18 fl oz stock
300 g / 10 oz vialone rice
salt and coarsely ground pepper
butter
50 g / 2 oz Parmesan

This is a tasty risotto, perfect in the winter months when the only fresh vegetables in the markets are frost-bitten and unappealing.

—⁂—

Make sure you wash the dried peas well – there is often some gravel mixed in with them when they are sold loose – and leave overnight to soak.

Next day, sauté the chopped onion in the oil and butter and when it is light brown, add the drained split-peas and cover with stock. Cook on a moderate heat, adding more stock from time to time, until the split peas become very soft and the mixture is creamy. This may take up to an hour.

Add the rice and more stock and continue to cook until the rice is *al dente*, about 10 to 12 minutes, stirring regularly so that nothing sticks to the bottom of the pan. The final consistency should be *all'onda*.

Add a knob of butter, before serving with grated Parmesan and a little coarsely ground pepper. Serve hot – after all, this is a winter dish.

Risi e porri
Leek risotto

Serves 4
300 g / 10 oz vialone rice
500 g / 1 lb leeks
60 ml / 2 fl oz olive oil
50 g / 2 oz butter
1 garlic clove
1 litre / 1¾ pints weak stock
or boiling water
salt
50 g / 2 oz mature Parmesan

The vegetable markets of the Rialto are always bursting with fresh produce and the leek is omnipresent. It is a humble relative of the onion, with its white bulbous root and long green leaves. Eaten together, from root to tip, leeks represent a balanced combination of yin and yang, according to followers of Eastern philosophy. Venetians will use just about anything to make risotto.

—⁂—

Cut off the muddy tips of the roots and the ends of the leaves of the leeks and then wash and cut into pieces some 4 to 5 cm (about 2 in) long. Heat the oil and butter with the garlic clove and remove the garlic when it has turned golden. Add the leek and cook slowly for at least 20 minutes.

Add some salt and then the rice. When this is well mixed with the disintegrating, soft leeks, add ladlefuls of either weak stock or boiling water, and cook until the rice is *al dente*. Add some grated mature Parmesan to serve.

Riso a la pilota
Husker's rice

One of the most original ways of preparing rice comes from the plains of Verona and Mantua, where great stretches of land are given over to rice paddies. The first time I ate this dish I was reminded of Arab couscous (which is made using granules of durum wheat rather than rice). Whoever invented *riso a la pilota* must have had family links with Lucca or Genoa, places of infamous tightfistedness: the slow cooking on a very low heat works perfectly but it does raise the suspicion that one of the concerns was to save energy! Actually, this dish seems to have come from those employed to husk (*pilare*) rice. This was done using a huge paddle wheel, like that at the Old Ferron Rice Works. More than 7 metres in diameter, this particular piece of industrial archaeology has survived in perfect working order – partly due to events during the Second World War.

The entire area of *Isola della Scala* (in the plains to the south of Verona) was heavily bombed by the allies – except, that is, for the immediate neighbourhood of the Ferron Works that stood close to a camp holding English prisoners of war. Many local families, terrorized by the bombing raids, sought shelter in the the old building, where they carried on business as usual: one man ran an *osteria*, another continued working as a blacksmith shoeing horses and other draught animals; there was also a tailor and a barber's shop. All in all, the old factory quickly became a bustling community, known as *Piccola Italia* (Little Italy). After the Armistice was signed in 1943, the husking works also became a shelter for English and Italian soldiers trying to escape the Nazis and fascist militia. And in recognition of the services it provided, Little Italy received a special award from the Allied Supreme Command.

Rice husking in the factory never ceased throughout those difficult times; for many people, all that stood between them and starvation was indeed the local crop of *vialone* rice. My own father recalls how it was cooked in large aluminium pans which were brought to the boil and then – in order to save fuel – placed in crates packed with sawdust, where they continued to simmer gently.

This recipe requires good-quality rice with an evenly sized grain, preferably large-grain *vialone* or *arborio* variety. The result is rice that is neither too *al dente* nor too soft (as they tend to cook it in Tuscany). This can then be served with whatever sauce or dressing you choose. In the Verona area *riso a la pilota* is usually served with a sauce made using chicken livers, pepper and other spices.

———✖———

Serves 4

4 litres / 7 pints water
450 g / 1 lb vialone or arborio rice
a paste of flour and water
salt and pepper

Sauce
30 ml / 1 fl oz olive oil
1 onion, chopped
450 g / 1 lb chicken livers,
trimmed and chopped
1 tsp curry paste (optional)
half a glass of white wine

Fill a large pan with salted water. When it boils, remove from the heat and pour the rice into the centre of the pan; this works best with a funnel so that the rice falls directly to the bottom of the pan and gradually forms a cone that reaches to just above the level of the water. Now place the lid on the pot and – to better conserve the heat – seal it completely using a simple water and flour paste. Leave to one side for 45 minutes. When you remove the lid, the rice will be cooked perfectly because, instead of being bounced about by boiling water, each grain will have rested in its original position while absorbing the moisture from around it.

To make a chicken-liver sauce to accompany the risotto, fry the onion in the olive oil in a frying pan until softened and beginning to turn golden. Add the chicken livers and turn them in the pan juices over a medium heat until sealed all over, then add the curry paste, if using (it softens the bitter taste that livers sometimes have), and the wine and cook until the livers are done: about 5 minutes.

Risi conzi
Creamed rice

Serves 4
400 g / 14 oz vialone rice
1 litre / 1¾ pints water
125 g / 4 oz creamy butter
100 g / 3½ oz medium-mature
Parmesan
salt

This is perhaps the simplest of all Venetian dishes and is closely related to a northern Italian dish that many consider of Lombard origin: *riso in cagnoni* ('dog rice'), which is basically nothing other than boiled rice. The Lombard version, by contrast, uses melted butter flavoured with a sage leaf.

Boil the rice in salted water. When it is *al dente*, drain almost completely and place in a deep bowl with several knobs of creamy butter. Mix vigorously and, when all the butter is melted and mixed evenly, add the finely grated Parmesan.

Risoto con radicchio di Treviso
Radicchio risotto

Serves 4
45 ml / 3 tbsp olive oil
50 g / 2 oz butter
fresh rosemary sprig
1 onion, finely chopped
200 g / 7 oz pancetta,
finely chopped
500 g / 1 lb Treviso radicchio
a glass of white wine
1 litre / 1¾ pints beef stock
300 g / 10 oz arborio
or vialone nano rice
50 g / 2 oz Parmesan

The sunny verdant hills of the Veneto are the home of radicchio, which, initially, was picked wild and has since been transformed into several cultivated varieties. With its aromatic flavour, radicchio lies at the heart of a broad segment of the gastronomy of the Veneto. Traditionally, Treviso radicchio is the real master of all the others, with its triumphant lance-like, curling striped purple leaves. It can now be found in food markets all over the world. Its various relations include the red and variegated radicchio of Castelfranco (the birthplace of Giorgione) – which seems more of a flower than a salad green – as well as other red radicchio varieties from Chioggia, Verona and the Po delta.

—⁂—

Heat the oil and butter with the rosemary sprig to flavour them and then remove the rosemary and fry the finely chopped onion until it is golden. Add the finely chopped pancetta together with about four-fifths of the radicchio, cut into pieces 2 to 3 cm (about 1 in) long. Add the wine and cook on a low heat.

When the radicchio and *pancetta* are cooked and the wine has evaporated, add some beef stock and the rice, which must cook for approximately 15 minutes. The risotto should not be too thick but *all'onda*. Add grated Parmesan, according to taste. The remaining fresh radicchio leaves should be used to decorate each serving.

Risi e verze
Rice and savoy cabbage

Serves 4
60 ml/4 tbsp olive oil
40 g/1½ oz butter
½ onion, finely chopped
400 g/14 oz young Savoy
cabbage, finely chopped (discard
the tougher outer leaves)
250 g/8 oz vialone rice
1 litre/1¾ pints weak beef stock
salt and pepper
50 g/2 oz Parmesan

When autumn temperatures drop and one can feel winter approaching, large Savoy cabbages from the Trento area begin to make their appearance in the markets. Pale green and crinkly, their outer leaves are tightly wrapped together against the cold. Inside is a heart of yellowish leaves that can also be eaten raw as a salad. Savoy cabbage is used as a side-vegetable with strong-flavoured dishes, and in Venice, cabbage risotto is very popular.

———⁂———

Melt the butter and oil in a pan, then add the finely chopped onion and sauté until golden brown. Add the finely chopped cabbage. Add a little water and then place the lid on the pan and leave the cabbage to simmer for a minute or two to soften it.

Add the rice and the diluted beef stock. Add salt and pepper to taste and stir continually, until the rice is *al dente* (10 to 12 minutes). When ready, mix in the grated Parmesan.

Risi e cavoli
Cauliflower risotto

Serves 4
500 g / 1 lb (1 medium-sized)
cauliflower
½ onion, chopped
30 ml / 2 fl oz olive oil
75 g / 3 oz butter
1 garlic clove
1 fresh sage leaf
300 g / 10 oz arborio rice
1 litre / 1¾ pints stock
salt and pepper
50 g / 2 oz Parmesan

This is another wintry dish for when the landscape of the Veneto starts looking like something out of a fairytale, with fog enveloping fields, vineyards and farmhouses, and cauliflowers from the south are in plentiful supply.

Strip away the outer leaves of the cauliflower and break it up into florets. Sauté the chopped onion in the oil and butter with the garlic clove and sage leaf to flavour. Remove the garlic and sage after a couple of minutes and then add the florets and sauté on a low heat for about 15 minutes, until they take on a light golden colour.

Now throw in the rice. When it is well coated in the cooking juices and the grains have become slightly shiny, add the beef stock a little at a time, stirring constantly and making sure that the risotto doesn't ever get too dense. Add the grated Parmesan at the end and, if desired, some pepper.

Riso co' la ua
Risotto with raisins

Serves 4
1 garlic clove
25 g / 1 oz fresh parsley, chopped
60 ml / 4 tbsp olive oil
150 g / 5 oz raisins
350 g / 12 oz arborio rice
salt
600 ml / 1 pint water
50 g / 2 oz mature Parmesan

The use of raisins and sultanas in Venetian cuisine is testimony to the city's long links with Byzantium, where the climate meant there were abundant supplies of dried grapes. In Venice itself sultanas tend to be more popular, because they do not have seeds; a good children's snack. Whereas this risotto used to be common in Venice, a sign of the city's predilection for rather sweet dishes, it is now unusual. Malaga raisins can be used instead, and this dish can also be made with pine nuts, cooking it with milk rather than water.

Sauté the garlic clove and chopped parsley in the olive oil. When the clove is golden brown, remove it and add the raisins. Then add the rice and a little salt and stir well to coat the rice grains. During the cooking, add the boiling water a little at a time, stirring continually. Before serving, mix in a good handful of mature Parmesan.

Risi e bisi nel giorno di San Marco
Pea risotto for the Feast of St Mark

The feast day of Venice's patron saint, St Mark the Evangelist, falls on 25 April. Coming close to Easter and the advent of spring, the feast day became an occasion to celebrate the end of winter and the reawakening of the natural world. Stately celebrations during the glory days of the Venetian Republic traditionally included a magnificent banquet at the Doge's palace, to which the doge invited the procurators of St Mark's, patricians of the Great Council, state bureaucrats, military figures and foreign ambassadors. The menu of exquisite, refined foods and fine wines allowed for some simplicity, with one of the key dishes being the traditional *risi e bisi* – a pea risotto made using the very first peas of spring, renowned for their tenderness and sweetness. The dish is celebrated in these words by the Venetian poet Domenico Varagnolo:

> To bless the holy Spring,
> which makes a garden a paradise,
> all I need is a soup bowl,
> a soup bowl of our own *risi e bisi*…
> There, in hundreds of tiny little globes,
> I savour a tender green jewel of the earth
> scattered in a white sea of tender smiles.

As these lines make clear, a substantial quantity of *bisi* was needed to make the dish, but sometimes too few had ripened in time for the feast. So, to make sure that the traditional *risi e bisi* could be available, the state administrators always arranged a reserve delivery of peas from Liguria, where the winters are shorter and spring arrives much earlier. On behalf of the Serenissima, a transport of pea plants was arranged, during which the plants were nurtured and watered all along the route so that the peas would stay fresh. These caravans of *bisi* travelled halfway across Italy and, in less than a week, arrived at the edge of the lagoon, where they took ship for Venice. By hook or by crook, the Doge had to have his *risi e bisi* for the celebration of St Mark's Day.

This combination of rice and peas became a celebrated feature of Venetian cuisine, so much so that there is a local saying 'Every *riso* has its *biso*' (for every grain of rice, there's a pea). However, to make a good *risi e bisi*, small and tender peas are essential: ones that melt in your mouth when you eat them raw. Furthermore, you must also have a great deal of patience for shelling the tiny peas. Still, the final result is well worth it.

———— ✦ ————

Serves 4

½ onion, chopped
50 g / 2 oz butter
60 ml / 2 fl oz olive oil
50 g / 2 oz salt-cured
pork belly, diced
1 kg / 2¼ lb sweet fresh
garden peas, shelled
30 g / generous 1 oz fresh
parsley, chopped
1 litre / 1¾ pints beef stock
250 g / 8 oz vialone rice
50 g / 2 oz Parmesan
salt and pepper

Sauté the chopped onion in butter and oil in a low-sided pan until it is clear and glossy. Add the diced pork belly and the peas, then the chopped parsley, making sure that the mix does not start to stick. Season with salt and pepper and add a glass of beef stock, over a high heat so that the liquid evaporates quickly. Now add more stock and then the rice, stirring continually to prevent the risotto from sticking to the bottom of the pan. Add further stock during cooking until the rice is ready, making sure that the mixture remains distinctly runny. When ready, stir in the Parmesan.

A further refinement of this dish involves boiling the empty pea pods, then scraping the insides of the shells with a spoon and adding this green paste to the pea mixture. Do this only if the peas are organically produced as otherwise all the pesticide residues will have concentrated here. As peas are particularly susceptible to pests, farmers are inclined to use an abundance of chemical agents.

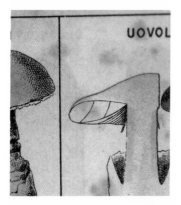

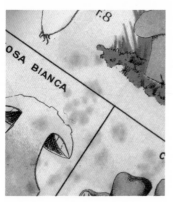

Risoto coi fonghi
Mushroom risotto

A true 'staple' of Venetian cuisine, mushroom risotto comes in two versions, one for autumn and one for winter – that is, with fresh or dried mushrooms.

When the storms of late August – the so-called *burrascate della Madonna* – lower the temperature and heavy rains fall in the alpine foothills, one can start hunting for the glorious wild mushrooms that are renowned throughout northern Italy. Good mushrooms not only grow wild, but they can also be cultivated in caves. In the hills around Vicenza there are numerous caves, quarried first by the Romans and then by those who built the region's famous Palladian villas. They were sometimes used as prisons – the local town of Costozza takes its name from the Latin 'to guard' – but also as wine cellars and even as shelters for the local population in times of war. The political situation in the thirteenth century was very turbulent due to the expansionist programme of Ezzelino III da Romano, feudal lord over lands stretching from Verona to Padua, who set his sights on Costozza as well. To escape this ferocious warlord, thousands fled to the hills, taking shelter in the *Grotto della Guerra* (Cave of War). To no avail: the tyrant pursued the refugees into the caves and slaughtered them. I wonder whether this massacre could be the origin of the extraordinarily fertile soil to be found there. And mushrooms are not the only produce associated with caves. At a luncheon in a villa directly above one of these grottoes, my grandfather was served an unforgettable dish of fried bats!

But to get back to the risotto, this works best when the mushrooms are fresh – best of all are *porcini* (ceps). Never use ones you have picked yourself unless you are confident that you can recognize them as edible or can consult a mycologist. Out of season however, one can achieve perfectly satisfactory results with cultivated mushrooms (white or chestnut) or dried mushrooms, or a mixture of the two.

Serves 4

250 g / 8 oz fresh porcini
or chiodini (honey mushrooms)
which must be market-certified,
if you are not an expert,
or 150 g / 5 oz dried porcini
75 g / 3 oz butter
½ onion, chopped
½ garlic clove, chopped
350 g / 12 oz arborio rice
1 litre / 1¾ pints beef stock
25 g / 1 oz fresh parsley, chopped
salt and pepper
50 g / 2 oz Parmesan

If you are using dried mushrooms: soak them for half an hour in boiling water. Then strain and set aside the soaking liquid. Sauté the mushrooms in half the butter. Then add a little of the soaking water and cook them for a further 30 minutes.

Clean and wash fresh mushrooms and then slice and sauté over a moderate heat in a little butter.

In another fairly large saucepan, sauté the chopped onion and garlic in the rest of the butter and, when it is golden, add the rice. Mix the rice well with the onions and butter before beginning to gradually pour in the boiling stock and stir all the time to make sure nothing sticks as the risotto softens. When the rice is cooked it should still be firm.

Add the mushrooms and chopped parsley to the risotto, check for seasoning and add more salt and/or pepper if necessary. Just before serving, stir in the grated Parmesan.

A still life by the metaphysical painter, Filippo de Pisis, active in the first part of the twentieth century, who lived in Venice for the latter phase of his life.

Risi e sparasi
Asparagus risotto

Serves 4
200 g / 7 oz green asparagus
(tips plus chopped sections
of the thin stalks)
60 ml / 2 fl oz olive oil
60 g / generous 2 oz butter
500 ml / 18 fl oz stock
25 g / 1 oz canned
chopped tomatoes
300 g / 10 oz best-quality
large-grain vialone rice
salt
60 g / generous 2 oz Parmesan

The delicately flavoured asparagus makes a surprisingly tasty rice dish. Use either just the tips of fat asparagus spears or longer sections of the thinner dark green ones; white asparagus shouldn't be used. Though the method is similar to other vegetable risottos, this one must be served in an even more liquid state.

———— ✸ ————

Sauté the asparagus tips in the oil and butter. When they have deepened in colour, add the stock, tomatoes and the rice and cook until the rice is *al dente*. Ladle out the dish while it is still rather liquid and warm and sprinkle with Parmesan.

Risoto de branzin
Sea bass risotto

Serves 4
500 g / 1 lb sea bass,
cleaned and scaled
1 bay leaf
1 garlic clove (optional)
1 shallot, chopped
30 ml / 1 fl oz olive oil
75 g / 3 oz butter,
plus extra to serve
300 g / 10 oz large-grain
vialone rice
fish stock
small glass of dry white wine
salt and a few whole peppercorns

The great Po river flows into the Adriatic forming a massive delta with numerous small serpentine waterways, flanked by reeds and rushes, where the breeze across the waters brings an evocative salty smell from the marshes, stimulating the appetite for one of the Po delta's great delicacies. This is a risotto made with sea bass, a large silver-grey fish that is a fast and voracious swimmer – considered the 'shark' of the valli, where it avidly devours the small fish and fry that are raised in the enclosed waters at the corners of the lagoon.

———— ✸ ————

Cook the sea bass in slightly salted water to which you have added a few peppercorns. When almost cooked (10 to 15 minutes), take from the water and, when cool enough to handle, remove the fish from the bones (in medium-sized chunks). Now place the head, skin and bones back in the water in which the fish was cooked, add the bay leaf and, if desired, a garlic clove. Simmer to make a rather reduced fish stock.

Sauté the chopped shallot in the oil and butter and then add the fragments of sea bass and the rice, pouring in a small amount of fish stock at a time until the rice is cooked. Just before removing from the stove, sprinkle with the white wine, and stir in a knob of butter.

Risoto de mar
Seafood risotto

Serves 6
½ onion, finely chopped
1 garlic clove
60 ml / 2 fl oz olive oil
50 g / 2 oz butter
half a glass of white wine
300 g / 10 oz white bream
300 g / 10 oz scorpion fish
300 g / 10 oz red mullet
1 kg / 2¼ lb mussels
1 kg / 2¼ lb clams
500 g / 1 lb canestrelli (or make up
the quantity with ordinary clams)
400 g / 14 oz arborio rice
about 6 cups of fish stock
(including the leftover liquids from
cooking the fish and mussels)
salt
25 g / 1 oz fresh parsley (optional)

Given the understandable secrecy each cook observes with regard to his or her own seafood risotto, the ingredients can vary – and should vary according to what's best at the market. This version of the tasty dish draws upon the best fish and shellfish available at the Rialto fish market. The *canestrelli* (pectin clams) mentioned below are like small, smooth scallops.

Sauté the finely chopped onion and whole garlic clove in the oil and butter until golden brown; then remove the garlic so as not to offend the more sensitive modern palate. Add the white wine and a little water and simmer the white bream, scorpion fish and red mullet for 30 minutes. Remove the fish when cool enough to handle, take away the head, skin and bones from the fish and break the flesh into medium-sized chunks. Set aside, together with the strained cooking liquid.

In another pan at a high heat, toss the mussels, clams and *canestrelli* for a few minutes so that the shells open. Discard any that do not open. Place the molluscs and any cooking liquid (which is best strained to get rid of any sand) in a pan with a little of the fish stock and the rice, cooking at a lively heat and stirring continually until the rice grains are well coated. Add the remaining fish stock gradually and keep cooking until the rice is *al dente*. Add the chunks of fish flesh near the end of the cooking time. If desired, add finely chopped parsley in the last couple of minutes of cooking.

Risoto col nero
Black cuttlefish risotto

Serves 4
*300 g / 10 oz medium-size,
tender cuttlefish (2 per person)
½ onion, chopped
½ garlic clove
60 ml / 2 fl oz olive oil
50 g / 2 oz butter
25 g / 1 oz fresh parsley
or swiss chard, chopped
350 g / 12 oz arborio rice,
well washed
2 cuttlefish ink sacs
500 ml / 18 fl oz fish stock
salt and pepper*

With its unusual taste and peculiar, intense colour, no self-respecting – that is, superstitious – Neapolitan would dream of eating a dish of jet black risotto, but it is a great favourite with Venetians, who are attracted rather than deterred by its flavour and appearance.

———— ∞ ————

Remove the eyes, bones and stomachs of the cuttlefish but set aside the ink sac, being very careful not to burst it (you do not want to spray black ink all over the kitchen). Skin the body and tentacles under running cold water and then cut the cuttlefish into regular strips or pieces.

Now sauté the chopped onion and half a garlic clove (if desired) in oil and butter until it turns a good golden colour, then remove the garlic, add the cuttlefish and cook at a moderate heat for a few minutes, adding salt and pepper and the finely chopped parsley or chard. Stir continually so the cuttlefish does not stick to the bottom of the pan and cook for 30 minutes.

Now add the rice and the ink sacs. As the liquid is gradually absorbed, gradually add more boiling stock or hot water until the rice is perfectly cooked. Serve *risotto nero* on white or cream-coloured plates, to accentuate its visual impact. Check the seasoning before serving but, as with many fish risottos, this is better without Parmesan.

This risotto can also be made with smaller, baby cuttlefish and without their ink sacs. Clean thoroughly and cook the baby cuttlefish as described above, but without cutting them into pieces and sprinkle generously with white Frascati or Marsala. After half an hour, add the rice and continue to cook as described above with hot water or stock.

Ivano, one of our neighbours, finds it easy to smile in between his many tasks as a fisherman.

Risoto de scampi
Scampi risotto

Serves 4
400 g / 14 oz medium-size scampi,
shelled
100 g / 3½ oz butter
25 g / 1 oz fresh parsley, chopped
½ onion, finely chopped
400 g / 14 oz arborio rice,
well washed
1 litre / 1¾ pints fish stock
salt and pepper

Though originally native to the seas of northern Europe, and usually identified as 'Norwegian shrimp', scampi have become assimilated into Venetian cuisine thanks to their delicate taste – rather similar to that of lobster. As we will see later, there are various Venetian ways of preparing scampi: grilled, fried, boiled (and served with mayonnaise). However, my favourite recipe involving scampi is a risotto that is so good it is very difficult to resist a second helping. Tastier than prawns and shrimp, the scampi must be very fresh; otherwise, when cooked, they become rather bitter. As with oysters, they should be eaten when the month has 'r' in its name. But that seems to be a tradition honoured more in the breach than the observance: throughout the year, fine, plump, brightly coloured scampi are one of the boasts of the Rialto fish market.

Sauté the scampi with a little butter, parsley, salt and pepper and then set them aside, to be added to the risotto only when the rice is cooked.

Meanwhile, prepare the rice separately in the usual way: sauté the onion in the rest of the butter; add the rice, gradually pour in small quantities of stock. When the rice is almost ready, check for salt and throw in the scampi, stirring vigorously for a minute or so. Some cooks use beef bone marrow instead of butter, and, when the rice is still cooking, throw in a generous handful of grated Parmesan (even though the use of cheese in fish dishes is not usual).

Risoto de peoci
Mussel risotto

Serves 4
2 kg / 4½ lb quite large mussels
60 ml / 2 fl oz olive oil
½ onion, chopped
1 garlic clove
350 g / 12 oz arborio rice
25 g / 1 oz fresh parsley, chopped
4 cups fish or weak meat stock
salt and pepper

To other Italians, the Venetian name for mussels – '*peoci*' – comes as rather a shock, given that it might be misunderstood as the word for 'louse'. Even the Italian word, *cozze*, has negative connotations – it is the term used to describe a girl of less-than-average beauty! The local mussels are smaller than those found on the Ionian and Tyrrhenian coasts, but they seem to acquire a more substantial taste where the salty and lazy waters of the Adriatic meet the expanse of the lagoon; and that's not just my (patriotic) opinion, but demonstrated by the enormous quantities of these mussels that are exported from Venice every day. Mussel populations have developed in rich numbers all around the Venice lagoon and especially at the inlets and along the Lido shores. Clinging on to rocks, wooden piles along the navigation channels, boat moorings, ropes, concrete jetties and sea walls, mussels form what look like bunches of black bananas. The centre for mussel harvesting is Malamocco, which, in the eighth century, was briefly the seat of ducal power.

───※───

Clean the downy external part that enables the mussel to cling to surfaces, scrub away sand and dirt from the dark ebony shells using a metal brush. Then wash them in very salty water (unless buckets of seawater are available).

Place the mussels in a large pan over a high heat so that the shells open and release their liquids. After 5 minutes remove from the stove and discard all unopened shells. Strain any residual sand from the cooking liquid. Set aside 20 or so of the largest and plumpest mussels, still in their shells, to garnish the dish when served. Remove the remaining mussels from their shells.

Sauté the onion in the olive oil with the whole garlic clove. When the onion is golden, remove the garlic clove and stir in the rice over a moderate heat. Add the mussel liquid gradually and then use boiling-hot fish stock; if you do not have any, use weak meat stock or even plain boiling water. When the rice is almost cooked, add the mussels and the chopped parsley and cook for a couple of minutes. Season with salt and pepper and serve, using the mussels that have been set aside to decorate.

A version of this risotto with clams is prepared in a similar way. Once the clams have opened, strain their cooking liquid to remove residual sand; then add the clams and cooking liquid to the risotto pan, with the rice and cook all the ingredients together.

Risoto de schie
Grey-shrimp risotto

Serves 4

1 kg / 2¼ lb schie or small shrimps
25 g / 1 oz fresh parsley, chopped
1 garlic clove
60 ml / 2 fl oz extra virgin olive oil
50 g / 2 oz butter
350 g / 12 oz vialone
or arborio rice
1 litre / 1¾ pints light beef stock
salt

This local variety of small grey shrimp is native to the lagoon and has a special distinctive flavour. Usually, *schie* are boiled, shelled and then served as an antipasto with oil and lemon juice; or lightly fried in oil with parsley and garlic. They taste wonderful as an antipasto either way; but if boiled you have to use your hands to remove all the shells and it is a laborious process. The advantage of deep-frying them instead is that the end result is crisp and tasty and can be eaten whole, shell and all. You can also make a risotto with them.

───⚬⚬⚬───

Boil the *schie* in unsalted water for a few minutes, until a solid foam forms on the surface. Drain and crush the shrimps in a mortar, then pass through a cloth or fine sieve.

Sauté the parsley and garlic clove in the oil and butter and, when this is golden, remove the garlic and add the puréed *schie*, the rice and some of the light beef stock. Cook on a moderate heat, stirring continually and adding stock as required until the rice is ready. This risotto, in contrast to the other versions, should be dense and rather thick.

Cavroman risoto
Lamb risotto

Serves 4

50 g / 2 oz butter
1 onion, finely chopped
500 g / 1 lb older lamb on the bone,
preferably shoulder
250 g / 8 oz tomatoes, skinned,
seeded and chopped
1 cinnamon stick
300 g / 10 oz arborio rice,
well washed
1 litre / 1¾ pints beef stock
50 g / 2 oz mature Parmesan
salt

'Cavroman' is a Venetian term for 'stew'; perhaps this recipe descends from Venice's links with Dalmatia and Albania and the widespread use of mutton. Whatever the origin, it is very tasty and filling, so can be served without a second course.

───⚬⚬⚬───

Sauté the finely chopped onion in the butter and, when it is light gold, add the pieces of lamb on the bone – a shoulder cut works best because the meat is especially tender and plump. Cook on a moderately high heat until browned, then add the skinned and seeded chopped tomatoes, a pinch of salt and a cinnamon stick and cook for a long time on low heat (1½ to 2 hours, depending on the size of the lamb pieces).

When the lamb is soft but not yet falling off the bone, remove it from the pan and bone it with a sharp knife. Return to the pan and add the rice. Pour in some stock and cook, adding more stock as required; when the rice is *al dente* add the grated mature Parmesan. Enjoy with a full-bodied, strong red wine.

Risi e luganegha
Sausage risotto

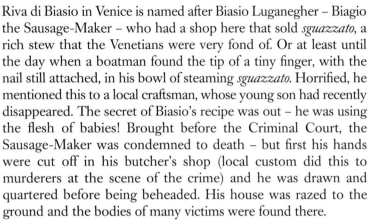

Serves 4
6 best-quality sausages
30 ml / 1 fl oz olive oil
60 g / generous 2 oz butter,
plus extra to serve
½ white onion, finely sliced
350 g / 12 oz arborio rice
half a glass of dry white wine
1 litre / 1¾ pints beef stock
75 g / 3 oz Parmesan,
plus extra to serve
salt

Riva di Biasio in Venice is named after Biasio Luganegher – Biagio the Sausage-Maker – who had a shop here that sold *sguazzato*, a rich stew that the Venetians were very fond of. Or at least until the day when a boatman found the tip of a tiny finger, with the nail still attached, in his bowl of steaming *sguazzato*. Horrified, he mentioned this to a local craftsman, whose young son had recently disappeared. The secret of Biasio's recipe was out – he was using the flesh of babies! Brought before the Criminal Court, the Sausage-Maker was condemned to death – but first his hands were cut off in his butcher's shop (local custom did this to murderers at the scene of the crime) and he was drawn and quartered before being beheaded. His house was razed to the ground and the bodies of many victims were found there.

If you still have an appetite after this little story, this is a particularly tasty risotto, based on the myriad special varieties of sausage available in the town of Treviso especially and indeed throughout Italy (some more heavily flavoured with herbs than others). However, the *luganegha* used in risotto are not the same sort of sausages you would use for a second course; the choice of meats is different, as is the *dosa*, the secret mix of herbs and spices within it. We use short fat sausages made expressly by the local butcher for risotto; they are 100-per cent pork, without any seasonings, but you can use any best-quality sausage.

— ∞ —

Cook the *luganeghe* in an open pan with the oil, butter and the finely sliced white onion. Add very little salt, if any, since the sausage will be salty. Cook at a moderate heat and, when the onion is golden brown, halve and set aside two sausages and cut the others into small pieces. Return these to the pan and add the rice. Mix thoroughly for a minute or so, making sure that the sautéed onion and sausage blend well with the rice. Add half a glass of white wine and cook, stirring frequently. When the wine has been absorbed, add the beef stock, stirring it in a little at a time and making sure that the rice does not stick to the bottom of the pan.

When the rice is ready – it must be very smooth – remove from the stove, adding a knob of butter and a generous handful of the grated Parmesan. Stir in energetically. Bring the risotto to the table already served in bowls, with each portion topped by one of the reserved half-sausages – and further grated Parmesan.

Risi e figadini
Rice and chicken livers

Serves 4
6 chicken livers
75 g / 3 oz butter,
plus extra to serve
3 fresh sage leaves
1 litre / 1¾ pints chicken stock
1–2 tbsp canned chopped tomatoes
½ onion, chopped
1 carrot, chopped
1 celery stick, chopped
30 ml / 1 fl oz olive oil
300 g / 10 oz large-grain
vialone rice
75 g / 3 oz Parmesan
salt

You can say what you like about the innovations in the way food is now distributed, delivered and sold, but there is one unmistakable advantage to it: you can buy as many chicken livers as you need without having the chicken itself – so you are free to make chicken-liver risotto without being obliged to have a chicken dish as your main course as well.

———— ∞ ————

Wash the livers and chop them into pieces, then sauté lightly in half the butter, with the sage leaves. Cook for just a few minutes and add a pinch of salt.

Colour the stock with a little of the canned chopped tomatoes and bring to the boil.

In a third pan, sauté the chopped onion, carrot and celery in the oil and remaining butter; then add the rice. Cook, adding ladle upon ladle of stock as necessary and stirring frequently. Halfway through the cooking, add the livers with their cooking juice. When the rice is *al dente*, stir in a knob of butter and plenty of grated Parmesan. Serve immediately.

Risoto co le secole
Beef risotto

Serves 4
300 g / 10 oz sècole or lean,
high-quality braising steak
75 ml / 2½ fl oz olive oil
75 g / 3 oz butter
½ onion, chopped
1 celery stick, chopped (optional)
1 carrot, chopped (optional)
300 g / 10 oz vialone rice
1 litre / 1¾ pints beef stock
50 g / 2 oz very mature Parmesan
salt and pepper

This is best made with the pieces of beef that are called '*secole*' in Venetian: small fragments of the very tender and tasty meat that is found clinging to the vertebrae of the animal. So unless you are more than a good client – a good friend – of the butcher, you will have to pass on this particular titbit and buy some braising steak instead.

———— ∞ ————

Sauté the beef fragments (or chopped steak) in the oil and butter with the chopped onion, celery and carrot; add salt and pepper if desired and leave to cook slowly for a couple of hours.

When the *secole* are tender, add the rice and then begin to add beef stock as required. Remember this should be a very liquid risotto. Before serving, mix in 2 good handfuls of very mature Parmesan.

Risoto all'isolana
Veal and pork risotto

Serves 4
150 g / 5 oz butter
300 g / 10 oz lean,
boneless veal, diced
100 g / 3½ oz lean,
boneless pork, diced
fresh rosemary sprig
1 litre / 1¾ pints meat stock
600 g / 1¼ lb vialone rice
150 g / 5 oz good-quality Parmesan
salt, pepper and ground cinnamon

The lands between Verona and Mantua have produced not only *riso a la pilota,* but also this recipe, which makes the most of the very special characteristics of short-grain *vialone* rice, a local speciality. The name comes from *Isola della Scala,* where recently a competition was held to find the most authentic recipe for this dish. There was much debate over whether it should be made using *tastasal* (pork loin) or veal: in the following recipe, I have gone with those who championed a mix of pork and veal!

Using about half the melted butter, sauté the diced lean veal and pork together with a little cinnamon, a small pinch of pepper, salt and the sprig of rosemary (remove when the cooking is finished). Then add a little meat stock and cook gently, making sure that the meat is golden rather than dark brown. Continue to cook while preparing the rice.

Bring the rest of the stock to the boil and add the rice. When it is about three-quarters cooked, add half the meat sauce and a little of the grated cheese, mixed with more cinnamon and the remaining (melted) butter. Mix gently, turning over the contents in the pan. When the rice is completely cooked, add the rest of the meat, with more grated Parmesan, and mix well but not too vigorously.

Reassuring meat wrapping used by our favourite butcher printed with the rhetorical question: 'conosci quello che mangi?' and 'Conosci chi ti vende quello che mangi?' (Do you know what you're eating?' and 'Do you know who sells you what you eat?').

Risoto a la sbiraglia
Police patrol's chicken risotto

This dish is known as 'Police patrol's chicken risotto' in a derogatory reference to the policeman's profession, although the dish is tasty and one of the boasts of Venetian cuisine. The origin of the name is uncertain; perhaps it refers to a deplorable habit of cops on patrol in the countryside, who were not above making off with a couple of chickens to prepare this nourishing dish and warm themselves up during the long winter nights on duty. The name might also refer to the fact that in the mid-eighteenth century, when the power of the *Serenissima Repubblica* was waning, the Veneto became an area of transition between conflicting states and was frequently raided by foreign armies; it is possible that famished French or Austrian soldiers in the region allowed themselves a bit of poaching. Known in other parts of Italy as '*risoto alla cacciatora*' ('hunter's risotto'), this is a substantial dish that makes a second course unnecessary. Here is one of the less complicated versions of the dish; although a certain care is needed in the final stages.

Commestibili esentati

Serves 4
½ onion, finely chopped
75 g / 3 oz butter
500 g / 1 lb tender young chicken
(poussin or spring chicken) pieces,
chopped into small pieces
1 litre / 1¾ pints beef stock
350 g / 12 oz vialone rice
75 g / 3 oz Parmesan
salt and pepper

Sauté the finely chopped onion in most of the butter and, when it has become light golden, add the chicken. Add salt and pepper and then mix in another cube of butter while it browns over a medium heat. When the chicken is well browned, after 12 to 15 minutes, add some of the beef stock (or boiling water), together with the rice. Stirring continually, add stock as required and, when the dish is nearly done, add a generous handful of moderately mature Parmesan, to give flavour and bind the risotto together.

Here's another version that is even more hearty, but all the ingredients aren't necessarily found in a typical farmyard! First boil the chicken, together with 500 g / 1 lb of stewing beef, a white onion, a ripe tomato, a celery stick and two young carrots (all chopped). To facilitate the cooking process, ensure that the water in the pot covers the chicken. When the meat is ready and falling away from the bone, remove the chicken from the pan and bone it using a sharp knife. Take half of the chicken and chop the meat into medium-sized pieces; the other half of the chicken can be used later for a galantine.

Meanwhile, leave the broth left over from cooking the chicken to simmer and reduce with just the beef and vegetables in it. Then set aside the beef and discard the vegetables. Use the broth to cook the risotto.

Add the chicken pieces to the sautéed onion (as per the previous recipe). Half a glass of strong white wine or a shot of cognac is optional at this stage, while the chicken browns and before adding the rice and the beef broth, a little at a time. Take care to remove the surface scum and lumps of chicken fat that emerge during cooking.

For a lighter version of the dish, use boiling water in the latter phase of cooking. Add a good quantity of grated Parmesan 2 or 3 minutes before you remove from the heat and stir in. Serve the risotto in shallow bowls so that it does not lump together and cools quite quickly. If the rice stays hot too long, it not only burns your tongue when you eat it but also continues to cook on the plate, becoming soggy.

Opposite: *Giovanni Grevembroch produced a huge number of watercolours depicting the details of eighteenth-century life and customs of Venice. This is how the poultry sellers of the day brought their produce to town.*

Risoto con le quagie
Quail risotto

Serves 4
4 oven-ready quail
4 slices of lardo *(cured pork fat)*
or pancetta
½ onion, finely chopped
60 ml / 2 fl oz olive oil
50 g / 2 oz butter
fresh rosemary sprig
fresh sage leaf
half a glass of dry white wine
1 litre / 1¾ pints stock
350 g / 12 oz arborio rice,
well washed
salt and pepper
50 g / 2 oz Parmesan

Sometimes the advantages of modern life clearly outweigh its drawbacks. For example the ease with which we can now enjoy the fine, delicate flavour of quail thanks to the huge quail farms in Japan and air freighting.

———— ✖✖✖ ————

If necessary, burn off any remnants of feathers from the birds by holding over a naked flame and set aside their livers and hearts for later use, if you have them. Season the quail, wrap each one in a slice of *lardo* or *pancetta* (not too thick) and tie in place with butchers' string. *Lardo* is similar to cured fatback bacon and must not be confused with lard.

Sauté the finely chopped onion in a heatproof casserole with the oil and butter – plus some rosemary and one sage leaf to enhance the flavour. When the onion is golden brown, remove the sage and rosemary and add half a glass of dry white wine and the salted and peppered quails (together with their livers and hearts). Turn the quails regularly, so that they cook throughout and brown evenly (30 minutes or so).

Take the casserole from the heat, remove the quail and set aside to cool. When you can handle them, take the meat from the bones (keeping the breasts whole). Set the breasts aside in a warm place with a little of the juice from the pot to keep them moist.

Return the casserole with the remaining cooking liquid to the stove and add the pieces of quail meat and a little stock. Add the rice, stirring well, and continue to cook, gradually adding the rest of the stock and stirring frequently until the rice is *al dente*. Add the grated Parmesan at the end.

To serve, place a quail breast (still warm) on top of each serving of the risotto, together with some of the cooking juices.

Some people prefer to cook the quails separately in the oven for 15 minutes, and then place them whole on each plate of risotto. But I think it is unfair to make one's guests struggle with the small quails' bones while the rice is getting cold. Anyway, the rice cooked with bits of quail meat and part of the juice from the bird is much tastier.

The fork

N MAY of the year 1000, Doge Pietro Orseolo II inflicted a great defeat upon the Narentan pirates who infested the waters of the Adriatic. This victory was commemorated every year after that with a state banquet on Ascension Day, for which occasion an eighteenth-century historian records the following articles of silverware being removed from the strongboxes of the city Mint: 757 round plates, 63 serving dishes, 70 bowls, 25 soup dishes and fishplates, 180 salad bowls, 20 ice buckets, 12 coffee-pots and just 300 sets of cutlery. The relatively low number of eating tools is due to the fact that at the time it was customary for most guests to bring their own knives and forks. The practical advantages of this are borne out by the fact that ambassadors and important personages were served at table by their own attendants, who brought with them a 'canteen' that contained cutlery and drinking vessels (thus cutting down the risk of illustrious guests being poisoned).

The use of table forks began in Venice much earlier than in other European countries. In fact, this particular instrument of tableware appears to have been introduced around the year 1000, when Maria, niece of the Byzantine emperor Constantine VIII, used a double-pronged gold fork at the banquet celebrating her betrothal to Giovanni Orseolo, the 19-year-old son of Doge, Pietro Orseolo II. Other historians claim that the use of the fork began about 70 years later and credit it to the wife of Doge Domenico Silvio.

The actual origin of the fork is also difficult to determine, though there is no doubt that it dates back to antiquity. Certainly, primitive peoples had more basic etiquette than ours and the fork would have been superfluous at the great banquets of Homer's day, in which fruit and vegetables played a large part.

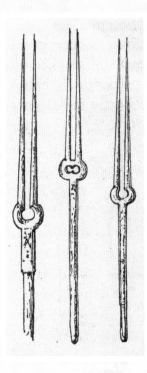

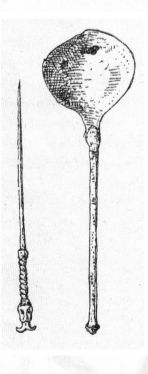

In Rome, the end of the Republic and the advent of the Empire brought with it a taste for ostentatious display. Gone were the days when the consul Fabritius sat by his fire to cook himself some beets. The simple lifestyle of the past gave way to widespread indulgence in luxury and excess. The aim now was to dazzle guests with a display of expensive and rare tableware in gold and silver. These pieces might include *murrhine* glass drinking vessels worth millions of *sestertii*, or *ligulae*, implements whose very name suggests they were tongue-shaped. (The form may also have been inspired by the old Roman sword which, in its turn, had been modelled on the shape of a bay leaf and fixed to the end of a shaft of wood.)

Then with the fall of the Empire in the West and the beginning of the barbarian invasions, many civilized practices – including the use of the fork – went into decline. The aristocracy disappeared, as did the taste for refined living. For many centuries to come, people would entirely forget about the refined tableware that had been used by the Roman patricians. In the Empire of the East, however, things were different, and the use of such luxury items continued.

The Crusades brought the nobility of Italy and other European countries into renewed contact with this world of the East; and when the crusaders returned home, they took with them the custom of eating with the *ligula* or fork. The flourishing of arts, literature and trade heralded further lifestyle refinement. Utensils were still to be found only rarely, and never outside the homes of the rich. Most people continued to eat with their fingers and – what is even more off-putting for us – from the same plate, which might perhaps be shared by up to four or five guests.

Types of fork were definitely in use in fifteenth-century Florence, as shown by Sandro Botticelli's painting of the wedding of *Nastagio degli Onesti*, which was commissioned by Lorenzo de' Medici – Lorenzo the Magnificent – as a wedding gift for the Pucci family. One member of that family, Antonio, is known to have commented that he could tolerate the fact that, before drinking from a glass, people simply wiped their lips on the back of their hand but he certainly could not tolerate those who ate in a slovenly manner or shared their plate with several others. If people at the time had realized that the frequent epidemics were due not to the malign influence of the stars or the ominous passage of comets, but rather to matters of hygiene, there is

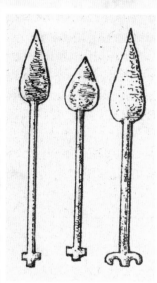

little doubt that a far greater number would have found this sharing of plates unacceptable. The introduction of individual plates, as well as forks, would have been rather more effective than the procedures which, since the days of Pythagoras and Hippocrates, philosophers and physicians had proposed as ways of avoiding contagion.

The delight in the refined and the *recherché* was characteristic of a later age, when gentlemen frequented learned academies, sported massive wigs and reflected a taste for the effete, the mannered and the precious. Now, the humble fork, which generations had done without, became an indispensable item of tableware, establishing itself first in Italy then in other countries of western Europe.

Travelling in Italy in the early seventeenth century, an English servant recorded that throughout the peninsula he came across the custom of using a small fork, something that he had never encountered in any other part of Christendom. The implement had also been adopted by a large number of the foreigners living in Italy. The forks of the period were mostly iron or steel; but some were in silver, used only by gentlemen. Having praised the use of the fork to his fellow-countrymen and introduced them to its use, the Englishman earned himself the nickname of *Furcifer* (bearer of the fork).

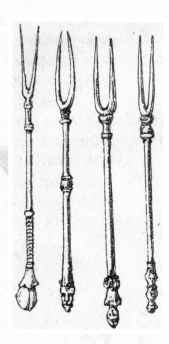

When Catherine de' Medici moved to the French court, she took with her the Florentine custom of using forks. The practice then established itself at the court of Charles V, who amassed a notable collection of forks. In Paris itself, the fork became one of the local oddities at the inn *Le Tour d'Argent*, where Henri III of Valois – son of Catherine de Medici – used a fork for the first time. Henri III was in Poland when his brother Charles IX died and he became king of France. His rather lackadaisical return to take up his crown brought him to Rovigo in the southern Veneto, where one of the most noble families provided him with magnificent hospitality at the Palazzo di Roncade (designed by Michele Sanmicheli). In recognition, Henri III knighted Antonio Roncade and authorized him to add the white cross of the Valois to his family arms. The cutlery used by the king is still jealously conserved at the Accademia dei Concordi.

For some time, the fork was seen as a mere extravagance; even the Sun King, Louis XIV, himself preferred to use his fingers, and was only persuaded to accept forks when his court moved to the magnificence of Versailles in 1684.

Caution regarding use of the humble fork had long been voiced by the Church and clergy. The austere St Peter Damian may have believed in the apparition of the dead and his own ability to return to earth nine centuries after his own death; he may also have preached that self-flagellation and fasting were the ways to attain spiritual perfection; and may even have carved wooden spoons as a hobby – but he nevertheless considered the fork to be an invention of the Devil. This fervent ascetic went so far as to claim that it posed a threat to one's eternal salvation and exhorted one and all to shun the diabolical implement. Such urgency was superfluous because in those days (1007–1072) there were few who were willing to follow the example of the Byzantine princess who had recently introduced Venice to the use of the fork. Most people considered the implement to be unnecessary and effete, finding it much more convenient to use the five fingers with which Mother Nature had supplied each hand. Meanwhile, things were no better in Africa, as one can see from this comment written by my ancestor, the navigator Alvise da Mosto, whose record of his 1457 navigation along the coast of Africa contains the following observations:

> Of the manner of life and eating in Budomel. As for the manner of living – that is, of eating – it is governed as I described above regarding the King of Sanega, whose wives every day send him many arrays of foods one by one. This style of life is followed by all the Negro lords and their men of account, for whom the womenfolk do the shopping; and they eat on the floor, bestially and without any manners. And no one eats with these Negro lords, except for the Moors who read them the Law and one or two of their principal Negroes. All the lesser folk eat together in tens or twelves; they place a basket of food in the middle and all put their hands therein. They eat a little at a time, but they eat frequently: four or five times a day.

Religious superstitions continued to put up strenuous resistance to progress, including the introduction of the fork, and it was only in the eighteenth century that the ecclesiastical authorities re-examined the debate regarding this infernal implement, the use of which was still forbidden within the walls of monasteries and convents. In reality, it was only during the course of that century that the fork became the everyday item of tableware that it is today.

Pasta, gnocchi & soups

Pasta, gnocchi & soups

Italians are particularly orderly in the way that they eat; most meals are a sequence of clear-cut courses. We even say '*parla come mangi*' ('speak like you eat') when we think someone is being too pretentious or talking hot air and should be more down-to-earth. Every Italian can be expected to eat methodically and sensibly. One of the bastions of a square meal, however modest, is the *primo piatto (*first course). Following on from risottos, this section includes many other first-course staples: pasta dishes (usually made from wheat flour, with and without fresh eggs), gnocchi (from potatoes) and various soups. Moreover, a few of the dishes described can be served as *piatti unici*, that is, complete meals, even by Italian standards.

The close links with the Near East have left their traces in Venetian cuisine – for example, the use of pine nuts and sultanas in the preparation of fish '*in saòr*' (marinated) with vinegar and onions. However, the most obvious influence is the use of spices, which, in the most vibrant stage of Venice's history, was a veritable status symbol. Byzantium was the source of the legendary *brodo nero* (black soup), a lethally rich stew of 'high' game birds cooked with cured pork fat, cloves, sugar, vanilla, poppy seeds, ginger, cinnamon, pepper, sultanas, almonds and pistachios. It is no coincidence that a number of seventeenth-century reports regarding the demise of certain noblemen give the cause of death as 'indigestion'!

It was another link with the East that enabled Venice to stake its claim as the origin of that Italian staple, pasta. Since this dish is so important in Italian cuisine it was perhaps inevitable that, among others, the Venice region should vie for the honour of being the first to have introduced it. Venice has advanced claims that pasta had been brought to Italy from Cathay by Marco Polo. According to that traveller's *Milione* – so called because contemporaries claimed his accounts of experiences in the East contained a million tall stories – the Chinese had been making pasta for centuries, using either rice or sago flour. According to Marco Polo, the Chinese 'national dish' had long been pasta served with a sort of chicken stew, and there is no denying that the rather dark, thick pasta that he describes is fairly similar to the Venetian *bigoli*.

Although flattering to Venice, it is hard to deny that pasta was also being used in Italy a long time before Marco Polo. According to reputable scholars, it originated in Sicily, where durum wheat – the essential ingredient – had been grown since ancient times;

the Sicilian term *maccarruni* figures in popular expressions that predate the Middle Ages, such as '*cascari lu maccarruni 'nta lu furmaggiò* – literally, 'the macaroni falls into the sauce', or in other words, have some pasta with your sauce rather than vice versa! Boccaccio's *Decameron*, written in the fourteenth century, is a true celebration of the pleasures of life; and along with the amorous adventures and misadventures that the writer delights in, there is mention of succulent macaroni rolling down the gentle slopes of a mountain of grated cheese.

In the Veneto, women produced not only *bigoli* – made using a *bigolaro*, a piston-like contraption that forced the pasta out through a sort of sieve – but also hand-mixed egg pasta, which was first kneaded, and then worked using a special wooden spoon (the *mescola de le lasagne*) and finally rolled out on a wooden board. These sheets were cut into various forms (*tajadele*, *lasagne*, *lasagnete* or *paparele*) that were hung to dry on special rods; the off-cuts or the bits that went wrong were used in soups. In Venice, the traditional *bigoli in salsa* was eaten at Lent and in the run up to other religious festivities, whilst the very similar *bigoli con la sardela* was all one ate for dinner on Christmas Eve in Verona.

Up until relatively recently, bread and pasta were a rarity in the kitchens and dining rooms of this region, especially following the First World War when there was abject poverty due to the devastation of much of the area by fighting around the Piave river. Pasta was considered a treat for religious and family celebrations. The most exceptional treat was egg pasta because eggs laid by the farmyard hens were generally reserved for use as 'currency' in paying for the daily or weekly shopping. Inevitably, supplies of flour dwindled to almost nothing in the period immediately before the new harvest was gathered and during those weeks there was obviously very little bread and pasta, so people survived on polenta with vegetables (plus a little butter and cheese).

The *arte* (professional guild) of pasta-makers was founded rather late in Venice, in 1638, but from then to the end of the Republic and beyond the *Arte dei lasagneri et fabbricatori si de menueli come in altri pastumi* (The Guild of the Makers of Lasagne and Other Pastas) continued to grow, with new shops being opened all the time. The *lasagneri* not only sold pasta but also flour for use by those who wanted home-made pasta or pastries. There were also a number of *fritoleri*, who sold lasagne and macaroni dishes made using oil, butter and, sometimes, lard but the usual mix in Venice was oil and butter, with lard being used only rarely. Pasta came in various types: *subioti* (small macaroni), *lasagne* and *bigoli* (thick, wholewheat spaghetti). Shorter, more coarse-cut types of pasta were used in the more rustic dish of *pasta e fagioli*.

One of the traditional dishes in the Veneto, *pasta e fagioli*, is also common in the rest of Italy give or take the inevitable regional

Opposite: *Rejoicing in the wheat harvest in the 1930s, somewhere in the Veneto.*

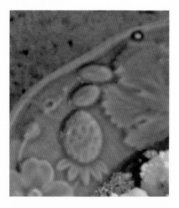

variations. Prepared with slight variations even within the Veneto region, this has always been considered a humble dish and was judged according to its density. For peasants, boatmen, gondoliers and others whose working day had perhaps started at dawn it was a real treat to see your spoon 'stand up' in the dense soup of beans and pasta – an indication that the dish could satisfy the hungriest of men. In Venice and Chioggia, for example, the soup is made particularly thick by forcing some of the cooked beans through a sieve and leaving some whole; the pasta used is generally *linguette*, *subiotini* or *tirache* and must never be egg pasta. Around Padua, on the other hand, the dish is almost always made with egg-pasta tagliatelle, whilst in Treviso the recipe is similar to that in Venice but is thickened using one or two potatoes (in the countryside the soup is also served over raw radicchio dressed with oil, vinegar and pepper). When you move farther inland, towards Vicenza and Verona, *pasta e fasioi* tends to become thinner, almost a bean soup with very little pasta added (*tagliatelline*, *linguette* or dark *bigoli*). And up towards Belluno and Feltre in the foothills of the Dolomites – the source of *lamon* and Santa Giustina beans – the dish is made with rice instead of pasta.

As for the origin of the recipe, it dates back at least a couple of hundred years, when the large and tasty beans introduced from the Americas began to displace the smaller, black-marked beans then being grown in Europe. The newcomer was immediately appreciated by the peasants of the Veneto and cheap but highly nutritious beans – together with polenta – became the staple diet of generations.

Some special ways of preparing beans came about by accident or due to force of circumstances. For example, one version of bean soup is known as '*zuppa col brusin*' (burned soup) and is due to the fact that it had to be cooked in the pot for hours and hours. The dish was eaten by those who gathered the reeds that were then bound into bundles to line the ceilings of buildings throughout the Veneto. These workers set off very early in the morning in their flat-bottomed boats to cut reeds in the tributaries of the Po that flow into the lagoon or, further south, directly into the Adriatic. As the work also involved the women of the house, there was no one to prepare food during the day, so the beans and rice were left to soak overnight in a pan of water and then placed on the embers of a riverside fire just before the workers set off. Enclosed by stones, these embers would continue to glow for hours on end and when the reed-cutters came back the soup was cooked. Given the fact that no one was there to stir them, the beans burnt slightly, forming a sort of crust on the bottom of the pan, which gave the dish its distinctive flavour of *brusin*.

Gnocchi Padovani
Padua-style gnocchi

Serves 4
500 g / 1 lb potatoes
500 g / 1 lb Italian 00 grade flour
100 g / 3½ oz polenta
50 g / 2 oz fresh breadcrumbs
3 eggs, beaten
150 g / 5 oz butter, melted
salt
400 ml / 14 fl oz water

Padua has one very special recipe for gnocchi, which is more complicated than usual but does make this traditional first course seem quite out of the ordinary.

⎯⎯⎯ ⨳ ⎯⎯⎯

Steam and peel the potatoes as described in *Gnocchi Veronesi*.

Mix equal parts of flour and steamed potato with the polenta, breadcrumbs, salt, beaten eggs and melted butter. Mix very carefully to make sure the ingredients come together evenly into a fairly solid paste. After rolling the mix into long 'fingers', cut short lengths and flatten them into the typical gnocchi form with your fingertip against the prongs of a fork.

Cook in boiling water, removing each *gnoccho* with a slotted spoon as it floats to the surface. Serve with butter and grated Parmesan or a meat *ragù* or tomato sauce.

Pestariei
Gnocchi from the Dolomites

Serves 4
250 g / 8 oz Italian 00 grade flour
400 ml / 14 fl oz water
400 ml / 14 fl oz milk
salt

From the Cadore area, *pestariei* are a first course of almost Franciscan simplicity, being a sort of gnocchi made using flour and milk.

⎯⎯⎯ ⨳ ⎯⎯⎯

Mix the white flour with a little water and break up the dough to form small gnocchi, shaping them using your hands. Cook in a salted mix that is half milk and half water. As they rise to the surface, remove them from the pan with a slotted spoon. Serve hot, in bowls.

Canederli
Salami gnocchi

Serves 4

500 g / 1 lb dry bread, cut up
bowl of milk
100 g / 3½ oz smoked pancetta,
finely chopped
100 g / 3½ oz salami,
finely chopped
a little finely chopped fresh parsley,
chives or onion
grated nutmeg
Italian 00 grade flour
4 eggs
salt
1 litre / 1¾ pints beef stock

The quality of the pork fat that the family pig would yield only became apparent when the slaughtered animal was cut open. The thickness of the layer of fat that was then revealed and brought either broad smiles or expressions of glum disappointment: if the layer was thin, obviously, the cured pork fat would not last as long – a serious blow for a family that, in certain periods of the year, had nothing but *lardo* to eat with polenta.

Naturally, a part of the animal that was even more appreciated than the *lardo* was the *pancetta*, cured either flat or in rolls. The slivers of salted meat running through the fat made this a real treat, and *pancetta* is simply delicious, sliced and eaten between two thick chunks of bread.

One typical dish of the Cadore area is *canederli*, a sort of gnocchi whose strong flavour comes from the salami and *pancetta* used in preparing them. This dish is very filling and fits the category of *piatti unici* (main course).

―∞―

Soak the dry bread in a bowl of milk and then add the *pancetta* and salami, together with parsley, chives (or finely chopped onion), nutmeg, salt and one egg per person. Mix in enough flour to make a fairly dense paste. Using a wet wooden spoon, form rather large gnocchi (ping-pong ball sized, or larger) and boil them in stock or salted water for 30 minutes.

Reduce the stock to a sort of gravy to serve with the *canederli*, together with mustard or horseradish; the perfect side dish is green salad or thinly sliced and dressed raw green cabbage.

Gnocchi Veronesi
Verona-style gnocchi

Serves 4
*1 kg / 2¼ lb floury, yellow-fleshed
potatoes, e.g King Edward,
Golden Wonder, Kerr's Pink,
Duke of York, unpeeled
200 g / 7 oz Italian 00 grade flour
salt*

For the meat sauce
*½ onion, chopped
1 carrot, chopped
1 celery stick, chopped
100 g / 3½ oz braising beef, cubed
60 ml / 2 fl oz olive oil
40 g / 1½ oz butter
400 g / 14 oz peeled, de-seeded
and chopped fresh tomatoes
or canned tomatoes
1 litre / 1¾ pints beef stock
or water
a handful of chopped fresh parsley
fresh sage or rosemary leaves
salt and pepper*

**Alternative serving
suggestion**
*100 g / 3½ oz butter
100 g / 3½ oz Parmesan*

Verona is the home of wholesome, home-made gnocchi. At least, that is what the local people say and they may not be entirely wrong: my foraging experiences over the years have found gnocchi made in other cities of the Veneto that are tasty, while the ones in Verona are always truly delicious. A few commemorative events reflect the supremacy of Verona gnocchi: *gnocchi sanzenati* (San Zeno Gnocchi) were originally a carnival dish, part of a tradition that dates back more than 400 years when on the last Friday before Lent, the dish is served in the famous Piazza in front of the church of San Zeno.

Verona-style gnocchi are generally served with a sauce of horsemeat, cooked for a long time with fresh tomatoes. For those who don't eat horse, one can make a simple beef *ragù* or even serve just with butter and lots of finely grated Parmesan.

———

To make the meat sauce, first fry the onion and other vegetables in the oil and butter until the onion is golden brown. Add the meat and brown well on all sides. Add the tomatoes and enough stock or water to cover, put in the herbs and season with salt and pepper. Bring to the boil and then simmer on a low heat for 2 to 3 hours, until the beef is tender.

The secret of great gnocchi is to steam the potatoes rather than boiling them, so they are drier, and to mix the cooked potatoes with as little flour as possible (otherwise the end result may be rubbery and indigestible). When the potatoes are tender (which may take 30 to 40 minutes) leave until cool enough to handle and then remove the skins. Sieve the steamed potatoes and mix into a smooth paste with the flour and a pinch of salt. Roll the paste into sticks as thick as your finger, then cut these sticks into lengths of about 2 cm (1 in) and slightly flatten them with your fingertip against the back of a grater or on a fork.

Cook in boiling, salted water for 3 to 5 minutes – the gnocchi are cooked when they rise to the surface and should then be removed immediately from the water.

Serve the gnocchi with the meat sauce poured over them, if you made it, or with plenty of melted butter and grated Parmesan.

Bigoli in salsa
Thick spaghetti with sauce

Serves 4
200 g / 7 oz white onion,
finely sliced
75 ml / 2½ fl oz Tuscan olive oil
75 g / 3 oz salted anchovies
and/or tinned sardines, boned
400 g / 14 oz bigoli
(thick wholewheat spaghetti)
salt and pepper
1 litre / 1¾ pints water

During the time of the late and much-lamented Venetian Republic, this was a very common dish during Lent. A type of thick, dark spaghetti made from whole wheat, *bigoli* have a name that is misleadingly like that of the *bigolanti*, boatmen who used to transport drinking water to the various islands of the lagoon because the wells in the *campi* (squares) of Venice and the other islands never held sufficient volumes of fresh water. In fact there is even a canal in Venice called the Rio dell'Acqua Dolce, which takes its name from the fact that it was the landing-stage for the boats that brought fresh water from the mainland for Venetian wells. When they constituted a guild in the fourteenth century, these water-carriers took as their patron saint San Costanzo, because – it was said – the lamps before images of this saint burned on water alone, without any need for oil or other fuel.

Obviously, Venice's water requirements nowadays are met by the mains… and just like the *bigolanti*, *bigoli* themselves have become rather hard to find.

To prepare the sauce, lightly brown the finely sliced onion in the oil; then add a little water (which boils away) to complete the cooking, leaving the onions very soft. Mix in the boned sardines and anchovies, cut into pieces and mash them up some more with a wooden spoon as you stir the mixture over a moderate heat. Add a little pepper (but no salt) and cook until the sardines break up almost completely.

Cook the *bigoli* in boiling, salted water until they are *al dente*. Drain, then mix in a serving bowl with the warm sauce. But if you have a particularly large frying pan, first mix the *bigoli* with the sauce over medium heat for a minute or two; this maximizes the flavours.

I prefer the so-called winter version of this dish, which includes a handful of raisins and pine nuts in the anchovy salsa. A bayleaf in the pan while the ingredients cook also adds flavour to this extremely rich and satisfying dish.

Spaghetti con le vongole
Spaghetti with clams

Given that it's spaghetti, this cannot be a very traditional Venetian dish; but it is one of which I am immensely fond. My children, too, love it – as much as they enjoy collecting the clams themselves, a treasure that is to be found in the mudflats of the lagoon, in sands along the coast of the Lido or at the 'Bacàn'. This is a splendid set of sandbanks in the lagoon, off the island of Sant'Erasmo, known as the Venetians' beach, where families moor their boats in ankle-deep water while they sunbathe and collect clams. It lies near the sixteenth-century Forte di Sant'Andrea, which throughout much of the history of the Venetian Republic looked out onto the shipping lanes used by galleys, galleons and fishing boats; it must also have been a perfect vantage-point from which to watch the defeat of the ships that Napoleon sent against the city. Those vessels have gone now – as has the view of the sea. All you can see these days from the Bacàn is a huge 'island' of cement and rock, created so that the Lagoon can continue to accommodate menacing oil tankers and obese cruise ships. To this end, work has begun on a project that intends to separate Venice from the sea by a gargantuan system of mobile barriers that may – perhaps – one day work, though not before the harsh economic costs have been felt as well as incurring ecological damage.

Commercial clam fishing in the Venice lagoon and along the Adriatic coast is extremely lucrative and consequently there are many 'pirates' who illegally harvest clams using damaging motorized systems attached to the bottoms of their speed boats, which churn up the mud and collect the suspended clams. Not only do they irreversibly damage the lagoon habitats where clam stocks would regenerate, they also sneak into areas which are off-limits according to the authorities, like the waters around the industrial zone of Marghera which contain higher levels of toxic contaminants but, because of the warm factory effluents, produce clams that are larger and seem more succulent. So make sure your clams are supplied by a reputable source or buy them in a regulated fish market.

Serves 4

1 kg / 2¼ lb clams
2–3 cloves garlic
100 ml / 3½ fl oz olive oil
handful of parsley
500 g / 1 lb spaghetti
salt
1 litre / 1¾ pints water

Buy fresh clams and then leave them to purge in salted water for about an hour or so. Sauté the garlic clove in olive oil until golden brown if you plan to remove it. Alternatively chop it finely before cooking begins. Add the well-drained clams and cook on a high flame for about 5 minutes, until all of the shells have opened; discard any shells that do not open, as they should not be eaten. Shell half of the clams, setting aside the other half for decoration. Return the shelled clams to the pan with the oil. Add the finely chopped parsley and salt. Cook the spaghetti and drain, then tip it into the pan (for this dish it must definitely be cooked *al dente*). Stir together the spaghetti and the clam mixture for at least a minute, then serve immediately, garnished with the unshelled clams.

Though I prefer this recipe, some people add a few crushed small tomatoes to the shelled clams in the oil; others prepare a tomato sauce by sautéing 2 to 3 garlic cloves in oil and then adding tomatoes to cook for 7 to 8 minutes. The procedure is then the same as for the recipe above. If you really want to, you can also add a pinch of *peperoncino* or pepper after you have added the chopped parsley and the salt, before adding the *al dente* spaghetti. Again, stir together clams and spaghetti for a minute or so before garnishing with the unshelled clams. Whichever recipe you choose, don't allow the unshelled clams to go cold while you are mixing the sauce with the spaghetti.

Spaghetti alle vongole *at a Venetian* trattoria *with the cultural attaché of the Portuguese embassy from Rome, some years ago, while planning a trip to the Cape Verde islands (I still haven't made it there).*

Bigoli co' l'anara
Thick spaghetti with duck

Serves 4

For the bigoli
300 g / 10 oz wholewheat flour
75 g / 3 oz butter, melted
3 duck's eggs, beaten
a little milk
salt

For the sauce
1 young duck and its livers
1 litre / 1¾ pints water
60 ml / 2 fl oz olive oil
25 g / 1 oz butter
½ onion
1 carrot
1 celery stick
2 fresh sage leaves
pomegranate or lemon juice
salt and pepper
75 g / 3 oz Parmesan

As already mentioned, it is fairly difficult to find *bigoli* as they used to be. Only in the Vicenza area and some places near Verona are they still produced using the age-old *bigolaro*, a cylindrical press in which the pasta dough is forced down through holes from which it emerges like the writhing locks of the Gorgon. This pasta is great with the full-bodied flavour of duck.

To make the *bigoli*, tip the flour into a mound on a clean work surface. Make a well in the middle of the flour with your fist and add the butter, eggs, milk and a pinch of salt. Using a fork, beat together the eggs and milk and begin to incorporate the flour from the sides of the well. Keep pulling the flour into the eggs – it will look messy until all the flour has been incorporated. Start kneading the dough with both hands, working it into a cohesive mass. Remove the dough from the work surface, scraping up and discarding any dried, crusty bits. Lightly flour the work surface and continue kneading for 3 more minutes. The dough should be elastic and a little sticky. Continue to knead for another 3 minutes, remembering to dust your board when necessary. Wrap the dough in plastic cling film and allow to rest for 30 minutes at room temperature before rolling and cutting it.

Using a special *bigolaro*, force the paste out and leave the *bigoli* to dry and harden in a safe place. If you don't have one, use the thickest spaghetti cutter that comes with an ordinary pasta machine.

For the sauce, place the duck in a pan with a lot of salted water, together with the onion, carrot and celery. Bring to the boil and then leave to simmer for an hour.

Remove the duck and vegetables and set aside. Strain the stock and then bring to the boil and use it to cook the *bigoli*; remove and drain before they get too soft and place in a bowl.

Meanwhile, prepare the sauce with the duck livers. In a frying pan, sauté the livers with some oil and butter flavoured with salt, pepper and sage, so as to have a rich-coloured sauce. Add some of the duck meat, chopped finely. Some add a little pomegranate juice to the sauce to sharpen it (lemon juice is a valid substitute). Pour this sauce over the *bigoli* and add plenty of grated Parmesan before serving.

Pasta e fasioi
Pasta and beans

Serves 4
300 g / 10 oz dried lamon beans
1 onion, chopped
1 carrot, chopped
1 celery stick, chopped
40 g / 1½ oz lardo, chopped
60 g / generous 2 oz pork rind,
or a ham bone, or pig's trotter
150 g / 5 oz dried tagliatelle
(not fresh pasta)
salt and pepper
Tuscan extra virgin olive oil,
to serve

Like rice, the other ingredient which some have said could be the heraldic emblem of Venetian cuisine, beans are not actually native to this area. They were originally brought to Italy from central South America by the Spanish at the beginning of the sixteenth century.

Throughout the Veneto, there are numerous versions of *pasta e fasioi*. Not only does each area employ a different type of pasta for this traditional soup – broad *tagliatelle* in Vicenza, *bigoli* in Verona, *subiottini* (small *maccheroni*) in Venice or *fettuccine* elsewhere in the region – but the base of the soup changes: in some areas it is a cream of bean soup with just a few intact beans; in others, the beans are cooked in a very thick broth.

And although *pasta e fasioi* belongs to the region's peasant cuisine, it is a universal favourite, especially among those who should probably eat the least! Failure to eat it can be fatal: Bertoldo, the hero of a local folktale, eventually dies because he does not get to eat his dish of 'turnip and beans'. A good *pasta e fasioi* should be dense enough for a spoon to stand up in it.

The dish is much quicker to prepare with fresh beans but it can also be made using best-quality dried beans that have been soaked in fresh water for at least 12 hours. If the *lamon* beans are hard to find, any large white or red beans can be used instead.

———— ✥ ————

Soak the beans overnight in cold water. Rinse and drain.

Place the onion, carrot and celery in a pan of water with the cured pork fat and, to add flavour, the pork rind, ham bone or pig's trotter. When using pork rinds, boil them first for 10 minutes separately to get rid of the excess fat. Add the beans and cook on a low heat for a number of hours, carefully removing the froth or fat that comes to the surface. Towards the end of cooking, to thicken the broth, remove some of the beans and pass them through a sieve before returning the paste to the pot. Add salt and pepper and the pasta and cook until the pasta is still *al dente*.

Before serving, remove the rind, cut it into thin strips and place a piece in each bowl. *Pasta e fasioi* should be served tepid, when the surface is almost forming a skin, onto which you pour a little extra virgin olive oil and freshly grind some pepper.

One of the tastier varieties of this dish is the *lasagne e fasioi balotoni nostrani col pistelo* (lasagne with local beans and *pistelo*), which originated in Este, a pretty little town that stands at the foot of the Euganean Hills near Padua and is famous for its ceramics. What gives the dish its very special flavour is the *pistelo*, the part of a pig's leg below the knee that is first cured in salt for 20 days or so.

Casunzei ampezzani
Mountain ravioli

Serves 4
275 g / 9 oz Italian 00 grade flour
2 eggs, beaten
700 g / 1½ lb red turnips
and/or beetroot
125 g / 4 oz butter,
plus extra to serve
salt and pepper
1 litre / 1¾ pints water
poppy seeds, to serve

Cortina stands in a most picturesque, sunny, broad valley in the Eastern Alps, surrounded by the towering rocky peaks of the Dolomites. After the War of the League of Cambrai, this area ceased to be part of the dominions of Venice, and remained an isolated part of the Tyrol for four centuries, right up until 1918. It was so isolated that even Italian wine was unknown here and the local drink was the strong and warming grappa, which smugglers brought in via perilous mountain routes. These *casunzei* are a typical local dish – filling, tasty and perfect in icy weather. There are various versions, with grated cheese (possibly *pecorino*), ricotta, breadcrumbs or eggs being added to the turnip filling.

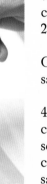

Make the pasta first. Mix the flour, eggs and some salt into a paste with enough cold water to achieve the desired smooth and elastic consistency and roll flat, making sure it is not too thin (about 2 mm is fine). Set it to one side on a table or marble work surface.

Boil the turnips and beetroots until soft and then peel them. Grate them coarsely and sauté in a pan with the butter and some salt and pepper.

Cut the pasta using a round cutter with serrated edges, about 4 cm (1¾ in) in diameter and place a spoonful of the filling in the centre of each round. Fold over and seal the edges carefully, then squash slightly in the centre so that each raviolo looks like a cockerel's comb. Cook the *casunzei* for 4 to 6 minutes in boiling, salted water.

Served with a generous sprinkling of ground poppy seeds and abundant melted butter, this dish is heaven at lunchtime on the ski slopes; or rather eating the ravioli is evocative of being high up in the snowy peaks!

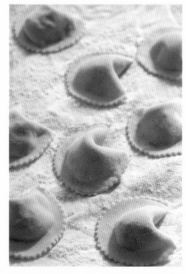

Paparele e figadini
Papardelle and chicken-liver sauce

Serves 4
250 g / 8 oz Italian 00 grade flour
2 eggs, beaten
salt

The refined cuisine of Verona includes this excellent first course – so delicious that even the Montagues and Capulets might have been tempted to forget their feud to enjoy it together.

———— ∞ ————

Sauce
175 g / 6 oz chicken livers, chopped
40 g / 1½ oz butter
1 litre / 1¾ pints beef stock
50 g / 2 oz Parmesan

Mix together the flour, eggs and a little water or milk and salt to form a dough. Roll flat (not too thin, about 2 to 3 mm thick) on a board. When it has 'set', dust it with flour and roll it up loosely. Then cut the roll into slices about 1 cm (½ in) wide to form the long *papardelle* strips. Unroll these and leave to one side.

In a pan, sauté the chopped chicken livers in the butter and then, when they are cooked, pour in the stock and bring to the boil. Then add the *papardelle,* which require just a few minutes cooking time. Serve with plentiful grated Parmesan.

Another *papardelle* dish, also from Verona and typical for the feast day of San Zeno, is made with a sauce of sautéed peas and *pancetta.*

Sguazeto a la bechera
Butcher's stew

Serves 4
300 g / 10 oz tripe
200 g / 7 oz lung
300 g / 10 oz oxtail
100 g / 3½ oz spleen
1 celery stick, chopped
1 onion, chopped
1 carrot, chopped
salt
1.1 litres / 2 pints water
25 g / 1 oz mature Parmesan

Perhaps this very tasty dish would be more accurately described as a soup. Its name – from the Venetian word for a butcher (*bechero*) – is probably due to the fact that only a butcher's shop would provide such a wide selection of what some would regard as 'offal'.

———— ∞ ————

Having washed the tripe, spleen, lung and oxtail very thoroughly, boil them for 15 minutes or so to get rid of any unpleasant tastes. Wash them once more in cold water and then place in a pan full of water together with the celery, onion and carrot. Simmer slowly, periodically removing the scum and fat that comes to the surface. When ready add salt and a handful of grated Parmesan.

Manestra de zuca
Pumpkin soup

Serves 4
½ onion, chopped
30 ml/2 tbsp olive oil
25 g/1 oz butter
25 g/1 oz lardo, diced
1 garlic clove
3 large potatoes, thinly sliced
400 g/14 oz pumpkin, skinned,
seeded and thinly sliced
200 g/7 oz subioti or subiotini
(small macaroni)
salt and pepper
1 litre/1¾ pints water
50 g/2 oz Parmesan

Seemingly a very simple and mundane vegetable, the pumpkin figures in various recipes from the Veneto that build upon its taste and its rich, smooth texture (rather similar to the pulp of chestnuts or sweet potatoes). Not all types of orange pumpkin are suitable for making soup, so you should buy *zucca barucca* or *zucca chiozzotta* – the tastiest types. Butternut squash is a good substitute.

Sauté the chopped onion in oil and butter with the cured pork fat and garlic clove. Then add a few large potatoes and the pumpkin. As soon as the mixture begins to take on a golden colour, add salt and pepper and cover with water. When it comes to the boil, add the pasta and leave to cook for 15 minutes, stirring frequently. Serve the pumpkin soup with lots of grated cheese and, if desired, fried or toasted *crostini* (diced bread). A hard and mature sheeps' milk *pecorino* cheese can be used instead of Parmesan; it has a decisive flavour that contrasts well with the smooth, soft pumpkin.

Manestra de orzo
Cream of barley soup

Serves 4
125 g/4 oz pearl barley
300 ml/½ pint milk
300 ml/½ pint water
25 g/1 oz butter
25 g/1 oz plain flour
25 g/1 oz Parmesan
2 egg yolks
salt and white pepper

This nourishing soup is particularly suited to cold, rainy days in the mountains, when one really appreciates a hearty bowl of warming soup at the fireside. Like many other dishes from alpine areas, where the open hearth was largely given over to the mixing of polenta and the turning of roast poultry on a spit, it is not labour-intensive.

Rinse the barley then cook in boiling salted water for about 1 hour.

Meanwhile, mix together the milk, water, butter and flour, stirring vigorously. Now add the grated Parmesan, the egg yolks and salt and pepper.

When the barley is almost ready, pour in the creamed mixture, making sure no lumps form and that the barley does not stick to the bottom of the pan. Simmer for a few minutes, so that the cream thickens, but it should not form a skin. The soup can be served as it is or poured over fried or toasted bread.

Sopa de coa
Oxtail soup

Serves 4
1.2 kg / 3 lb oxtail
1 onion, sliced
1 carrot, sliced
a few celery leaves
fresh parsley sprig
fresh thyme sprig
1 bay leaf
1 litre / 1¾ pints water
salt and pepper

For its distinctive and robust flavour, oxtail is considered a real treat and is indeed one of my all-time favourite dishes. We normally have it on 4 October, the Saint's day of San Francesco d'Assisi (although his love for animals may have reduced him to being a vegetarian)!

———⚬⚬⚬———

If necessary, skin the oxtail and then cut it into regular chunks. Clean thoroughly in running water, or at least rinse the pieces many times, so that the tail gets thoroughly cleaned. Increasingly, oxtail is sold ready-cleaned, however.

Place the oxtail pieces in a medium-sized pan together with the sliced onion and carrot, some celery leaves and the parsley, thyme and bay leaf. Season with salt and pepper, cover with water and bring to the boil. Allow to simmer slowly for 4 to 5 hours until all the pieces of oxtail are well cooked and the stock has been substantially reduced. Serve with slices of toasted crusty bread.

Panada
Bread soup

Serves 4
300 g / 10 oz dry bread
1 litre / 1¾ pints beef stock
pinch ground cinnamon
60 ml / 2 fl oz Tuscan olive oil,
plus extra to serve
75 g / 3 oz Parmesan
salt

Before becoming one of the most prosperous areas in Italy, the Veneto was one of the poorest. This dish, rather like the Tuscan *pancotto*, uses dry bread as its main ingredient. The result is delicate and smooth, and was much appreciated back in the times of my grandparents' generation.

———⚬⚬⚬———

Place slices of old, dry bread in a pan and cover with beef stock flavoured with a little cinnamon and some good Tuscan olive oil and leave to stand. Thirty to 40 minutes later, once the bread has thoroughly absorbed the liquid, cook on a very low heat for about 45 minutes, stirring frequently but gently so as to reach a velvety consistency. Check the seasoning and add salt only if necessary. Before removing from the heat, mix in a good handful of grated Parmesan. Serve with a little olive oil poured on top. Some people also like to mix in a raw egg at the end.

Sailing the seas

HOUGH cooking on board ship or boat used to be a complicated matter, the results were not as basic as many believe. On the *bragozzi* that sailed out of Chioggia, small fish were fried and served with polenta, which might also be eaten with fish – generally sardines – *in saòr*. The most common pasta dishes or soups were those with beans or seasonal vegetables. And there was also meat: salted beef or pork conserved in a mix of mustard and vinegar, salt and honey. The stock extract used in making the pasta dishes was produced by cooking odd cuts of meat and offal to form a dense gelatine that was then dried; this was the origin of the 'stock cube' that we use nowadays.

The cooking on merchant ships, which also transported passengers, was more elaborate. Fish was used in lasagne or a sort of salted fish 'pie' made with cheese. This latter dish was prepared by frying the fish in boiling oil, then mixing it with ox brains, fish pulp, boiled eggs and soft cheese. The mixture was then seasoned with pepper, marjoram, rue, wine and oil and then simmered slowly – perhaps with a few extra eggs, too. Malmsey wine, salad and mutton were also served on board, and the most appetizing dishes included Cremona mortadella, Milanese *cervellata* (made with ox brains), *piasentin* (a type of cheese from Piacenza), Parmesan, Treviso-style tripe, Modena sausage, Genoese pasta (perhaps *trofie* with pesto), song thrushes, geese and quails – all heavily spiced, of course.

But it was not always like this. For a long time, travelling by sea, with many months between one port of call and the next, meant living on the ship's biscuit which filled the kitchen galleys. The oarsmen on a Venetian ship were almost all freely enlisted men. They had the right to four cups of wine per day, plus a bowl of soup or pasta, half a kilo (a pound) of beef or pork, Sardinian cheese, tuna in oil and almost 700 grams (1½ lb) of ship's biscuit; this latter was also used to make soups. One such soup – *panada* – played an essential role in satisfying the crew's perpetual hunger. It was made with ship's biscuit and dressed with a little oil, salt, garlic and – if available – stock and dried leaves of rosemary and sage.

The few oarsmen who actually were convicts were fed *frisopo*, which they claimed was disgusting and inedible. When, for some reason, supplies of ship's biscuit had run out and it had not been possible to obtain new stores, the broken pieces and crumbs were gathered up from the bottom of the galley cupboards, and these formed the main ingredient of *frisopo*, a much less appetising version of *panada*. From this term derives the word '*frisopin*', which towards the end of the Republic was used for the soldiers serving on board ship; clearly, given the poor state of the crumbling Republic's finances, these men, too, were fed a soup based on ship's biscuit.

The best such biscuit was produced by the *pistori* (bakers) at the Venice Arsenale, where one ancient bread oven still exists. The recipe was handed down from father to son, so with the end of the Republic – and the death of the last *pistor* to serve within the shipyards – this jealously guarded secret was lost forever. Bought by other navies as well – who appreciated its high quality – the Venetian *biscotto* never went bad or mouldy, nor did it become worm-ridden. For example, in 1821 several quintals of Venetian *biscotto* were found walled up in the storerooms of a Venetian fortress on the island of Crete. They had been there since the island fell to the Turks in the mid-seventeenth century and yet when the *biscotto* was found – almost 170 years later – it was still edible. This tradition of ship's biscuit still lives on in Chioggia, where bakers produce tasty small ring biscuits known as *bussolai* that will keep for several months.

As for water, ships had to replenish stores every three days, because the water on board became putrid; the crew also took advantage of these stops to obtain fresh food. Some ships even carried livestock on board, in an enclosure towards the stern, for slaughtering when needed. One problem Venetian galleys did not have was scurvy, the plague of all navies. This was probably due to the fact that their ships' supplies included not only barrels of wine and oil but also containers of lemon juice.

Of course, the key ingredient for preserving fish and meat was salt. In Roman days, the placid lagoons of the Veneto had already become valuable sources of salt. Later, the State imposed a monopoly on the trade and production of salt, with the main deposits being located in the area of the Po delta, where swamps and marshes alternate with the open waters of lagoons. As well as being essential for human and animal life, and for the conservation of fish and meat, salt was a key ingredient in the *garum* and *allec* the Romans used in making sauces (these were rather similar to our own stock cubes). Cassiodorus, a Roman senator and historian of the sixth century, wrote of the Veneti: 'their main source of wealth is salt, because the man is yet to be born who does not need salt… Everyone searches for gold… But there is no one who can do without salt, which serves to make all foods agreeable.'

For many centuries, control of the salt trade was of great strategic importance; and by the tenth century Venice was poised to impose its monopoly on the trade in salt from the Po estuary. This was the resource that supplied the Venetians with the means to acquire what they could not grow or produce themselves. It was as good as ready money for the early settlers here – a role that one sees in other parts of the world, as well. In a passage from his account of his travels, one of my ancestors, the mid-fifteenth-century navigator Alvise da Mosto, has this to say about the markets he had seen in western Africa:

> All those who own the salt lay out piles in a line, each indicating his own pile. And thus having made the said piles in a line, each marks his own, and then the entire caravan moves back half-a-day's journey. Then come another people of Negroes, who do not want to be seen or to speak to others. And they come with large boats, so that they seem to come from some islands. And having disembarked and seen the salt, they leave a quantity of gold by each pile and then they go away, leaving both the gold and the salt. And when they have left, the Negroes who own the salt come, and if the quantity of gold satisfies them, they take the gold and leave the salt; if the quantity of gold does not satisfy them, they leave said gold with the salt and go away again.

And thus this bargaining-at-a-distance would go on until both parties were satisfied.

One salt-producing centre was in the north of the lagoon, around the Isola della Salina. Here, as late as the middle of the nineteenth century, Cavaliere Astrue di Montpellier set up an important sea salt plant, which continued to function right up until the First World War. Murano, too, was a place of salt production. First settled in Roman times, Ammuranium later attracted refugees from Altino and elsewhere who were escaping from the invading barbarians. These newcomers constructed mills and introduced a precise system for the production of salt. A special sort of lock was created with a gate that rose to let salt water in and then closed to contain it in small ponds, where the heat of the sun caused evaporation and produced a salt-rich solution. This was then channelled into even shallower ponds, where the last remaining water evaporated, leaving crystallized salt. Having been ground by rollers, these salt crystals were shovelled into sacks that were then stored ready for trade.

A photo I took in Pellestrina about 20 years ago of a fisherman and his sardine catch.

Polenta

Polenta

Ultimately a staple for humble households throughout the Po valley, polenta seems to have been introduced to the area via Venice, through commerce. Maize – a novelty discovered in America – was traded by some itinerant merchants. Perhaps it was the very colour – a yellow normally associated with the yolk of an egg or with exotic flowers – that first enthused the peasants of the Veneto, amidst the flat and interminable plains intersected by monotonous lines of poplars, mulberry trees and canals, overhung by weeping willows. Given that fresh bread was only available about once a week, polenta would have brought a note of festivity to mealtimes. And, during the greyest winter months when there were few fresh vegetables, polenta could be served with a triangle of strong cheese, meat sauce or even just milk to provide a nourishing meal.

Then there is the very softness of polenta, which made it popular not only with children, but also with old people in an era when dental care was not what it is today and the aged lacked the teeth they needed to chew harder food. Much cheaper than bread, polenta also had the added advantage that it was served hot – something that was very important in the cold and humid countryside of northern Italy.

It is not known for sure whether polenta was first introduced via Venice, but it is certain that the best polenta is not to be found in Venice. The humidity and sea air mean that finely ground maize flour quickly goes lumpy so coarsely ground polenta is used instead, which does not have the same softness. Some areas of the Veneto also produce white maize flour for polenta, very similar to the mealie-meal that is practically the national food of southern Africa. White polenta is better than yellow for some dishes, even if only because it looks better on the plate. I'm also sure that many of those who claim to have an opinion on the matter would actually be unable to tell yellow from white polenta, were they to taste it blindfold!

While polenta looks simple to make, it requires skill and an awareness of the many ways in which it can be prepared: there are those who like it so thick that you can cut it with a knife and grill it in slabs like toast and those who prefer it to be much more liquid; those who eat it cold and those who only eat it hot. Whatever the result you desire, true polenta should be made in a *caldina* or *caldiera*, a large copper pot gleaming on the inside but smoke-blackened on the outside. Nowadays, of course, people mostly use an ordinary pan, but this definitely changes the flavour; experts dismiss the result as nothing but 'pudding mix'.

For good old-fashioned polenta, fill a pot up to two-thirds with salted water; adding a spoonful of olive oil helps to prevent the mixture from forming lumps. When the water boils, pour in the maize flour with your left hand while you stir clockwise with your right (never change direction). The flour thus absorbs the liquid evenly and does not form lumps. Let the polenta bubble away slowly, stirring constantly while making sure that it does not stick to the pan or burn. It is ready when it falls easily off the wooden spoon. There is also an instant polenta mix, available in supermarkets; while the results are less tasty, it is sometimes convenient to have polenta that is ready in 5 minutes rather than 45.

Most commonly, polenta is served with fish, game birds and 'Venetian-style' liver; though, in fact, it goes with nearly everything for breakfast, lunch or dinner. Indeed, polenta could be served with almost anything and figures in a little nursery rhyme sung to children when trying to cajole them into eating: 'Fish bones for the cat, bones for the dogs, polenta for people, millet for birds and din-dins for children.' The most appetizing polenta-based dishes are described over the following pages.

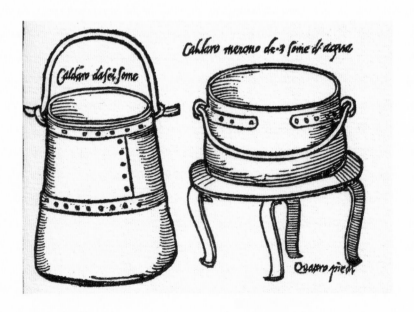

Copper cooking pots like these are still used in our kitchen.

Polenta fasolà
Polenta with beans

Annoyed that his parishioners had neglected to make offerings of produce to the church, year after year, the parish priest of San Quirico (near Vicenza) decided one day to seek revenge: he took the statue of the patron saint from the high altar and hid it in a field of wheat. When the parishioners asked about the disappearance, he answered that the saint had become tired of not receiving any offerings and had left town. Gradually the news spread, and the frightened parishioners went back to the priest to ask him to do something to get the saint to return. 'Let's go to look for him,' said the cleric and the next day a long procession wound its way through the fields and meadows of San Quirico. Led by the priest, the people chanted promises to San Quirico of 'beans and fodder and more beans too'. Having walked the length and breadth of the fields, they eventually came to where the priest had hidden the statue and with great jubilation carried it back to the church. From that moment on, the priest was never short of beans.

The name given here for this popular dish comes from Padua. In Venice it is called 'bean sauce' and in the Po delta area, *gli sbirri intabarrati* ('cloaked policemen'). Though it may seem time-consuming, this dish is actually quite easy to prepare.

Serves 4

*300 g / 10 oz dried beans,
such as* lamon *or flageolet*
100 g / 3½ oz pancetta, *chopped*
½ onion, chopped
30 ml / 1 fl oz olive oil
50 g / 2 oz butter or lard
chopped fresh rosemary and sage
300 g / 10 oz polenta
salt

Soak the beans for at least one night.

Next day, cook the beans in a thick-bottomed saucepan with the chopped *pancetta* and onion for a few minutes in the oil and butter or lard. Add plenty of hot water and a sprinkling of rosemary and sage. Cook on a low heat for at least 4 hours. If too much of the liquid is absorbed, add some more water.

When the beans are done, season with just a little salt (remembering that the *pancetta* is already salty) and gradually sprinkle in the polenta, cooking for at least a further 45 minutes. The mixture must never be allowed to get too dense. It should be served piping hot with – or after – dishes with a particularly strong flavour: game, pork, mutton stew, *pesce in saòr* (marinated fried fish).

A similar version of this dish is known as *i sughi de fasioi* and was popular among the poorer people in the Veneto, who often used to serve a single dish (*piatto unico*) for their main meal, rather than have the traditional division of a meal into first course, second course, fruit or dessert.

Sauté chopped onion and celery in oil and butter until they are golden brown. Add the beans – preferably fresh – and cover them with water and boil until they are tender. Do not add the salt until later, as the skins will harden. Drain the beans and set to one side. In a copper pan, prepare a normal polenta and when it is about half ready add the beans and stir gently, so that they do not break up. Do not let the mix set too much. This is a very substantial dish, best served with a strong white or good red wine.

The late-eighteenth-century engraver Zompini's depiction of a street seller offering polenta to some hungry looking boys in one of the campi *of Venice (*left*) and Pietro Longhi's notorious domestic painting of polenta being prepared. When the cooked polenta was poured onto the wooden board the ladies superstitiously thought it was a sign of providence if any air bubbles formed in the process.*

Schiz
Baked cheese

Serves 4
500 g / 1 lb schiz
or any other young,
slightly firm, cheese,
e.g. halloumi
or a fresh Lancashire
or Wensleydale
150 g / 5 oz butter
150 ml / ¼ pint double cream
pinch of salt

The main ingredient here is *schiz*, a slightly curdled cheese that is one of the traditional products of the mountains of the Belluno area and is particularly suited for dishes that are as simple as they are tasty. The cheese itself originates in the rustic setting of the summer pasturelands of the alpine foothills, where the herders make this non-salted and slightly pressed cheese, which is ready to eat immediately. *Schiz* is produced in large forms and can be found in markets throughout the Belluno area and in various places around Treviso; it is sold in rectangular chunks that are ideal for slicing and serving at home. It can also be conserved in the freezer. One of the best *schiz* now available – a real boast of Veneto cheese-makers – comes from the Busche Dairy, a cooperative that combines a number of producers in the Feltre valley and has in recent years made a real name for itself with the quality and variety of its produce.

Schiz is served in trattorie and mountain refuges throughout the Belluno and Feltre mountains. It emerged as a dish during the period immediately after the war, when the farmers carried the milk taken from the few family cows to the dairy in order to make cheese. The curd that oozed out of the moulds was cut away, carefully collected and taken home with the newly formed cheese. While the cheese would be left to ripen in the cellar; the surplus curd, known as the *schiz*, was cut into strips and cooked in a pan. It constitutes a humble but very nutritious meal and the name derives from the fact that when it is on the fire it spurts *schizzare* (drops of whey).

Cut the *schiz* into slices about 1.5 cm thick x 12 cm long x 8 cm wide (½ x 4 x 3 in). Melt the butter in an ovenproof pan and then sauté the slices of *schiz*, until they become a light golden brown on both sides but do not stick together.

Preheat the oven to 180°C /350°F /Gas Mark 4.

When the *schiz* slices are the right colour, pour over the cream, season with salt and bake in the oven for 20 minutes or so. The best way to serve baked *schiz* is with polenta and a fine, full-bodied local red wine with a rich bouquet – for example, a well-aged Merlot or Cabernet.

Polenta conzada
Polenta and cheese

Serves 4
*350 g / 12 oz very fine
yellow polenta
300 ml / ½ pint milk
300 ml / ½ pint water
100 g / 3½ oz hard cheese
150 g / 5 oz ricotta cheese
125 g / 4 oz butter, melted
salt*

Polenta – that is, any mixture prepared using ground cereals – is obviously very ancient and was first made when humankind discovered how to use two stones to grind a crude sort of flour. The Greeks made *poltos* and the Romans *puls*, using spelt, a close relative of wheat that was common at the time, or buckwheat. In the mountains especially it remains an essential part of the daily diet. In peasant homes, it is generally served firm – in past times it had to be a substitute for the bread which mountain-folk could ill afford; the cheese (an indispensable complement to polenta) served with it could be soft, smoked or mature.

The day in the mountains begins early, at 6 am, when only the first glimmers of light can be seen in the valleys. Before setting off for the day, the workers' fuel is provided in the form of slices of polenta, slightly toasted on the embers of the fire and then dunked in a bowl full of warm milk. This not only tastes good but also provides the energy necessary to undertake yet another day of hard work – even if work such as chopping wood and tending livestock has increasingly been superseded by operating ski lifts in the winter months.

This particular *polenta conzada* (literally, 'flavoured polenta') is traditional in the Cadore area in the heart of the Dolomites, and is still served in the more isolated villages and farmhouses.

—⊗⊗⊗—

Using very fine yellow maize flour and equal parts of milk and water with a little salt, mix and cook a very soft polenta. With a large wooden spoon that has first been dipped in water, form small gnocchi of polenta and divide between four bowls. At the bottom of each bowl, and over each layer of gnocchi, sprinkle grated cheese, ricotta and lots of melted butter. The number of layers depends on how hungry you are.

Opposite: *Polenta is often incorporated in the snacks offered at the Venetian* baccari *(taverns and bars).*

Polenta pastizada
Harvester's polenta

Serves 4
400 g / 14 oz yellow polenta
75 g / 3 oz butter
150 g / 5 oz Parmesan
salt

Sauce
1 onion, chopped
1 carrot, chopped
1 celery stick, chopped
125 g / 4 oz butter,
plus extra to serve
250 g / 8 oz boneless veal, diced
200 g / 7 oz sopressa (soft
salami), chopped
200 g / 7 oz fresh mushrooms,
sliced
1 glass of dry white wine
500 g / 1 lb canned
chopped tomatoes
150 g / 5 oz chicken livers
salt
Parmesan

The maize harvest in early autumn used to be a great celebration for the peasants; a moment of relief following the exertions and trepidation of harvesting the yields from a year on the lands. After the day's work, the entire family – or numerous families – got together in the arcaded ground floor of the farmhouses and, by the light of oil lamps, set about the *scartocciatura* (stripping away the husks from the cobs). If neighbours came to give a hand, it was customary to serve griddled slices of pumpkin together with a glass (or two) of vino novello. The session often ended with a dance in the fresh autumn air, with the exchange of furtive glances amongst the young and the occasional furtive embrace too. Of course, 'polenta today, polenta tomorrow' meant that the ingenious cook was always on the look-out for a different way of serving up this basic foodstuff. The following is a very tasty and filling *piatto unico*.

Make a medium-consistency polenta and lay it out (2 cm / ¾ inch thick) on a marble slab. When it has cooled, cut it into more or less regular slices and lay these in a wide ovenproof dish that has been well greased with butter. Preheat the oven, ready for browning the cheese (or you can use a hot grill).

To make the sauce, sauté the chopped onion, carrot and celery in about 75 g / 3 oz butter. When golden, add the diced veal, the *sopressa* and the fresh mushrooms. Cook for 15 minutes and then pour in the white wine and tomatoes. Add salt and cook for a further 25 minutes. At the last moment, add the chicken livers, having first sautéed them separately in the remaining butter. Pour over the polenta.

The *polenta pastizada* should be topped off with some knobs of butter and Parmesan, and then lightly browned in a hot oven or grill. Serve straight from the oven in the same dish. Make sure you have a good set of pot holders, or carefully wrap a napkin around the edge of the dish!

Polenta a boconi
Layered polenta

Serves 4
200 g / 7 oz very fine white
or yellow polenta
200 g / 7 oz sugar
pinch of ground cinnamon
200 g / 7 oz butter, melted
salt

Bundles of brushwood blazing in the grate were like a refreshing tonic for the exhausted worker returning from the fields. In the evening, the entire family huddled around the hearth, as if their closeness to each other would relieve them of the physical weariness and melancholy of their hard lives on the land. Chilled to the bone and exhausted, they instinctively sought consolation from human contact, from the blaze of the fire and from the polenta steaming away in the polished cauldron.

As the old man of the family diligently stirred the pot, there was an opportunity for talk. The brushwood crackled and spat, and each person offered his terse account of a day that seemed to have passed as slowly as a prison sentence. At last, the polenta, as golden-yellow as the sun, was ready. A dish that cheered up one and all – from the very young to the toothless old – this was the staple for these folk and had been ever since the seventeenth century, when the maize crop in the Veneto began to outstrip wheat.

First brought from the New World by Columbus and the Spanish, maize gradually spread across the continent – from Spain to Venice and the rest of Italy. The plains of the Veneto – from around Verona and Padua in the west to Friuli in the east – proved to be well suited to the cultivation of both white and yellow maize, and the crop was an immediate success. Plantations stretched into numerous drained and reclaimed marshy areas, products of the Venetian Republic's far-sighted and wide-ranging agricultural policies, which it had pursued since the 1400s. However, polenta could be dangerous – it was so filling, the poor neglected their intake of fruit and vegetables and this increased the risk of *pellagra*, a disease caused by a vitamin-deficient diet.

The following is a simple dessert that mothers in the Veneto countryside have lovingly prepared for their children over countless generations.

After finishing school, I went camping in the mountains and one of the things we did was make polenta on an open fire.

―――❧―――

Using very fine white or yellow maize flour, mix a medium-consistency polenta in a (preferably copper) pot. When it is ready, remove from the heat and – using a wooden spoon that has been held in very hot water – place a layer of the polenta in a damp bowl. Sprinkle abundantly with a mixture of sugar and cinnamon and then drip melted butter on top. Repeat the layers until all the polenta is used up.

Trades & professions

ILLS had stood in the area of Ponte dell'-Astichello near Vicenza since ancient times; powered by waterwheels, some of them were even erected on platforms that floated on the river itself. One day, a woman with a whiff of sorcery about her came to one of these mills. Familiar with the rumours about her, the miller found a way of keeping her there by saying that he could not deal with her corn until he had served other customers. The woman complained but eventually took her sack to a corner of the mill and sat there to wait. The miller, too, waited and waited, until the 'witch' fell asleep. And when midnight struck, a little mouse emerged from the mouth of the sleeping woman and scampered away. At that point the miller tried to wake her, but – dead to the world – she was stone cold and no longer breathing. Just before dawn, however, the mouse returned, ran up into her lap and then disappeared into her mouth, at which point the woman's colour came back and she started to breathe normally. Certain now of the truth of the rumours, the miller gave her a mighty slap, waking her with: 'Ugly Witch, now I have unmasked you!' At first, the woman cried but then she thanked the miller because, as everyone knows, 'a witch unmasked is a witch undamned.'

By the eighteenth century, Venetian cuisine was firmly based on long-standing traditions, which had survived in part thanks to the efforts of the *Associazioni dei Mestieri* (Association of Crafts and Guilds). The *arte prima* within the city was that of the *pistori*, who made bread. From the Middle Ages onwards baking had been subject to a wide range of public legislation aimed at guaranteeing and regulating the quality of flour, the way dough was mixed, the different baking methods used and the price of the various kinds of bread. If a *pistor*'s bread was found to be of poor quality, it was cut into chunks and then thrown down the steps of the Rialto bridge; if he was found to be selling underweight loaves, he was fined; and if the bread was not properly certified or properly baked, it was confiscated.

When my father was young, bread played a central role in the Venetians' diet. Of almost legendary importance, it enjoyed a sort of 'aura' that distinguished it from other foodstuffs and he still recalls the experience of making bread himself:

> One day it was the turn of my brother and I to be introduced to the secrets of baking. At the wooden board in the kitchen, our teacher used flour, water and yeast to carefully explain to us the theory and then showed us the practice of bread-making. With our short fingers, we kneaded the dough as best we could, forming little oval bread buns which we then baked and ate. I don't think it was wonderful bread; but the insatiable appetite we had at that age made anything edible.

Throughout the Veneto, the city communes and lordships of the Middle Ages had passed laws to guarantee that everyone would find good-quality bread – and that policy was continued by the Venetian Republic. The flour had to be approved by the *Ufficio ad Bullam Panis* (Bread Licensing Office) and each day bakers' shops had to post the official price list for bread in a clearly visible place. A good number of Venetian bakers (around 20) worked in St Mark's Square, because the state wanted to be sure of ready supplies right in the centre of the city. A further 25 were located in the Rialto area; the commercial heart of the city, this hummed with activity at every hour of the day and night. Wooden structures backing directly on to the Bell Tower, the 20 shops in the Square sold their produce through an open hatch or *balconade*; counter assistants, dressed in *traverson* (an apron) and sort of chef's hat, thus became known as *balconieri* and shop attendants are still called that today in Venice. Just like nowadays, the bakers turned out various types of bread, which included *albus* (white bread) and *tota farina* (wholemeal bread).

The flour was stored in an *albuol* (a sort of trough beneath the kneading table) with a sliding top, on which the kneading was carried out. The shaped loaves were then left to 'prove' until they were ready for baking, when they

Nutrimento soave
(lattaia)

were slid into the oven on the flat disk of a long-handled oven shovel known as a *palo da pan* or *palo da biscoto*. A vaulted structure with air holes for ventilation, the oven had a small central door with an even smaller door on the right for governing the draught to the fire; under the open area at the front of the *altare* (oven) there was ample space to store wood. The bakery workers included the *acquariol*, responsible for supplies of fresh water, the *pistor* – who actually kneaded the bread, put it in the oven and calculated the baking time – and the fire stokers, who had long wooden-handled pokers to adjust the fire at each new addition of fuel. When they were removed from the oven, the crusty loaves were placed on special baker's shelves or baskets to cool. In the countryside, where bread was made at home (generally on Saturdays), the cooled loaves were then placed in the *arca*, a sort of bread chest that had a central section for the week's supply of bread and a side compartment for flour.

Another ancient tradition was the production of *pan biscotto* in Venice. A basic part of the supplies for soldiers, this was also produced for ships' passengers, in quantities according to the length of the voyage. Such 'ship's biscuit' became famous because it never got eaten by worms or tasted stale. Within the city itself, there was also *buffetto*, a type of luxury bread that was produced only by a handful of bakers and was usually bought only for the old or for the sick. It was a very fine and very white bread, made using the best-quality flour, sometimes with small additions of butter and sugar; however, during times of shortage or famine, production of *buffetto* was suspended.

The first refinery to extract sugar from molasses successfully was set up by a *spezier de grosso*, a druggist whose typical products included candles, coated almonds and almond oil. Though only the *spezieri de fino* (or *spezieri di medicine*) were veritable apothecaries, any type of *spezier* had to go through a long period of training before he could open his own shop. The State, in fact, required such people not only to complete a five-year apprenticeship and then spend three years as a *spezier*'s shop boy, but also to pass a very tough examination before the *Collegio degli Speziali* (College of Druggists and Apothecaries).

At the sweet end of the baking market were the *scaleteri* or *ciambellai*, confectioners who sold their produce in the streets, usually a tray of doughnuts or cakes made using pepper and honey. This category of tradesmen was subject to a wide range of regulations, some of them rather strange. For example, they were not allowed to carry more than one tray of goods at a time, they could not sell cakes in churches during Confirmation ceremonies nor model cakes in the forms of women, horses, cats or birds.

As for the *fritelle*, they were practically the Venetian Republic's 'national cake' and were made in the street by *fritoleri*, whose square-shaped wooden stalls were dotted around the city. The dough was mixed on a large wooden table in view of one and all, then the *fritelle* were fried in oil, pig fat or butter contained in large dishes that rested on tripods. When ready, they were laid out on decorative plates, alongside displays of such prized ingredients as pine nuts, raisins and citrons.

Opposite: *A milk seller (top) and a Venetian sugar refinery, using sugar-cane brought from Venetian lands in Cyprus, according to Grevembroch.*

Fish

Fish

The Greek word for fish – *'icthys'* – was taken by the early Christians to be an acronym for *Iesous Christos Theou Yios Soter* (Jesus Christ, Son of God, the Saviour) and this explains why the fish symbol appears on the walls of Palaeo-Christian catacombs. And for the terrorized Veneti seeking shelter from invading barbarians, fish provided salvation: the waters of the lagoons that stretched from Aquileia to the Po delta not only kept their enemies at bay but also supplied abundant stores of food. From that moment onwards, fishing and hunting played a fundamental role in the history of the Veneto. After the collapse of the Roman Empire, these activities became the prime source of food, rather than a supplement to agriculture. Without fish, there is no way that the communities who took refuge in the lagoons could have survived.

Given that fishermen in the open sea are at the mercy of the elements, the very activity of fishing takes on an almost religious aspect; it involves venturing into the unknown and then returning with a catch that determines their fortunes. For the peoples who lived along the coasts or shorelines, boats were like horses, enabling them to go out to 'hunt' their livelihoods and come back with fish that could be eaten fresh or dried; be grilled or used to make soups. Even fish eggs could be salted and made into *bottarga* (dried fish eggs).

The Adriatic Sea is a plentiful source of tasty and varied fish, and over the centuries its generosity has been a key factor in shaping the customs, eating habits and traditions of the peoples who live along its shores. It is, for example, no coincidence that in Venice one of the nursery rhymes we sing to amuse children is all about fish: in turn, you touch the child's forehead, eyes, nose and mouth, then end by pulling gently on his ears, identifying each part of the face with a fish: *'Un'orada, do caparozzoli, Un rombo, Na cesta, Do sportele per el pesse!'* (One gilt head, Two clams, One turbot, One lobster pot and Two bags for fish!)

With their many islands, twisting canals, mudflats and open spaces of water, the lagoons that have formed at the mouths of the various rivers emptying into the Adriatic are a sort of hymn to freedom. Living in this varied world of land, air and water, man can move freely, propelled by just a few strokes of an oar. An essential complement to this liberty is the relative ease with which food can be obtained, either by fishing or by raising stocks to eat when the seasonal plenty of fish comes to an end. This tradition of *valli da pesca* (fish farms), which are simply closed-off areas around the periphery of the lagoon, goes back to the earliest settlements – even if fish caught in the open sea have a richer flavour.

The Rialto fish market reflects this plenty, with sea bass, turbot, gilt head bream, monkfish, dentex, red scorpion fish, grey John Dory and local goby fish. These latter are distinctive not only for their green and yellow stripes, but also for their special domestic arrangements: to accommodate his numerous partners, the male builds a nest with a single narrow entrance, then – when the young fish begin to hatch – it is he who acts as nursemaid to them. The local fishermen have an expression for the period from late June onwards when the goby settle down to this domestic contentment: *el go fa el leto* (the goby is preparing its wedding chamber).

Other signs of plenty at the Rialto market are gleaming sardines, sprats and mackerel; sinuous eels writhing around in metal vats; rich varieties of molluscs (cuttlefish, squid and baby squid, octopus, mussels, clams, razor clams, scallops); and numerous crustaceans such as bright red lobsters, the local black lobster with its monstrous claws, tasty spider crabs, mantis shrimp, scampi, shrimps, pink and blue-grey prawns and small local *schie* (grey shrimp).

The abundance of sea food in Venice and the surrounding area is reflected in the cuisine, characterized by a natural wealth of simple yet very tasty dishes: cuttlefish in its ink, fish *in saòr*, John Dory fillets, great selections of grilled fish, fish soup and wonderful risottos. It is a type of food that heralds celebration of any type – *la festa* – and around which friends and family gather to talk about life, hopes and affections.

Documents regarding food legislation in the Serenissima Republic include a list of tariffs that dates back to 1173, when Sebastiano Ziani was Doge, and reveal that from the Middle Ages onwards, the most common fish in Venice were trout, sturgeon, turbot, gilt head bream, red mullet, flounder, sole, eels, pike and tench. The most highly prized fish included bream and sea bass, whilst the smaller, cheaper fish included such local varieties as rock goby and *marsoni* (from the same family), which were all sold by the basketful. And, just like today, the best time for fishing was on a moonless night, when fish could be lured into nets by the lamps mounted on the front of boats.

Right up until the fall of the Republic, Venice had a large fishing community. In 1784, for example, the number of fishermen, boatmen, fishmongers and *valli* rangers totalled almost 20,000 (half of them resident in Chioggia, at the southern end of the lagoon, which had always been the centre for fishing in the Adriatic and farther east). These were communities of hardy men of stout character. In fact, fishing is still so important in the community as a whole that to describe someone as a 'fisherman' means nothing at all; for the term to have any significance, one has to say what type of fish the man caught (or catches), and from that one can also deduce the man's social and economic position. There were, for example, those who specialized in catching small sea bass or those who gathered the special local species of crab (*mazanete* or *moeche*). And, of course, each member of these communities paid particular heed to the 'fishers of souls' in their midst, happy to give thanks for the Almighty's assistance in facing the dangers of their work; the churches of Chioggia are full of naively painted votive plaques offered by those who survived perils at sea.

In eighteenth-century Venice, fish was a rarity in the households of the rich and noble, eaten only on fast days (and even then the small local fish were considered too humble for a patrician table). When you look at the recipe books of the day, all you find are mentions of fried fish, boiled fish and grilled fish, with the rare exceptions of *brodeto* (fish soup) and fish *in saòr* or *alla busara*. However, substantial quantities of fish were consumed by the rest of the city.

Fish served in patrician homes or at ducal banquets was of only the very highest quality, perhaps being brought in from rivers and lakes hundreds of miles away. That the doges were very demanding with regard to the fish they were served is demonstrated by the fact that the last Doge, Ludovico Manin, found time to decide personally who should be the keeper of the *Valli dell'Arsenale* fish farms that provided oysters 'for the comfort of the Ducal Family'. The remit for the position laid down that, in a number of instalments, the ducal kitchens would be supplied with more than 3000 dozen oysters. And that is without taking into account the supplies that were provided for the official dinners and State banquets, to which the Doge invited senators and ambassadors. The feast day of St Mark – Venice's patron saint on 25 April – was a particularly intense holiday that recalled the day in 999 (almost eight centuries earlier) when the Doge Pietro Orseolo II set sail from Venice to ensure the city's dominion over the Adriatic.

The plaque giving the price and the minimum and maximum size, which the Republic laid down for the various types of fish traded in the market, is still on the wall of the Rialto fish market. However, buying fish can still be daunting for the inexperienced. You have to take into account freshness, net weight and price according to season. In theory, it is best to buy fish in the morning from returning fisherman. Smell is also important: saltwater fish should have a hint of seaweed in their smell and freshwater fish should recall the smell of river reeds. The scales should be shiny, the flesh firm, the gills vivid red and the eyes particularly bright. If you follow the advice of a fishmonger you trust, you will quickly learn how to tell when fish is really fresh. And, having bought it, if you do not feel confident about your expertise in the kitchen, you can always follow the Venetian saying: 'Those who do not know how to cook fish, do it in the oven.'

Another important method of preparing fish is frying. Olive oil probably entered Venetian cuisine through the city's ancient links with Puglia, Sicily and the Greek islands. Naturally enough, one of the first ways in which it was used was to fry the fish that the lagoon and sea supplied in such abundance. Oil was transported in barrels from the hinterland to the very area in Venice where I now live; in fact, one of the alleys in my neighbourhood is called *Calle dei Botteri* (Coopers Alley). That this zone was long used for loading and unloading boats is shown by a decree of 1342 that sought to maintain accessibility for delivery boats and laid down that 'No privately enclosed area on the quayside from the landing-place of the boats up to Rio di Ca' Bellegno – that is, Ponte di San Cassan – is justifiable or permissible.' Walking around Venice, I have come across various other *Calli dei Botteri* scattered around various neighbourhoods.

Guild regulations required the city's coopers to make special barrels for the doge – and to provide certain public entertainments, including bull-baiting. A report concerning the night of 25 January 1511 recalls that the baiting of four bulls in *Calle dei*

A plaque at the fishmarket states the minimum permissible sizes for the various types of fish to be sold.

Botteri went on until 3 am, together with dancing and street theatre. Coopers had lots of work to do but they could also be a nuisance; a suit was brought against them by local residents complaining that their rest was disturbed by the continual rolling of the barrels along the streets, but without any mention of the late-night revelries!

People tend to eat less fried fish nowadays – preferring to avoid the smell it makes and watching cholesterol levels – but our grandmothers were very skilled in the art of frying fish, though they limited their use of boiling oil to the kitchen – unlike the ferocious widow who, in 1505, robbed her black-smith lover, then stabbed him whilst he was asleep, poured boiling oil over him, before finishing him off with a swipe on the head with a candlestick and finally setting fire to the house. Tried and convicted, she was punished by having her right hand cut off (in Campo Santa Sofia, at the scene of her crime) and was beheaded between the columns in St Mark's Square.

When I was small, there were still a few *frittolini* in Venice, shops serving good, crisp and tender fried fish. Now they have almost all disappeared along with their characteristic window displays of fish and a cloth-draped chopping board with a plump 'loaf' of yellow or white polenta. A huge pot of boiling oil was always ready on the stove, alongside trays of eels, cuttlefish rings, *schie* and other small shrimps. Both the fish and polenta were served wrapped in sheets of paper – and could either be taken home or eaten on the premises at bare tables with wooden chairs or benches. Unlike *osterie*, which had inventive and imaginative names, the *frittolini* were simply known by their owners' names. An even more basic version of these fry-shops were the *furatole,* which had a very humble clientele; perhaps the name comes from the Venetian *furabola*, which scholars define as 'barbaric' (the word's associations with darkness and obscurity made it particularly suited to pokey little places with smoke-covered, grimy walls). The regulations regarding these businesses gives some idea of how detailed Venetian commercial legislation could be: no clerks or ecclesiastics were allowed to run a *furatola*; the *furatoleri* were forbidden to serve foods reserved to *luganegheri* (sausage-makers) and were not allowed to serve food dressed with cheese, fine oil or other fats; nor could they serve even a splash of wine. Infraction of these rules resulted in a heavy fine and closure for up to a year.

But now let's look at the practical aspects of frying food. Some people prefer vegetable oil, claiming that it is lighter, less fatty and has a less invasive taste than its ancient rival. Others argue that, being more resistant to high temperatures, the molecules of olive oil do not break up during frying so that it is healthier. For myself, I prefer good-quality olive oil: its distinctive taste adds something to any dish – and particularly fried fish, for which you have to use a lot of oil.

To fry food successfully you need a sharp eye, experience and that *je ne sais quoi* that is possessed by all good cooks. The first trick is to keep the fish in the boiling oil for as little time as possible, just long enough for it to cook all the way through and become crisp on the outside. This is easier said than done and even an excellent cook can sometimes be dissatisfied with the results of his work. The second trick is to use small or medium-sized fish, and fry them a few at a time (unless you have a special deep-frying pan containing at least 10 cm/4 in of hot oil). Dropping the fish into the fat lowers the temperature momentarily, so if you put too much fish in at once, it simply sits there until the oil heats up again.

In the city's *trattorie* – and few surviving *frittolini* – the fried fish are generally sole, *passarin* (a tiny flat flounder), small goby fish, young eels, sardines and small local *noni*, alongside shellfish including scampi, prawns, shrimps, *schie*, small squid, cuttlefish and *canestrelli* (pectin clams). Washed, dried and dipped in flour, these are fried in boiling oil and then placed on kitchen roll to absorb excess fat. Sprinkled with salt and garnished with lemon, they are ready to be served.

Some images I took of the Chioggia fishermen in the 1980s.

Seppie col nero alla veneziana
Cuttlefish in its ink

Serves 4
800 g / 1¾ lb medium-sized cuttlefish
1 onion, chopped
75 ml / 2½ fl oz olive oil
75 g / 3 oz butter
1 garlic clove
glass of dry white wine
chopped fresh parsley
salt and pepper

A much less courageous and aggressive beast than its cousin, the reddish-brown octopus, the cuttlefish swims off at the first sign of trouble, releasing clouds of black ink to cover its tracks. This characteristic makes it a real delicacy, because its flesh remains tender and never becomes as tough and muscular as that of the octopus.

Along the Adriatic coast, the tides push this rather passive beast towards the sandy shallows, where – lulled into a contemplative mood – the oval-shaped cephalopod falls easy prey to the fishermen's nets and begins its journey to the kitchens of Venice. At this point, any ink that the cuttlefish did not release in its attempt to avoid capture becomes an important ingredient in a very tasty dish of extraordinary colour.

Prized in Venice, the dish is very similar to the traditional Spanish dish of cuttlefish *en su tinta*. The real secret to good *Seppie alla veneziana* is that the cuttlefish be small, young and freshly caught. However, as the most difficult part of the preparation is cleaning the cuttlefish itself, you might like to look for ones that are already cleaned, even if they are frozen, as this doesn't necessarily impact upon the flavour adversely.

—⁂—

To clean the cuttlefish, skin each one and cut away the mouth opening and the bone, and then gut the fish. Set aside a couple or so of the ink sacs. Now wash the cuttlefish several times in lots of water and cut it into strips.

In a pan, sauté the chopped onion in the oil and butter together with a whole garlic clove (remove the clove when it is golden). When the onion is light gold in colour, add the cuttlefish and sauté for 20 minutes or so before adding a glass of dry white wine and the ink sacs. Cover the pan and simmer on low heat until the cuttlefish become tender. Remove the lid, add chopped parsley, salt and pepper and leave to simmer some more, to reduce the liquid that the cuttlefish release during cooking. Some people also add a glass of brandy (having heated it to lower the alcohol level) or even a pulped tomato midway through the cooking, but these additions are not part of the traditional Venetian recipe. The dish should be served with soft, freshly prepared polenta, either yellow or white.

Another way of preparing cuttlefish, albeit fairly primitive, comes from the fishermen of Chioggia, who dry them in the sun during the summer, hanging on the decks of their boats, so that they can continue to be served during the winter. They can be eaten as they are, because they do not become as leathery as other dried fish. However, the best way to prepare them is to lightly grill them.

Rombo alla veneziana
Venetian-style turbot

Serves 4
1 kg / 2¼ lb medium-sized turbot
a little milk
1 lemon, sliced
*400 g / 14 oz average-sized
potatoes*
olive oil, for dressing potatoes
200 g / 7 oz green or black olives

Sauce

15 g / ½ oz plain white flour
150 g / 5 oz butter
300 ml / ½ pint weak stock
*100 g / 3½ oz mushrooms, stalks
removed and finely chopped, caps
sliced*
*chopped fresh parsley,
plus fresh parsley sprigs to decorate*
a glass of dry white wine
salt and pepper

Turbot served with potatoes and olives is now considered an archetypal Venetian dish, although there is little evidence that it originated in the lagoon.

———∞———

Clean the turbot and then cut off its head, tail and fins. Soak for a couple of hours in cold water, which will need to be changed frequently.

Cook the fish in salted water with a little milk and some slices of lemon for about 20 minutes. Boil the potatoes separately in salted water. In a third pan, make a white sauce by mixing the flour into the melted butter and then gradually add the stock and the finely chopped mushroom stalks, salt, pepper and plenty of chopped parsley. Add the white wine and then let it simmer to reduce.

Drain the boiled potatoes and dress them with some olive oil and chopped parsley.

To serve, place the turbot on a long dish surrounded by olives and potatoes and decorate with sprigs of parsley. Serve the sauce separately.

Bisato in tecia
Eel stew

Serves 4
750 g / 2½ lb medium-sized eels
60 ml / 4 tbsp olive oil
40 g / 1½ oz butter
1 garlic clove, finely chopped
*a handful of finely chopped
fresh parsley*
fresh sage leaves
2 shots of marsala or sherry
*250 g / 8 oz canned
chopped tomatoes*
salt and pepper

The more usual way of preparing the tasty yet fatty flesh of the eels caught in the *valli* is in a stew, served with polenta. In this case, the polenta should not be too soft and, preferably, should be made with white maize flour, which provides a good colour contrast with the reddish-brown stew.

———∞———

Gut the eels, cut off the heads and slice into sections 5 cm (2 in) long; this makes it easier to cook them thoroughly. Place the eel in a pan with oil and butter over a high heat until they turn the colour of amber. Then add the finely chopped garlic and parsley. Wait for the mix to become reddish-brown, then add a few sage leaves. Pour in the marsala and let it reduce a little before adding the tomatoes. Cook at a reasonably high heat for 20 minutes, so that the tomato is more reddish-brown than red. Serve hot, with polenta.

Fileti de sgombro
Mackerel fillets

A very simple dish, this too is typical Venetian fare.

Serves 4

1 kg / 2¼ lb medium-sized mackerel, cleaned and scaled
chopped fresh parsley
75 g / 3 oz butter
200 ml / 7 fl oz fish stock
salt and pepper

———— ∞ ————

Preheat the oven to 200°C/400°F/Gas Mark 6. Fillet the mackerel, place in a greased ovenproof dish and then sprinkle with parsley, salt and pepper. Add a few knobs of butter and moisten with some fish stock. Cook for 15 minutes in the oven, checking that the fillets do not dry out.

To serve, lay the mackerel fillets out in a star pattern on a warm plate and pour the cooking juices they have released over them. Or serve with a white sauce like that described in the recipe for *Rombo alla veneziana*.

Calamaretti fritti
Fried baby squid

Serves 4

500 g / 1 lb baby squid
fine plain white flour
oil, for deep-frying
salt
2 lemons, quartered, to serve

The baby squid of the Adriatic are amongst the finest you will find in the Mediterranean, their diminutive refinement matched by extraordinary taste. Most frequently they are simply fried with small shrimps, whitebait and other small fish. However, they can also be served on their own.

———— ∞ ————

Clean the baby squid and then remove the bone, which is a sort of small and rubbery triangular lamina. Wash and dry the squid; then coat lightly in flour and deep-fry in a pan of oil. Be careful during the frying because if the baby squid are fried for too long, they shrivel and become not only tough but also tasteless and indigestible. When the squid are golden, which should be less than 10 minutes, remove them from the pan and, like any fried fish, place on paper towels to absorb the excess oil. Sprinkle with lots of salt and serve with lemon quarters.

Marsoni fritti
Fried *marsoni*

Serves 4

600 g / 1¼ lb marsoni or whitebait
olive or vegetable oil,
for deep-frying
salt
2 lemons, cut into wedges, to serve

'*Marsoni friti e polentina, un fià de vezena e vin de spina*' ('fried *marsoni* and polenta / A bit of Vezzena and draught wine'): according to the saying, the best way to enjoy the unmistakable aroma and flavour of *marsoni* is deep-fried, accompanied by Vezzena, one of the classic cheeses of the Asiago highlands in the Vicenza area. The name probably derives from the fact that these small fish are most abundant in March (*Marso* in dialect). The fish are easiest to catch where rivers like the Piave pass from the mountains and begin their descent towards the gentle plains. Whitebait would be a good alternative, although it is a marine rather than freshwater fish.

⎯⎯⎯⎯✼⎯⎯⎯⎯

Wash the *marsoni* thoroughly under running water and dry carefully. Coat them in flour and fry for a few minutes in boiling hot oil. Serve hot, with a lot of salt and lemon wedges to squeeze over.

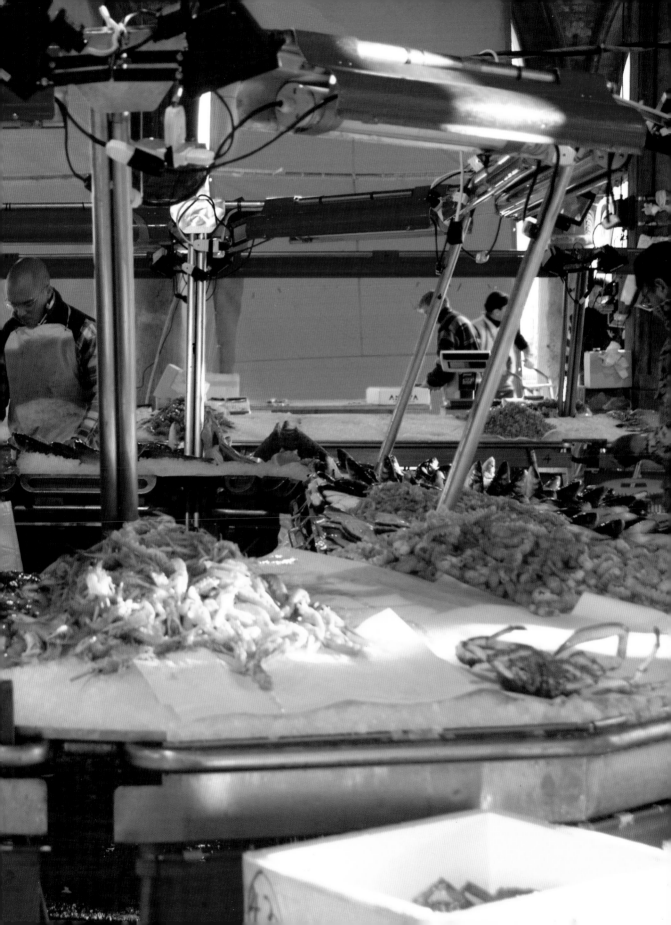

Bisato sulla brace
Grilled eel

More than elsewhere in the city, Campo San Luca was the place for burning the effigy of *La Vecchia* (The Old Woman), which took place halfway through the Lent period. This custom dates back to 1721 when a boy from the old pharmacy in Campo San Luca was executed for the murder of a prostitute; outside the pharmacy had been a sign depicting an old woman. The celebrations that accompanied the immolation of this effigy included 'eel-bobbing'. The eel in question was in a large tub of black-stained water, but the real difficulty was that you had to catch it with your teeth!

Between October and January, the bellies of young female eels begin to turn a silvery colour and flashes of black dots appear along their flanks, indicating that they are now fully adult and it is time for them to begin their migration. Many, however, will not get very far; they are caught in the *valli da pesca* (traditional fish farms) that dot the coast from the Po delta up past Chioggia and Caorle to Grado and then served up in the region's restaurants, especially the delicious *trattorie* along the Sile, Livenza and Brenta rivers.

The migratory urge of the eel is a very powerful one, driving this strange serpent-like fish to swim great distances – and even to drag itself across dry land – to get back to the Sargasso Sea where it was born and now, having reached sexual maturity, where it will breed and die. From this area of ocean – the very same as the mysterious 'Bermuda Triangle' – the microscopic young eels will subsequently set out in the opposite direction, swimming with the Gulf Stream until they reach the mouths of Europe's rivers some three years later. It is an incredible natural phenomenon, the scale of which is given by just one figure: in 1667 a total of one and a half million kilos of eels were caught at the mouth of the river Arno, measuring between 2 and 12 cm (1 and 4 in) long. And there is a further mystery: recent studies have been unable to detect the passage of the eels through the Straits of Gibraltar from the Mediterranean into the Atlantic. So how do they pass from one sea to the other?

Another open question that can cause hours of happy debate around the dinner table is whether the Veneto *bisato* is superior or inferior in taste to the freshwater eel. I favour the *bisato* and the large eels of the salty or brackish *valli da pesca* because they have a longer interlude before they undertake that amazing 10,000-mile journey. Only young eels live in fresh water; no adult eel has ever been found swimming up a river, whereas eels in the fish-runs can live for more than 10 years; there is even one recorded case of a female living in a fish-run for 55 years. In fact, what is known in the Veneto as *bisato* is never the male of the species, because these almost never grow beyond 50 cm (20 in) long. Still, this matriarchy is of little interest in the kitchen, because – as with most fish – there is a tendency to talk about the *bisato* as if it were an asexual being.

The fishermen's dwellings out in the *valli* are similar in structure to the traditional rural houses in the Veneto countryside, apart from a few differences reflecting their functions. The walls are traditionally hung with hunting and fishing equipment rather than agricultural implements; more fishing equipment is kept in the large wooden boathouses that project out over the waters. The space of the single ground-floor room is taken up by various worktables, and at the centre stands a large raised fireplace. It is here that the fishermen prepare one of the specialities of this area: grilled eel.

Many gourmets argue that the best *bisato* is that prepared in *tecia* – that is, in a stew – but since I had grilled eel, caught fresh at a *valli*, I can no longer agree. Of course, the beautiful scenery may have had a certain influence on my judgement together with the company of friends and the incredibly skilful keepers who, using a torch, could locate the eels in the muddy shallows and capture them with a forked stick. Then after the hunt, we all went back to the keeper's cottage, where a brightly burning fire of bound twigs and wattles was waiting to welcome us.

———— ◦❀◦ ————

Serves 4
2 fresh eels, filleted
(order these from your fishmonger)
salt

Heat the barbecue until the coals are covered in fine white ash. Place the eel fillets skin-side down on the barbecue and cook for 10 to 15 minutes; the skin protects the eel from the embers and the heat makes it shed nearly all its fat, giving the meat a very delicate taste. The result is wonderful.

Light and tender, this goes perfectly with glass after glass of white wine. Meanwhile, the fire roars and you enjoy the ever-lasting magic of being out here in the lagoon, with *valli* stretching as far as the eye can see, boats rocking gently on the water and the glow of the sunset in the distance.

Another popular way of preparing eel is rather simple but requires a baker's oven – or even a kiln. *Bisato sull'ara* was a favourite among the glass-blowers of Murano; its name in Venetian refers to the *ara* above a glass kiln where the newly created vases were placed and left to cool very gradually. The eels would be placed here on a bed of bay leaves to cook. Since eel has become less popular, the glass blowers prefer instead to use the *ara* to cook pig's trotters and lentils!

Renga salada
Salted herring

Serves 4
*4 good dried salted
or smoked herrings
500 ml / 18 fl oz milk
60 ml / 2 fl oz olive oil
1 onion, finely sliced in rings
a few bay leaves
pepper*

This slim fish, with its light blue and whitish scales, was originally a native of the seas of the north. In the Veneto, herrings used to be the Lenten dish *par excellence*. For example, a *Sagra della Renga* (Herring Feast) is still held on Ash Wednesday at Ponte Albano near Motta di Livenza, deep in the countryside. The last revellers go home bearing a large herring on the tip of a bamboo cane, the very symbol of the end of Carnival and the start of a period of abstinence. According to popular tradition, the herring would be cleaned, rubbed with oil and grilled before being hung from the lamp above the kitchen table. Everyone in the house simply rubbed their slice of toasted polenta against the fish to give it a bit of flavour during the parsimonious Lent period. Herrings can also be a real treat if prepared properly.

Wash the herrings and boil for 10 minutes or so, then place in a fresh pan in the cold milk or in fresh boiling water and leave to soak for about an hour, until the fish is tender and has lost a lot of its salty taste.

Remove the bones and divide the herrings into fillets, then place in a terrine with the oil, the finely sliced onion rings, some bay leaves and a twist of pepper. Leave the herrings to marinate like this for three to four days. Some people include finely chopped parsley and garlic in the mix.

Another herring delicacy is the roe, washed and placed in a jar with a lot of oil, pepper and other herbs. They are rather like caviar. Both the roe and the herring should be served with polenta and a light wine – light because you will need to drink quite a lot, given the saltiness of the herrings.

Variation

Serves 4
*4 good dried salted herrings
60 ml/2 fl oz green olive oil
25 g / 1 oz fresh parsley, chopped
½ garlic clove, finely chopped*

The above recipe is redolent of herring's north-European origins; in the Veneto it is also prepared in the following way:

Place the large salted herrings in boiling water for 5 minutes so that they lose their surface salt and soften up a little: remove and dry, then place on a moderately heated grill for about 10 minutes until well cooked. Remove and bone. Divide the fish into fillets and dress with green olive oil, parsley and some fragments of garlic. Set aside in the refrigerator and serve two or three days later.

Branzino al sale
Sea bass cooked in salt

Serves 4
*2 sea bass, weighing
about 400 g / 14 oz each
fresh thyme and parsley sprigs
1 garlic clove
2 kg / 4½ lb coarse grain sea salt
pepper*

The practice of cooking fish *al sale* (covered in salt), is an ancient tradition in the Venice lagoon, where the salt pans were already functioning before the end of the Roman Empire. Sea bass prepared in this way is one of the best versions but any medium to large fish can be used for this recipe. The result is surprisingly good, considering the simplicity of the method. The salt crust serves to seal in the fish juices.

Preheat the oven to 180°C / 350°F / Gas Mark 4. Gut, clean and rinse the fish well. Stuff the inside with thyme, parsley, the garlic clove and pepper. Pour half the coarse salt into an oven dish, place the fish on top and cover with the remaining salt. Be sure not to cover the eye with salt, so that you can check when the fish is ready. Cook in the oven for approximately 50 minutes, but check regularly – as soon as the eye turns white, the fish is ready.

Remove the fish from the oven and take off the salt crust and skin. Serve with Bercy sauce (a fish-stock-based velouté with shallots and a reduction of white wine, fish stock and seasonings), mayonnaise or a simple green sauce made with olive oil and parsley.

Gamberi di San Polo
San Polo prawns

Serves 4
800 g / 1¾ lb raw
freshwater prawns
1 litre / 1¾ pints water
75 ml / 2½ fl oz olive oil
25 g / 1 oz fresh parsley, chopped
chopped fresh oregano
dry white wine
salt, black pepper and
mild paprika

These renowned freshwater prawns come from San Polo di Piave, outside Treviso, near the source of the river Lia, in which they are fished. That these have long been considered a delicacy is demonstrated by an old fresco in the local church of San Giorgio, where – above the scene of the Last Supper – the artist added a clear depiction of some red prawns.

Unfortunately, the prawns fished from near the source of the Lia cannot meet the demand from local people as well as the numerous tourists attracted by this delicacy, so large quantities of similar prawns are now brought in regularly from the former Yugoslavia. These newcomers are then kept in special cages in the same waters, until it is their turn to be served up with the very tasty local sauce, which is a bright red-green.

Place the prawns in boiling water for 10 minutes or until they turn bright red. Drain and put them in a pan to sauté in olive oil with lots of chopped parsley. To heighten the taste, add a pinch of mild paprika, a little oregano, black pepper, salt and a splash of dry white wine. Cook for another 10 minutes, while the sauce reduces. San Polo Prawns should be served hot with a good yellow polenta, which makes a fine colour contrast, and some local white wine from Conegliano or Valdobbiadene. When prawns are not available, the recipe is almost as good with *canocie* (mantis shrimp) or scampi.

There is a certain ritual to eating San Polo prawns: you have to use your hands in order to pick apart the entire prawn. Every part contains some meat. As the Venetian expression says: *co no ghe xe gamberi, xe bone anca le zate* ('When there are no more prawns, the claws are good as well').

Scampi a la grela
Grilled scampi

Serves 4
20 large scampi
60 ml / 2 fl oz olive oil
chopped fresh parsley
salt and pepper

Of a brilliant pink colour that has the waxy hue of flower petals, scampi is a distant relative of the 'Norwegian Prawn', which arrived in the Mediterranean after emigrating from the rocky fjords of Scandinavia and passing the coasts of France, Spain and Portugal. Its name is of Greek or Byzantine origin, which is only fitting given that the last part of its journey up the Adriatic was through Byzantine territory: from Santa Maura and Corfu, the scampi moved onwards to Quarnaro and along the Dalmatian coast, where it found ideal conditions in the transparent, azure waters that rarely exceed 50 m (160 ft)in depth.

This is a very simple yet very successful Venetian dish. The secret is to use scampi that are both fresh and large. Once you get these home from the market, your job is practically done. The dish is not difficult to prepare, even if – as in so many things – practice makes perfect.

—⦿—

With a very sharp knife, cut the shells of the scampi along their bellies, from head to tail. Cut into the flesh to about half depth, so that the scampi is almost divided into two parts. Having opened them up, place under a hot grill with only a little olive oil, salt and pepper. When they are cooked (5 to 10 minutes on a barbecue or 10 to 15 minutes under the grill) place on a dish complete with shell – at least, that is the way aficionados prefer them served. Dress with more olive oil, pepper and a little finely chopped parsley.

Cotolete de sardele
Sardine cutlets

Serves 4
16 fresh sardines
plain white flour, for dusting
1 egg, beaten
dried breadcrumbs, for coating
very light vegetable or olive oil,
for deep frying
salt
lemon wedges, to serve

One of the cheapest and most unspoilt types of fish, the banal sardine is often overlooked. One way of making it more attractive – particularly to children, who do not like dealing with fish bones – is this recipe for sardine cutlets. My friendly fishmonger will fillet and clean a kilo of them for a modest €5 (£3). That's enough to feed the whole family plus a couple of school friends.

Cut the heads off the fish and then slice them open lengthways. Remove the bones but not the tail; the result is that the two fillets form a sort of butterfly cutlet. Coat in flour, then dip in a mixture of beaten egg and salt and cover with breadcrumbs. The cutlets should preferably be deep fried in olive oil, which is always tastier; but one can also use vegetable oil. Fry until golden brown, remove from the pan and leave for a couple of minutes on a paper towel to absorb excess oil. These *sardelle allinguate* (sardine tongues), as they are called in Sicily, should be served very hot with lots of lemon wedges and fresh salad.

Sardele a la greca
'Greek-style' sardines

Serves 4
500 g / 1 lb sardines
60 ml / 2 fl oz oil
25 g / 1 oz butter
25 g / 1 oz chopped fresh parsley
1 garlic clove
juice of 1 lemon
or 2 spoonfuls wine vinegar
salt

This simple recipe makes the most of the tasty, but sometimes underrated, sardine. It is prepared using the freshest fish, whose scales still have the distinctive silver flash.

Preheat the oven to 180°C / 350°F / Gas Mark 4. Gut the sardines, remove their heads and spines and cut the bodies into two fillets. Roll these into tight bundles and set upright in a pan containing the oil, butter, chopped parsley and a garlic clove; the pan should be packed tightly so that the rolls are touching. Now sprinkle with lemon juice or vinegar to reduce the oily taste of sardines. Add salt and bake in the oven for 20 minutes. Alternatively you can simmer the rolls very slowly in an uncovered pan for 15 minutes.

Baccalà alla vicentina
Vicenza-style stockfish

For centuries, *baccalà* – stockfish or salted codfish in the countries of Northern Europe – has been one of the tastiest offerings of Venetian cuisine, even if the origins of the dish are far from local and can be traced to the Lofoten Islands in the extreme north of Norway. The earliest inhabitants of that area – perhaps the Vikings themselves – had quickly learnt that to have abundant supplies of food all year round they simply needed to fish the enormous cod shoals within their waters, then dry the headed and gutted fish in the strong winds of the north. Hung up by their tails, the fish became as hard as wood and would keep for a long, long time. At last a solution had been found to the perpetual problem of hunger.

Sometime in the eleventh century, the Norwegians began to sell this dried fish in the rest of Europe, thanks to the skills of the German and Dutch merchants of the Hanseatic League, who very quickly established a monopoly in the sale of salt cod. And, ironically, the trade of these Protestant merchants was given a further boost by the Counter-Reformation Council of Trent in the mid-sixteenth century, which insisted upon a renewed severity of morals and fasting from meat on holy days.

In the Veneto, the origin of *baccalà* can be traced to the first half of the fifteenth century, when a Venetian *capitan da mar* (admiral), Pietro Querini, was shipwrecked in the waters of the North Sea and – together with 12 of his crew – he made it ashore to the island of Rost, the southernmost of the Lofotens (just below the 68th parallel).

Strictly speaking, *baccalà* is salt cod and *stocca fisso* is the term for stockfish but in Venice and the Veneto, unlike in the rest of Italy, *baccalà* and *stocca fisso* are used indifferently to refer to the same thing – stockfish. Once upon a time, before the discovery of saltpans in what is now Poland in the sixteenth century, salting was too expensive a procedure because the countries of the north did not have the sun and calm seas necessary to produce salt in large quantities. (The value of salt was not something that the Venetians needed to be told about, given that one of the sources of their fabulous wealth was the monopoly that they had established in their part of the Adriatic.) So, *baccalà* as salted cod came later. Being conservative, however, the Venetians and the people of the Veneto did not accept this new commercial variant (which is only a few centuries old) and continue to use the term in its old sense so all recipes derive from plain stockfish.

One of the tastiest ways of preparing *baccalà* is *alla vicentina*, a method that is now known and appreciated throughout Italy and beyond; visitors to the city are easily persuaded to try it. One such was Abbé Lane, the exuberant master of the cha-cha-cha, who having been served a meal of typical local fare – *pasta e fasioi* and *baccala alla vicentina* – commented, 'Good first course, great second course. Worthy of being one of the most famous dishes in the world.'

This method of cooking *baccalà* also gets rid of any residual toughness the fish may have even after being soaked in water. A good rule when buying *baccalà* is to go for the smaller, less rigid type – usually called *baccalà ragno* – which is easier to cook.

Serves 4
500 g / 1 lb dried stockfish
or salted codfish
250 ml / 8 fl oz olive oil
1 onion, chopped
handful of chopped fresh parsley
2 spoonfuls of white flour
3 salted anchovies, boned
300 ml / ½ pint milk
salt and pepper

If using salted codfish, rinse well in cold water. Then beat to tenderize the fish and leave it to soak overnight in cold water – change the water as often as sleep allows. Then carefully break up the fish and clean away the bones.

Using a lot of oil, sauté the chopped onion until it is very light brown, add the chopped parsley and the two spoons of flour for thickening. Then, add the cod, together with the boned anchovies, pepper and milk. Mix and then, without covering the pan, cook on a slow heat until all the milk is absorbed. Serve it hot with white or yellow polenta.

Baccalà a la capuzzina
Capucine stockfish (or codfish)

Serves 4
650 g / 2 oz dried stockfish
or salted codfish
1 garlic clove
25 g / 1 oz fresh parsley, chopped
60 ml / 2 fl oz olive oil
40 g / 1½ oz butter
1 litre / 1¾ pints milk
25 g / 1 oz each sultanas
and pine nuts
salt

If using salted codfish, rinse well in cold water before pre-soaking it overnight as described in the recipe for *Baccalá alla vicentina*. Boil for 15 minutes, then skin and bone the fish, and break into medium-sized pieces.

Sauté the whole garlic clove and the chopped parsley in the oil and butter and when the garlic is golden-brown, remove it and add the fish to the pan. Stir while cooking at a low heat, pouring in the milk, a little at a time. When the milk has been almost entirely reduced and the stockfish is almost cooked, add the sultanas and pine nuts. Add salt at the end, if necessary.

Fileti de sampiero
Fillets of John Dory

Serves 4
500 g / 1 lb John Dory fillets
plain white flour, for coating
1 egg, beaten
dry breadcrumbs, for coating
150 g / 5 oz good-quality
unsalted butter
2 lemons
salt

The local name for this large Adriatic fish – *Sampiero* – probably derives simply from the fact that St Peter is known to have been a fisherman. Looking rather like some of the more extravagant fish of the eastern seas, John Dory has undulating fins which end in long filaments. Averaging about 1.5 kg (3¼ lb), its grey, flattened oval body bears a distinctive dark marking – the size of a coin – on the side. Extremely tasty, it can be added to fish soup (the flesh from the head is particularly suited to this), but most frequently it is prepared in fillets.

———— ✺ ————

Wash the fillets and dry them thoroughly. Coat them first in flour, then dip in a mixture of beaten egg and salt before coating both sides in breadcrumbs. Fry the fish in plenty of butter, making sure that the fillets (which are quite thick) have enough time to cook thoroughly. When they have reached a fine golden colour, serve them on an oval plate with wedges of lemon to squeeze over.

This dish is often accompanied by baby artichokes and boiled new potatoes.

Broeto
Fish soup

Serves 4
500 g / 1 lb scorpion-fish, cleaned
500 g / 1 lb goby fish, cleaned
300 g / 10 oz schie
or small shrimps
½ lemon
2 tomatoes
600 g / 1¼ lb grey mullet
600 g / 1¼ lb monkfish
60 ml / 2 fl oz tablespoons
finest extra virgin olive oil
50 g / 2 oz butter
1 garlic clove
chopped fresh parsley
salt

French *bouillabaisse* and the *cacciucco* served on the Livorno coast of Tuscany are certainly more famous than this dish, which is so delicate and yet tasty, but based exclusively on the flavours of its seafood ingredients *broeto* is arguably superior. The saffron in the *bouillabaisse* and the pepper and paprika in the *cacciucco* both risk overwhelming the taste of the prized ingredients. *Broeto* is a very dense soup made using only the best the Adriatic has to offer, and, moreover, uses only carefully prepared pieces of fish so must be served without any annoying and distracting fish bones.

Scorpaena scrofa or *scarpene* (Venetian) is the same as *scorfano rosso* (Italian), scorpion fish in English. It is common in Mediterranean countries – there is no really good substitute except perhaps gurnard.

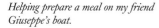

Clean the scorpion-fish, then combine with the cleaned goby fish and *schie* in a pan of water with half a lemon and two fresh tomatoes. Simmer for a good 30 minutes.

Strain, setting the cooking liquid to one side, and carefully clean the fish, discarding all the bones, skin, heads, etc. Pass the flesh and *schie* through a sieve. Strain the reserved cooking liquid and then stir in the dense 'purée'.

In another pan, simmer for 10 minutes the body of the monkfish and any pieces of flesh that you can get from its monstrous head. Add the grey mullet and simmer together for another 20 minutes. When they are ready, remove the head and bones of the mullet. Now sauté the garlic with the parsley in the oil and butter and then add the pieces of fish and sauté briefly. Then pour over the stock made with the strained fish purée, add a little salt and simmer for a few minutes.

To serve *broeto* in typically Venetian style, pour generous portions into large bowls over fried homemade bread.

Helping prepare a meal on my friend Giuseppe's boat.

Pesce in saòr
Marinated fried fish

The Venetian word *saòr* actually means nothing other than *sapore* (flavour) and refers to the fact that the use of good wine vinegar serves to heighten the taste of what, in effect, is marinated fish – a procedure that has been used throughout the Mediterranean since time immemorial.

The origins of the dish are simpler than one might think. In the days before refrigeration there was always the risk that part of a plentiful catch might go bad before it could be eaten – a sinful waste of God's bounty. One solution was to use oil, vinegar and onion to cook fish in a way that would preserve it for days on end without sacrificing its fragrance or flavour. According to a Venetian saying, the type of fish prepared *in saòr* defined one's social class: the poor used sardines, craftsmen and tradesmen used *passarini* (a type of small flounder) and the rich, sole.

Today the fish most commonly prepared *in saòr*, whoever you may be, are sardines, whose soft and smooth flesh combines wonderfully with this mix of onion, vinegar and raisins. Flounder and sole, meanwhile have moved on to a more 'noble' destiny, inspired by French cuisine. Nowadays in addition to the so-called *sarde de alba* ('dawn' sardines, caught immediately off the coast and brought straight to morning market), *papaline* (sprats; the name comes from the fact they are fished off the coast of what was once part of the Papal States) and, once again, sole and *passerini* with *schie* (the smaller local variety of grey shrimp) are used to make this dish.

Serves 4
650 g / 1¼ lb sardines, cleaned
a little flour
200 ml / 7 fl oz frying oil
800 g / 1¼ lb white onions, sliced
a glass of wine vinegar
50 g / 2 oz sultanas
pine nuts (optional)
salt

Cut the heads off the sardines and then coat them in flour and fry in a pan with a deep layer of oil, until golden. Drain, salt well and set aside. Into the same oil put the sliced onion and cook until soft, then pour in a glass of vinegar and cook until the liquid reduces a little.

In a serving dish, alternate layers of fried sardines and onions in the vinegar mix, with a sprinkling of sultanas, until the dish is full. The last layer should be onion and vinegar mix. Place the dish in a cool place for a couple of days, if you can resist! Prepared *in saòr*, the fish will keep for up to a week and tastes better and better with time. It can be eaten at all hours – even as a late-night snack with a bit of cold polenta.

Great feasts for ladies only

DORNED with coloured paper lanterns, flowers and sprigs of greenery all types of boats in the lagoon are transformed into floating 'dining-rooms' for the traditional supper eaten on the eve of the feast of *Il Redentore*. Held annually – on the eve of the third Sunday in July – to celebrate the end of the plague in 1570, this was and still is – an occasion illuminated by a marvellous firework display and, then as now, might end with a dawn dip in the sea at the Lido.

Several weeks might be spent in preparations for *Il Redentore*. The largish boat – generally a *peata* – was rented, equipped with tables and benches and then decorated. The plentiful food for the evening included such tasty and nourishing dishes as fish *in saòr* (sole, sardines and small local *passerin* fried and then marinated in strong vinegar mixed with fried onions and raisins), stuffed roast duck, the best fruit in season (including succulent red watermelon) and strong sweet wines from Cyprus, Greece and the coast of Puglia, with marsala from Sicily to accompany the traditional *fritole* (fried doughnuts) and *bussolai* (biscuits): all in all, a fine feast.

There was a time when certain *garanghei* (festive expeditions) were reserved solely for women of the humbler classes, giving them an evening away from husbands and beaux. One seventeenth-century gentleman – a certain Piero da Mosto – decided to invite himself to one of these ladies' occasions, but found himself out of luck. During the Easter celebrations, he – with two lady friends from the country and his sister – set out into the lagoon for a night-time picnic. Having bought some fresh fish from a passing fishing boat, they looked for somewhere to cook it.

His sister suggested calling upon their aunt, a nun at the convent of Sant'Anna. After sending a servant ahead with

the bucket of fish as a gift, they were soon welcomed by Sister Cherubina, who insisted that they come ashore. This, Piero's sister did not want to do; she wasn't very well dressed and was wearing clumsy boots. So they decided instead to take the boat up the narrow canal that ran alongside the convent cellars and keep their visit 'unofficial'. Sister Cherubina met them there and brought along her two cousins, Sister Nicolosa and Sister Costantina, making up a lively and happy party. However, within 15 minutes, the revellers were spotted by an agent of the local magistrate, who accused Piero da Mosto of having rather too good a time in the company of nuns. Thus the party was broken up – probably before the fish was even cooked – and Piero da Mosto found himself on trial.

Venetian women were as renowned for their beauty as for their lack of modesty. A certain Nicolò Franco da Benevento had this to say in 1542 about the beauty of Marina da Mosto, known as 'La Magnifica': 'A certain lady, Marina by name, the very mirror and essence of beauty, elegance, gentility and resolution. This fine lady goes about with an uncovered face, capturing hearts and affections and revealing what the heavens themselves cover to both warm and embrace the spirits.'

Others, however, were less complimentary about this lack of reserve, arguing that most of the city's noblewomen were revelling in 'the possession of a certain natural wit', which was enhanced by their delightful dialect and lack of interest in the things of the mind. While Venetian women were accused of 'crass ignorance' on the one hand, they continued blithely on their mission of amusement, surrounding themselves in gaiety right up to the final days of the Venetian Republic. A lifestyle of this kind is captured in a letter from an elegant Renaissance noblewoman, who however remains anonymous:

> My dear Checo, I assure you that I was delighted to hear news of you…. All the fun of the day is centred at Padua, with its famous opera house. I have no one at the moment, but there are many madly in love with me, whom I want to tell you about… Agostino Mosenigo, the Cavalier his brother, Ferigo Cavali, Momolo Morosini, Giusto Contarini, Vitor da Mosto [my own ancestor!], Momolo Giustinian, the brother of the king of France and a lot of foreigners. But, my love, I think of none but you, dear

heart. There is Alessandro Gritti who is courting me, and that relative of his, Ferigo Venier, and many others. But, be assured, they have no success and that I will always love you and I will never forget who loves me with his whole heart. Soon I am going into the country with my husband. Goodbye, my dear. Goodbye, dear heart. Love me truly. Your most affectionate friend, Cattina.

Of course, there were also ladies such as Maria Lippomanno, who took a serious interest in the arts, as well as elegant intellectuals such as Isabella Teotochi Albrizzi, whose cultural qualities were however insufficient to stop Lord Byron being dazzled – and then seduced away – by the notoriously beautiful Elena da Mosto (another relative of mine).

In Venice, Byron made the acquaintance of numerous women. He lived in one of the Palazzi Mocenigo on the Grand Canal – the very same building that had been the home of Anna Arundel, wife of the English general Thomas Arundel, whose 'friendship' cost Antonio Foscarini his life: for betraying the secrets of the Republic, this former ambassador to England, had to be 'strangled and strung up by the heels'. It was here that Byron wrote the first cantos of *Don Juan*. At one time he lived with Margherita Cogni, the wife of a baker, who, to escape the dire fate of having to return to her husband, amid tears and laments, threw herself into the Grand Canal from a gondola. However, with Elena da Mosto things went rather differently. One day, whilst at the theatre with Contessa Isabella Teotochi Albrizzi, Lord Byron told his companion sadly that, due to a pressing engagement, he would have to leave. The truth was that he was caught up in the turmoil and suffering of a new amorous intrigue. With a magnificent mane of hair and sea-blue eyes, Elena da Mosto was proving to be an insatiable and demanding lover – and the source of the only case of gonorrhoea that Byron did not catch from more 'mercenary' sources. (His cavalier attitude to these infections was such that he felt it was better to 'die in battle' when young than to live chastely.) Details of Elena da Mosto's attractiveness are described in a letter the poet wrote to his friend and confidant John Cam Hobhouse:

Venice. March 3d. 1818. My dear H. … Now for Venice.– Hoppner has got a son–a fine child.–The Carnival was very merry.–Madame Albrizzi's Conversazioni are greatly improved, there have been some pretty women there lately.– San Benedetto bas oratorios–Haydn & Handel–given by Andrea Erizzo.––My Whore-hold has been much extended since the Masquing began & closed–but I was a little taken aback by a Gonorrhea gratis-given by a Gentil-donna yclept Elena da Mosta–a lady who has by no means the character of being disinterested–but from some whim or other– positively refused money or presents from me (you may suppose I did not then know she was ill) I presume for the novelty's sake;–it is the first of such maladies–which I believe not to have been purchased…

In Renaissance Venice there were, in fact, two types of courtesans: the *cortigiana onesta*, who might keep a sort of intellectual salon, and the *cortigiana di lume*, a courtesan in the modern sense of the word, who plied her trade in the streets near the Rialto Bridge. There was even a *Catalogo di tutte le principale et più honorate cortigiane di Venezia*, which gave the names, addresses and rates of the best-known courtesans in Venice. One man who consulted this catalogue when visiting the city was the future Henri III of France, who during his time in Italy, met the beautiful and renowned Venetian courtesan Veronica Franco, with whom he passed many a pleasant hour, and to whom he is said to have declared in no uncertain terms:

> No more words! To deeds, to the battlefields, to arms! Come here and, full of most ardent desire, Braced stiff for your task, Bring with daring hand a piercing blade Let all armour be stripped from your naked breast.… Let no one else intervene in this match, Let it be limited to the two of us alone Behind closed doors, all seconds sent away… to eat with another mouth, sleep with another's eyes, move according to another's will, obviously rushing towards the shipwreck of your mind and your body – what greater misery? What wealth, what luxuries, what delights can outweigh all this? Believe me, among all the world's calamities, this is the worst.

Veronica Franco was probably the most famous *cortigiana onesta* of Renaissance Venice, combining refined literary and artistic tastes with beauty. She had been born in Cannaregio, a poor part of the city, of whose women it was said: 'The girls of Cannaregio eat polenta and millet; they haven't got a stove, because they have hocked even that'.

Meat

Meat

The huge antlered heads looming out of the white walls of castles made ancient traditions and legends regarding deer – and venison – as fascinating for me as a child, as were any of the tales involving the elves, gnomes and witches inhabiting woods and forests. Hunting of wild boar and deer was remarkable even in Roman times – as one can see from the bas-reliefs in the Belluno tomb said to contain the body of Domitia, wife of the Roman knight Flavius Ostilius, who is credited with founding the city. After killing a wild boar he was given the title '*vir unus*' (unique man).

From the Middle Ages onwards, the antlers of deer became trophies commemorating the deeds of local gentry who, over the centuries, were particularly proud of not only their hunting privileges, but also the more intimate privileges guaranteed by *jus primae noctis*. One of the keenest hunters of fallow deer was a woman – a former queen, no less. In the hills to the northwest of Treviso, Caterina Cornaro, ex-queen of Cyprus, established her court at Asolo in the sixteenth century. Over 20 years she embellished this domain with a splendid palace, two frescoed outhouses, extensive stables, two deep wells and a beautiful fountain – all in 100 hectares of land carefully laid out with laurel trees, vineyards, orchards and vegetable gardens. An important part of Caterina's life of delights was hunting, as depicted in a fresco over the arch in the central tower of her palace, in which she is mounted on a white horse as she hunts deer. The artist of this fresco might have been Giorgione, a painter for whom colour was of paramount importance in the creation of works that harmoniously combine figures and landscape to form images of obscure, fantastic meaning. Nowadays, all that is left of the frescoes is an image of a boat and the sinister legend, over the central well, which reads: 'the great well into which the queen had her paramours thrown.'

The deer had long been considered an emblem of power, and it often appears on heraldic crests. When a particularly magnificent specimen was killed, the carcass would be cut up into sections to be spit-roasted in the enormous fireplaces of smoky kitchens and then 'reassembled' before being brought to the banqueting table by stewards and attendants. The meat of the adult animals – those whose enormous antlers look like some sort of joke of nature – is rather tough and strongly flavoured. Therefore, people prefer the flesh of the younger animals and particularly of the poor fawns, whose meat is more delicate and tasty. Once upon a time, venison was almost always eaten roasted, stewed or in *salmì*; venison soup was also much appreciated. The antlers that did not end up gracing a castle's walls were cut up into small pieces and fried, or else ground into a sort of jelly, which was considered a true delicacy and served both savoury and sweet.

In paintings from all eras that show either important banquets or domestic meals, busy kitchens or carefully arranged still lives, the most commonly depicted meat is either poultry or game birds; it is much rarer to find larger animals featured (especially bovines). Even as late as the beginning of the twentieth century, a large part of bovine livestock was used for working in the fields. Oxen pulled carts and ploughs, while cows were used for lighter work (besides calving and for milk production). The animals were employed as long as they were strong enough, then slaughtered reluctantly when they were well past their prime. Even the tough meat obtained from these adult animals was a delicacy available to only a few people. Hardly anyone could afford to eat meat every day; it was a privilege to have a few morsels of meat on Sundays. Most consumers had to settle for offal or cheap off-cuts, the best pieces of meat being destined for the nobility. Furthermore, there was little selective breeding of bovines, so the flavour of the meat was unremarkable. You had to put up with what you got.

People ate an abundance of offal and giblets, which were considered to be imbued with great symbolic significance, as well as providing nourishment. By eating bits of the dead, it was thought that their life force would be communicated to the living, so life won out over the ever-present threat of hunger. What is more, because giblets and offal are soft and easily chewed, they were appreciated by those whose teeth had been damaged by age, scurvy and *pellagra* (a disease caused by vitamin deficiency). But innards and offal could not be kept for any length of time. This meant that, after years of loving care, when an animal was finally slaughtered, there was a period of a few days in which people could happily eat their fill. Not only was there abundant

One of Pietro Longhi's most famous paintings depicts duck shooting on the Venice lagoon. One can almost feel the chill of the winter's day in the valli da pesca.

food but also a variety of flavours. The most highly prized were the 'red innards': liver, lung, spleen, kidneys, tongue and heart. But there were also those who preferred the delicate flavour of the 'white innards': the head, brains and feet of a young calf all figured in tasty local dishes. One product that was particularly appreciated was salted tongue of beef, made using salt, saltpetre, garlic and various herbs and spices. As for oxtail, this continues to provide Venetians with a highly regarded dense soup and the recipe is included in this collection.

A pig's trotters and ears can be grilled; its kidneys cooked on the open fire, and the liver prepared in its reticulum. In Treviso, numerous dishes involve tripe, which were traditional midday fare for merchants and carters or a special delicacy served in the early hours of a wedding morning to the friends who were to accompany the bride and groom to church.

There were many chickens within the region, though few were actually served up as food on farms. Many went as 'tribute' to landowners and others were sold; eggs, too, were a source of cash. It was only at local festivities that the peasants got to eat chicken.

Records state that around 1780, approximately 15,000 bovines were eaten every year in Venice, mainly by the wealthy. This may seem a lot, but it pales somewhat when you look at the menu for the banquet held to celebrate Clement VI's election as pope in the fourteenth century. For that one meal 118 oxen, 1023 sheep, 101 calves, 914 kids, 60 pigs, 1500 capons, 3043 pullets, 7428 chickens and 1446 geese were slaughtered.

In Venice, meat was sold by *becheri* (butchers), whose stalls at the Rialto and St Mark's were designated annually. Towards the end of the seventeenth century, however, the public monopoly over retail sales of meat was relaxed and throughout the eighteenth century numerous butcher's licences were granted. Farmyard animals were sold by *pollaroli*, who came across the waters of the lagoon from the mainland with large quantities of chickens, hens, turkeys, pigeons and other domestic poultry, as well as such wildfowl as mallards, coots, quails, francolins, partridges, pheasants and geese. There were also egg-sellers and the *butirannti* who sold 'fine fat' – that is, butter.

Luganegheri (sausage makers) had a particularly important role. Forbidden to sell butter and fresh eggs but permitted to sell hard-boiled eggs, they could also deal in beef heads, feet, innards and entrails, which they bought from butchers and resold either cooked or uncooked. A late-eighteenth-century chart of *luganegheri* retail prices lists the following: 'Cooked Tripe: 6 *soldi* per pound. Stomach: 8 *soldi* per pound. Cooked Spleen: 10 *soldi* per pound. Cooked Feet: 4 *soldi* per pound. Meat of the Lower Belly and Neck: 28 *soldi* per pound. Cooked Tongue: 32 *soldi* per pound.'

When the city of Rovigo was under Venetian rule, all of its citizens were expected to maintain respect for public order and legal 'statutes'. There were, for example, inspectors of lodgings, officers responsible for the proper working of water pumps, syndics charged with running the local hospital and even overseers for the ghetto. However, only one such public figure enjoyed a full 40 days' holiday a year: the *estimatore alle carni* (meat assessor). There were generally two *estimatori*, appointed by drawing lots, and unlike all the other officials, they were excused from work for the entire period of Lent, when it was assumed that none of the citizens of Rovigo would be eating meat!

Returning to beef, it must be remembered that it was rarely eaten fresh, but was salted so that it could be consumed gradually, in small quantities, especially during winter. The Venetians have always had plenty of salt; indeed their trading empire was built on their monopoly over salt supplies. Once sold in Venice as one might nowadays sell caviar, *carne de Lampezzo* was a type of salted beef that was much appreciated in the region for its quality and flavour. It was imported from the d'Ampezzo valley, which after 1516 was no longer Venetian territory as a result of the War of the League of Cambrai. That war came about when Venice's power was at its height, and the Republic had made so many enemies that the Pope, the Holy Roman Emperor, the King of France and the King of Hungary (to name but a few) leagued together in the hope of humbling the city and seizing some of its wealth and dominions.

My father's shooting exploits never went further than a funfair – by hitting the target, your photo was taken!

One of my ancestors, Bartolomeo da Mosto, was engaged in trying to protect Venice and her territories at the time. First, while stationed in Dalmatia, he collected vital information through a network of spies. He found out that the armies of France and Spain were joining forces, and thus warned the Republic to take defensive measures. Subsequently, the crews of ships carrying oil and wheat from Puglia to Venice informed Bartolomeo that they had heard a French captain had armed swift mainsail galleys in Marseilles and the Pope – ostensibly enjoying good relations with Venice – had armed 16 light galleys at Civitavecchia. In May 1513, Bartolomeo was appointed as *Provveditore* (Governor) in Bergamo, from where he was better positioned to monitor approaching enemies and organize defences in the Po valley.

It was not until after the First World War that Cortina d'Ampezzo returned to Italy. It soon became known as the 'Pearl of the Dolomites' and today it is probably one of the most fancy mountain resorts. It is hard to imagine what it was like when the whole d'Ampezzano valley was a very poor area of scant resources – one of them being the salted meat that it exported to Venice. The local population survived on dairy products, vegetables and the few cereal crops that grew on the poor terrain of the lower mountain slopes. The cattle grazed on fresh pastureland and provided fine-quality, tender meat precisely because agriculture was so poor and, therefore, there was little draft work to be done in the fields. Generally, it was the women who tended the animals in the cowsheds, getting up before dawn to 'muck out' and do the milking. The milk was used to make butter, cheeses and ricotta. In the evening, the men, who had been out all day either in the fields or chopping wood in the forests, helped to prepare the large cuts of meat that would be salted to become the tasty *carne de Lampezzo*.

As for the ritual annual slaying of the family pig, this was an event that involved everyone in a peasant household. The atmosphere preceding the slaughter was a strange mix of festive anticipation and trepidation: everyone knew that the coming days called for frenetic work, but they also knew that they would be able to eat their fill. The slaughter of the pig followed a certain ritual and was generally carried out in the period between the middle of December and 17 January, the feast day of St Anthony Abbot – also known as *Sant'Antonio del porco* (St Anthony of the pig). He was not the only saint 'associated' with pigs: the feast day of St Thomas the Apostle (to whom Treviso dedicated one of its city gates) fell on 21 December and was often the day on which the pig was slaughtered, hence the expression *san Tomè el porco par el piè* (on St Thomas's Day the pig is taken by the feet). The slaughter and subsequent use of the various parts of the animal were rigorously regulated by the city's *podestà*, who had to ensure the quality and reputation of Treviso's famous *luganeghe* (sausages) would be maintained. For example, in an ordinance of 1382 the *podestà* forbade the use of meat other than pork in *luganeghe*; those contravening this order risked having their entire stock confiscated. As for the trade in pork meat, this never began before the beginning of January, so that the autumnal process of 'fattening up' the pigs would have been carried out completely.

On the last day of Christmas – the Feast of the Epiphany (6 January) – the fields around Treviso were ablaze with bonfires whose size reflected the status of the families gathered around them. Part of this celebration involved an invocation of good and plentiful harvests for the year to come: *Pane e vin, la luganega sotto el camin, la farina sotto la panera…* (Bread and wine, sausages on the fire, flour in the pantry…). When the fire had burned down, the embers were stirred with long hooked rods and the direction in which the sparks flew was taken as an omen. If they blew eastwards – towards Friuli – the interpretation was *ciò su el sac e va a pan* (put your bag on your back and set off begging); if the sparks went westward, however, the forthcoming year promised to be a good one.

Foremost among the tasty cured meats enjoyed in Venice is pickled pork tongue, which after simple boiling becomes a wonderfully tender dish. Then come *musetti* (a type of boiled sausage), various forms of salami, *ossocolli* (a particularly fat salami sausage), *pancetta* and *sopressa* (another fat, soft salami) – each flavoured not only with salt but also with carefully measured quantities of pepper and other (often secret) spices.

Most sausages in the Veneto are made from pork. Mild-flavoured and tender, even if a bit fatty, these are perfect for rice dishes, and adding flavour to a tasty and nourishing pasta sauces. Not all the ingredients are known; the producers keep some of them a jealously guarded secret. However, in broad terms, sausage contains *pancetta* (without the rind) ground together with salt, a pinch of saltpetre and the famous *dosa* (mix of spices); for the transparent, elastic casing of these medium-thick sausages, pig intestines are used. *Luganega* sausage is thinner and ideal for roasting and grilling. Particularly appreciated for its aroma, this is made using a mix of one-third pork shoulder and two-thirds lean *pancetta* without rind. The mincing process and the other ingredients are the same as above, except that the *dosa* of spices change, with a much greater proportion of pepper. Amongst the various *luganeghe* that are made in the Veneto using different types of meat, Treviso sausages have retained their high standing and reputation.

The different types of *sopressa* produced in Treviso enjoy a similar fame. Firm but tender, these salamis are skilfully made with a variety of mild or spicy mixes – but are inevitably good enough to convert even the most hesitant heretic. When in Treviso, the place to buy *sopressa* is the old Perissinotto grocery store within the Palazzo dei Trecento, which stands in a part of the main square that is known as *l'angolo dei soffioni* (breezy corner); the name is perhaps due to the draughts that blow through there or to the fact that this used to be the site of dog races for which the starting-signal was given by bursting an inflated paper bag. This *drogheria* (grocery store) continues a long-standing Venetian tradition of stores that sell imported spices from the East and make their own *rosolio* (sweet wine) and sugared almonds. The business dates back to the seventeenth century and is famous throughout the Veneto for the variety and quality of its mixed spices, which are still recognized as indispensable for the flavour and aroma of the Treviso *luganeghe*.

Up in Belluno, there is perhaps the greatest number of different sausages and salamis, which are perfectly suited to the bitter cold of these valleys. Together with the area's highly prized salted horsemeat, there are smoked hams, salamis made using horse and other meats, pickled tongue, fresh salamis and smaller salamis made of venison and chamois goat. In the Po delta, the queen of Veneto salted meats is the *bòndola*, made with pork and beef mixed with strong red wine, pepper and other spices (again the actual mix is a treasured secret). As for the Vicenza area, Trissino – where the architect Andrea Palladio spent his early years – produces a special cured ham, *parsuto com l'ossocollo*, Recoaro has its *parsuto coto* (roast ham), Sossano its *parsuto dolce* (sweet ham) – and, of course, there are *musetti* and *luganeghe*, which are here served with cabbage. Padua takes pride in its local *musetto* and *luganega*, including *musso*, garlic salami from Montagnana, and various small sausages that are good for grilling. As for the Verona area, it produces more garlic-rich salami, with special types of Valpolicella *sopressa* and yet more varieties of *luganaghe*, *musetti* and *ossocolli*.

Oca rostia co' pomi e castagne
Roast goose with apple and chestnuts

Serves 6

3 kg / 6½ lb goose (not too fatty)
50 g / 2 oz butter
200 g / 7 oz chestnuts
5 apples, peeled and quartered

Stuffing

600 g / 1¼ lb cooking apples,
peeled and chopped
250 g / 8 oz chestnut purée
1 egg, beaten
a few knobs of butter
salt and pepper

This dish still lingers in a few farmhouses in the Treviso area, reminiscent of the times when large, extended families would come together on foggy winter evenings.

Italian geese, as well as chickens, are characteristically smaller than elsewhere and less fatty and consequently this recipe may seem excessively rich. You can use less butter if you prefer and pour off the fat that collects in the tin every so often (it's very good for roasting potatoes).

———— ✣ ————

Preheat the oven to 150°C / 300°F / Gas Mark 3. First prepare the stuffing: cook the apples over a medium-low heat with very little extra water until soft. Strain off any cooking juices. Mix the apples, chestnut purée, egg, the knobs of butter and some salt and pepper. Then, after cleaning the bird carefully, fill with the stuffing and roast on a rack in a pan, for about 3 hours, basting regularly enough to avoid the meat becoming dry. Alternatively you can cook the goose in a casserole dish on the stove (as long as you turn it regularly).

Serve piping hot on a bed of apples cooked in butter and roast chestnuts.

Oca in onto
Preserved goose

Serves 6

a plump goose weighing
about 5 kg / 11 lb
coarse-grain salt
a few sprigs of fresh rosemary
a few sage leaves
olive or vegetable oil, if necessary

With its powerful neck and hard beak, the goose can be a fearsome creature when it loses its temper. Its dark flesh, however, is perfect for roasting or conserving as cold meats. This dish, which brings out its full flavour, makes a robust and tasty main course. It's not difficult to make, but does require some patience and application.

———— ✣ ————

Pass the goose over a naked flame to burn off the stubs of feathers. Cut away all the fat from under the skin and reserve it. Divide the goose into quarters. Boil the pieces for about an hour.

Melt the reserved goose fat over a gentle heat until liquid. When cool enough to handle, remove the meat from the bones and drain well. Put the goose in a large container that can be hermetically sealed and mix with plenty of coarse-grain salt and the fresh herbs. Then pour over the melted fat. If there is not enough, you can add olive oil or vegetable oil. Seal the container and set aside in the fridge for at least 2 months.

When opened, you can either eat the goose as it is (the salt will have preserved it perfectly) or you can fry it in its own fat with a little rosemary or sage.

Pollo rosto coi fasioi
Roast chicken with bean sauce

Serves 4
800 g / 1¾ lb dried beans, e.g lamon or
borlotti beans, soaked overnight
1 kg / 2¼ lb chicken with giblets
2 slices of lardo *or* pancetta
white wine, for basting

Sauce
50 g / 2 oz sopressa *(soft salami)*
75 ml / 2½ fl oz olive oil
2 salted anchovies, chopped
1 onion, chopped
1 garlic clove, finely chopped
chopped fresh parsley, basil and rosemary
half a glass of white wine
salt and white pepper

In the Venetian countryside boiled chicken was a highly prized dish. Served on a bed of rice (cooked in the water used to prepare the bird and then mixed with abundant Parmesan), it was part of a feast day or Sunday ritual, when the entire family gathered around the table and swapped news and stories. Such occasions helped to bond young and old, to bring together those who spent their lives within doors with those whom business took out into the wide world. For local people of a certain age, these associations mean that – quite apart from its gastronomic qualities – chicken remains a very noble dish. They remember when, in times of straitened circumstances, such poultry was the very embodiment of traditions and values.

Up into the Alpine foothills, traditions are different, with the summer markets offering very plump young chickens for sale. These are not for boiling but for roasting, and are often served with a bean sauce. Though it might seem a bit heavy for the time of year, the dish is usually served in the period between the Feast of St Peter and Paul (29 June) and the middle of July.

———⚬∞⚬———

Boil the beans in fresh, boiling water until tender (the cooking time depends on the type of beans and their age).

Prepare the chicken by covering it with the slices of *lardo* or *pancetta*, held in place with string or toothpicks, and season with salt and pepper, then pan- or spit-roast. Sprinkle frequently during cooking with white wine to prevent the meat from drying out. Check that the chicken is ready in the usual way: the juices should run clear when the thickest part of the thigh is pierced with a skewer.

Meanwhile, chop up the giblets with the *sopressa* and sauté in olive oil with the salted anchovies, chopped onion, garlic, parsley, basil and rosemary. Just before this sauce is ready, add the white wine and plenty of white pepper. Pour the sauce over the cooked beans and leave them for about an hour to absorb the sauce fully. Serve the bean sauce hot, in a separate jug.

Polastro in tecia
Chicken casserole

Serves 4

1 young chicken, weighing at least
1 kg / 2¼ lb, jointed into
6–8 pieces
60 ml / 2 fl oz oil
75 g / 3 oz butter
1 onion, finely chopped
1 celery stick, finely chopped
1 carrot, finely chopped
a pinch of ground cinnamon
2 cloves
250 g / 8 oz fresh porcini
mushrooms, sliced
1 glass of dry white wine
400 g / 14 oz canned
chopped tomatoes
beef stock, if necessary
salt and pepper

From the days of Charlemagne onwards, farmers had to raise 50 to 100 chickens per year to supply the kitchens of the local castle or prince. In the fourteenth century, Giacomo Dondi, known as Giacomo dell'Orologio, imported into the Veneto a new breed of chicken from Poland. This chicken was so welcome that it was adopted as the heraldic symbol of the associations devoted to St Anthony of Padua. The strutting breed became the most famous type of chicken in the Veneto. And having been considered more ornamental than anything else as a newcomer, its descendants were much appreciated not only for their size but also for the delicate flavour of their meat; even their eggs were of exceptional quality. By the end of the fourteenth century the reputation of the bird was such that, when the Paduans were defeated by the Venetians at Torre delle Bebe, not far from Chioggia, the treaty laid down that the vanquished would 'every year take 30 of their plump and fleshy chickens to Venice' – and that practice was still being observed in 1797, the year that the Venetian Republic fell. Even the giblets of the bird were used to make a fine *risoto coi rovinassi* ('leftovers' risotto). All that, however, is part of the past. The fine Padua chickens have been relegated to the yards of the few who are dedicated to safeguarding rare breeds, since the days of intensive factory farming and genetically engineered hybrids.

Still, given the abundance of poultry in our markets, you would think that preparing a good chicken casserole was a fairly straightforward matter. It isn't. As many of the birds available come from battery farms, they have none of the flavour of free-range chicken. However, it is still possible to get hold of a plump, young chicken that does have some real taste to it.

———— ∞ ————

Sauté the chicken pieces in a pan, with some of the oil and butter.

Meanwhile, sauté the onion, celery and carrot in the remaining oil and butter in a heatproof casserole. Add the browned chicken and its cooking juices. Add a little cinnamon, a couple of cloves, the sliced fresh mushrooms, tomatoes and the wine, with some salt and pepper. Cook on a low heat for about half an hour, adding a ladle of beef stock as required.

This chicken casserole should be served with freshly prepared coarse-grained yellow polenta.

If you are only able to get dried porcini, first soak them in boiling water for 30 minutes and then cook them separately, to prevent them from breaking up. Add them part of the way through cooking. Some people add a little flour at the end, to thicken the sauce.

Paeta rosta al magaragno
Roast turkey with pomegranate

Serves 4

1.5 kg / 3¼ lb tender young female turkey or turkey breast joint
60 g / generous 2 oz butter, softened
150 ml / 5 fl oz extra virgin olive oil
a few fresh sage leaves
4 pomegranates, seeds and pulp scooped out
salt and pepper

The walled and turreted medieval town of Marostica is credited with this princely dish – an honour worth contending for, as was the hand of the fair Leonora. She was the beautiful daughter of the local castellan, Messer Parisio, who, in 1454, found himself having to intervene in a violent dispute between Rinaldo da Angarano and Vieri da Vallonara, both suitors for Leonora's hand in marriage. Parisio refused to allow the two men to settle the question with a duel, threatening them with execution if they did so. The alternative he proposed led to the creation of Marostica's most famous feature: a massive chessboard laid out in the paving of its main square. A local chronicle describes how Rinaldo and Vieri fought their battle using 'large, living pieces… armed with all the noble insignia of the White and the Black.' The event became part of local tradition and still survives to this day, with chess games being played by people dressed as the various pieces.

But, to return to the turkey, a local proverb has it that it is best eaten when the mists of autumn are thick in the plains and uplands of the Vicenza area and 'when, in November, the must has turned to wine, the turkey is ready for roasting.'

———— ∞ ————

Preheat the oven to 180°C / 350°F / Gas Mark 4. Use a naked flame to remove any stubs of feathers from the turkey, then rinse and pat dry. Season inside and out with salt and smear with some of the butter. Place in a fairly deep casserole with the remaining butter, some of the oil and sage leaves, and roast for at least 3 hours.

Halve two of the pomegranates and remove the seeds. Heat them gently in a saucepan until the juices start to run and then strain. Remember to baste the meat with its own liquid every now and again. Halfway through the cooking, start to baste it with the pomegranate sauce as well.

Meanwhile, cut the giblets into small pieces and cook them in olive oil with the pomegranate seeds on a high heat, adding salt and pepper at the end. Once the turkey is thoroughly cooked, remove from the oven and cut into medium-size pieces, which you then return to the oven for a few minutes, after pouring over the cooked giblets and the juicy pomegranate seeds. Serve on a large dish sprinkled generously with the seeds of the remaining pomegranate, whose brilliant colour makes a fine contrast.

Alternatively, roast the turkey on a spit, covered with thin slices of cured pork fat and *pancetta*; this method also calls for regular basting with the juices that collect on the dish below and with pomegranate juice.

Faraona rosta
Pan-roasted guinea fowl

Serves 4
1 kg / 2¼ lb guinea fowl
50 g / 2 oz pancetta, *chopped*
60 ml / 2 fl oz olive oil
40 g / 1½ oz butter
paprika and other spices, to taste
200 ml / 7 fl oz stock
a glass of white wine
½ tomato, skinned,
seeded and chopped
salt and pepper

Guinea fowl are very popular in the Po delta. Oven-, pan- or spit-roasted, the flavour is similar to that of game; in fact, guinea fowl has to be 'hung' longer than normal poultry. But you must be careful not to leave it for too long, as some huntsmen do, because that can impair the aroma of the meat.

During the months of July and August, the entire Po delta is animated by village fairs; the highlights of which are performances inspired by local folklore, ballroom dancing, fireworks and merry meals in the open air served on long trestle tables under pergolas draped with grapevines, lasting late into the evening. Usually, the core of the meal is roast or stewed poultry, with one particular favourite being pan-roasted guinea fowl, a bird that combines the plumpness of poultry with the full flavour of game.

Remove feather stubs from the guinea fowl with a naked flame. Salt the bird, then put it in a heavy-based pan with the diced *pancetta*, oil, butter, salt, pepper, paprika and any other spices you care for, for example, cloves are a good accompaniment. Put on the lid. Gradually add the stock mixed with white wine and a little tomato while the bird cooks. The cooking should take at least an hour and the bird should be kept well covered by liquids so that the meat does not dry out. Serve the guinea fowl with boiled potatoes, seasonal greens and red wine.

Mazoro a la valesana
Mallard duck *valli*-style

Serves 4
2 oven-ready mallards
white wine vinegar
fresh thyme and marjoram leaves
peppercorns
60 ml / 2 fl oz olive oil
75 g / 3 oz butter
1 onion, chopped
4 filleted salted sardines
or anchovies, chopped
a glass of dry white wine

Hunting in the Venetian lagoon or on the waters of the Po delta is a fine pastime – even if, at the very beginning of the season, there can be so many eager huntsmen out there that you run the risk of catching more buckshot than game. There is something unreal about these wide expanses of water in the harsh days of winter. Crouched in your 'hide' waiting for the flocks of migrating birds, you enjoy a new awareness of the passage of time. Now and again, you feel a certain trembling of the heart when you remember that you are there to get these poor animals at precisely the moment when they are expecting to merely rest on their long and exhausting migratory flight south.

The sensory experiences of the day seem somehow separate from each other: the smooth glide of the boat with rhythmic waves in its wake that takes you out to your 'hide'; the pungent cold in the air; the crackling fire back at the *casone* (lodge) where you return, frozen but laden; the simple food prepared in the keeper's lodge. The day seems to have been a sequence of long silences; periods of waiting punctuated with short bursts of action. You feel yourself to have been part of a Nature that is both untamed and somehow 'to the measure of man'.

Spending time in one of these 'hides' is a long-standing tradition in Venice, as one can see in those wonderful eighteenth-century Pietro Longhi paintings of hunting in the lagoon. Of course, sometimes there is nothing to put in the game-bag. And it is a very special day when you manage to get a mallard with its distinctive white band around a petrol-green neck. This bird becomes a real delicacy when spit-roasted over the open fire in the keeper's lodge.

─────ತಿಂ಼ ─────

Leave the mallards to marinate overnight in enough vinegar to cover, with the thyme and marjoram leaves and some peppercorns to get rid of some of the gamey taste. Then brown the birds in 2 tablespoons of the oil and the butter. When ready, cut the birds into medium-sized pieces.

Sauté the chopped onion in the remaining oil in another pan and then add the mallard pieces. Mix in the fillets of salted sardines. Moisten with dry white wine and continue to cook over a moderate heat until the meat becomes tender. Be careful not to let it dry out. Serve with slices of grilled yellow polenta.

Anara col pien
Stuffed duck

This richly flavoured bird has long figured in Venetian cuisine: the lagoon provides a perfect habitat for ducks among the reeds in that transition zone where the mainland has not yet ended but the open expanse of water has not yet started. There are wonderful hiding-places for aquatic fowl (and their hunters). In springtime it is fun to observe proud mothers leading lines of eager ducklings in search of insects, small fish, crustaceans and strands of algae. With the slightest noise, there is a flurry of wings and mother duck soon has her young ones well hidden amongst the rushes, from where she ponders her next move.

The lagoon of Venice is not just the largest, but also one of the most important wetlands in Italy for wintering, migrant and breeding water birds. Wintering birds are those that breed in the far north, and then flee the harshness of central Europe to spend the winter in the Adriatic – duck species such as mallard, teal and wigeon fall into this category. Migrants are those which have wintered even farther south, sometimes south of the Sahara, and pass through the lagoon on their way north in spring, and again on their way south in autumn. Breeding birds are those which nest in the lagoon; they may also spend the winter on the lagoon, or may come to the lagoon from the south. Thus, the lagoon is a vital link in the global network of bird migration, and indeed one of the most important feeding stations where birds rest and refuel on their journeys along international flyways.

Wild duck – or '*osella*' in Venetian – has always featured prominently in the cuisine of Venice and the surrounding islands and the people of the Veneto have always been keen hunters, as well as fishermen. The hides – or *botte* – in which the huntsmen conceal themselves at the first light of dawn are dotted around the traditional fish farms in the lagoon. Having arrived here by boat, the patient and ruthless huntsmen spend hours – with a thermos flask and *sopressa* (salami) sandwiches – waiting for the ducks to be attracted by the floating wooden decoys.

During the centuries of the Serenissima, there was a tradition that the Doge would present the patricians of Venice with an annual gift of ducks hunted in the ducal reserves of the lagoon. And duck remains one of the centrepieces of the menu for the Feast of *Il Redentore*, held annually on the third weekend of July to celebrate the end of the plague in 1577 and indeed the opening of the shooting season. The festivities include an enormous firework display on the waters of St Mark's Basin; and certainly the best way to enjoy the show is from a boat, floating beneath the explosions of colour. Just as hotly anticipated as the fireworks, is the picnic that is enjoyed floating on the water in a boat. One of the traditional dishes is stuffed duck – the stuffing is particularly important because ducks are large-boned and therefore do not have enough meat to feed a large party. The dish requires a certain amount of work because of the number of ingredients involved.

———— ∞∞∞ ————

Serves 6

125 g / 4 oz chicken livers,
if duck giblets not available
50 g / 2 oz sopressa
(soft salami), chopped
50 g / 2 oz Parmesan, grated
fresh sage and rosemary
or other aromatic herbs
50 g / 2 oz fresh breadcrumbs
2 kg / 4½ lb duck, with giblets
60 g / generous 2 oz butter
fresh sage leaves
salt

Preheat the oven to 150°F / 300°C / Gas Mark 2. The stuffing uses the uncooked liver, heart and other appetizing innards, which are mixed with some chopped *sopressa* (salami) and grated Parmesan. Add the sage and rosemary or other herbs and the breadcrumbs. Fill the duck's body cavity and sew up the opening. Place in a large roasting dish, together with the butter, sage leaves and a pinch or two of salt. Roast for about 2 hours, while monitoring the heat and basting frequently, so that the duck is crispy on the outside, cooks evenly and does not dry out. Add some stock if the cooking juices run out.

The end result will be much appreciated by those you have invited to join you for the feast of *Il Redentore*, on a moonlit night in a boat decked in lanterns and vine leaves.

Glass foleghe *(coots) – perfectly accurately produced to scale.*

Oseleti scampai
'Escaped birds' skewers

Serves 4

250 g / 8 oz lean boneless veal
250 g / 8 oz lean boneless pork
100 g / 3½ oz calf's liver
100 g / 3½ oz pig's liver
50 g / 2 oz piece of pancetta
fresh sage leaves
100 ml / 3½ fl oz high-quality olive oil
glass of dry white wine
couple of ladlefuls reduced stock
salt and pepper

When hunting does not yield the results that the huntsman hopes for, one person who might well not be very disappointed is his wife – because she is spared having to work on difficult and fiddly dishes. Of course some hunters make up for what they don't shoot by buying it at the market. Or there is this tasty dish, made using other meats prepared in a way that makes them seem like game. This recipe for 'the ones that got away' features in regional cuisines all over Italy; but the Venetian version has some distinctive features.

———— ✦ ————

Cut the veal, pork, livers and *pancetta* into cubes the thickness of a finger and thread onto well-soaked wooden skewers (if possible, these should be boxwood, which gives the meat a special taste and does not absorb the fat from it). Each skewer should comprise: a piece of *pancetta*, a sage leaf, a lump of meat, a sage leaf, *pancetta* and then liver, alternating the two types of lean meat. Place the skewers in a heavy frying-pan in which you have heated the oil. Cook on a high heat, turning the skewers every now and again and sprinkling with wine and stock, which will add to the sauce. Serve very hot, still on the skewer and laid out on a bed of (preferably coarse-grain) yellow polenta. Either pour the cooking juices over them or serve separately in a sauceboat.

Sopa Coada
Roosting soup

Serves 4
3 plump, oven-ready pigeons
6 slices of pancetta
60 g / generous 2 oz butter, melted,
plus extra for frying
60 ml / 2 fl oz olive oil
1.2 litres / 2 pints chicken
or game stock
12 slices of dry bread
100 g / 3½ oz Parmesan,
finely grated
salt and pepper

There used to be a tradition in Venice that the confraternities and districts of the city would, on certain festivities, present the Doge with modest gifts such as fruit, cakes and other sweetmeats. One parish, however, presented him with a brace of wild pigeons, which one year escaped and took shelter within the vaulted roof of St Mark's Basilica. It was decreed that they were to be left free and their food paid for out of the Republic's coffers. Inevitably, these two birds reproduced and the number of pigeons around St Mark's increased; but, no matter how poor or hungry, no Venetians would have dared to touch the birds – a situation that only came to an end during the terrible Austrian siege of 1848–9.

This soup, literally called 'roosting soup' because of its lengthy preparation and slow cooking in the oven, comes from the Treviso area. There are numerous other permutations but the one given here is perhaps more traditional.

———∞———

Pass the plump pigeons rapidly over a naked flame to remove stubs of feathers. Then wrap them in slices of *pancetta* and place in a heatproof casserole with the melted butter, oil, stock and some salt and pepper. Brown on a high heat for 5 minutes. Then add the stock and pot-roast until tender, about 45 minutes.

Remove from the dish and set aside until cool enough to handle. Preheat the oven to 150°C / 300°F / Gas Mark 2.

Take the flesh from the pigeon carcasses and cut it into thin strips, then put the flesh back into the cooking juices left in the pot.

Fry the slices of dry bread in some butter until crisp and golden. Put a layer in an ovenproof dish; on top place strips of pigeon and sprinkle with the cooking juices and finely grated Parmesan. Repeat the layers until all the ingredients have been used up. Then pour a substantial quantity of cooking juices over everything and bake for about 30 minutes. If the stock reduces too far, add a little more. Turn up the temperature shortly before serving so that a slightly browned crust forms. After removing from the oven, liberally sprinkle more grated Parmesan on the *sopa coada*. Serve piping hot: you can also add a little more stock at this point.

Instead of pigeons, a variation of *sopa coada* from Mogliano, a town between Venice and Treviso, is made with chicken and veal cooked in tomatoes.

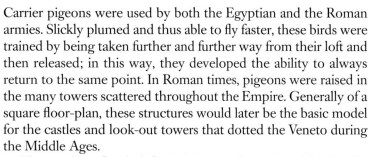

Toresani
Stuffed and spit-roasted pigeons

Serves 4

4 plump, young oven-ready pigeons, with giblets
100 ml / 3½ fl oz olive oil
50 g / 2 oz soft sausagemeat
50 g / 2 oz bread
25 g / 1 oz Parmesan, grated
8 slices of lardo *or* pancetta
12 slices of yellow polenta, cut into chunks
salt and pepper

Carrier pigeons were used by both the Egyptian and the Roman armies. Slickly plumed and thus able to fly faster, these birds were trained by being taken further and further way from their loft and then released; in this way, they developed the ability to always return to the same point. In Roman times, pigeons were raised in the many towers scattered throughout the Empire. Generally of a square floor-plan, these structures would later be the basic model for the castles and look-out towers that dotted the Veneto during the Middle Ages.

The number of such defences was greatly increased first by the Paduan 'tyrant' Ezzelino da Romano and then by the lords of Verona, the Della Scala family. The preferred sites were generally hill slopes or raised knolls. From the fourteenth century onwards, these structures were gradually incorporated in the villas of the Veneto (the Republic was very keen to substitute the ancient castles of the region – symbols of the hostile Holy Roman Empire – with contemporary villas). The remaining towers became known as *colombare* (*colombo* meaning pigeon) because they housed both carrier pigeons and those which were raised to be served up to the lords of the villa. To distinguish them from wild pigeons, these latter were referred to as *toresani* (*torre* meaning tower) and were particularly distinguished by their succulent meat.

Nowadays it is difficult to find genuine *toresani* pigeons, but the plump, young white pigeons from dove cotes are a good enough substitute. Never would I consider taking a Venetian pigeon for the pot; these are now more aptly called 'flying rats'! During the Second World War, however, my father remembers eating town pigeons on occasion, for lack of any alternative, but back then the pigeons' diet contained less urban waste than today.

Use a naked flame to burn off the stubs of feathers from the pigeons. Then cook the giblets and sausagemeat together to make the stuffing; mix with the bread and grated Parmesan. Use this mixture to stuff the pigeons. Once stuffed, the pigeons are placed on the spit and draped with slices of *lardo* or *pancetta*; on the same spit thread chunks of polenta. Cook on a continuous but moderate heat, basting occasionally with oil, salt and pepper. The turning of the spit and the sprinkling with the oil (to keep the birds moist) are the most delicate parts of the cooking process.

The juice that the birds release should be collected in a dripping-pan and served together with the birds on a large dish. If you do not have a spit, you can do the pigeons in a casserole on the stove or in the oven, making sure to turn them frequently. The result is equally tasty.

Fasan col pien
Stuffed pheasant

The Bible describes mankind's earliest forms of nourishment: 'and God said, "Behold, I have given you every herb bearing seed, which is upon the face of the earth, and every tree, in which is the fruit of a tree yielding seed; to you it shall be for meat."'(Genesis 1.29). Thus in the beginning man ate nothing but the fruits of the earth. He only began eating meat after the Great Flood, which was when acquiring food first became a problem. However, not all places were like Eden. There were deserts afflicted by droughts, mountain areas at the mercy of snow and glaciers... so not everyone could live on fruit, honey, beans, eggs, herbs and roots.

In the Neolithic Age, man became a hunter and the flesh of his prey became the very basis of his diet for a long time. Then, around 10,000 years ago, the development of agricultural techniques meant that the relative importance of hunting gradually diminished and the practice gradually became a status symbol, a pastime for the privileged.

The 'fashion' for hunting still persists albeit beginning to fade out due to shortages in the necessary 'raw material'. The heyday of hunting was definitely in the Middle Ages, when kings and emperors, lord and barons organized the great hunts depicted in paintings. A clear sign of power, such events were the most exclusive of pastimes.

It was in the landscape of the gentle foothills of the Treviso area, where castles, bridges and rivers appear in the medieval backgrounds of Giorgione's paintings, that men discovered the full taste of game. And foremost among the huntsmen's prey was always the plump and rich-flavoured pheasant. A bird of truly oriental plumage, its name derives from the fact that the pheasant was originally a native of the river Phasis in Colchis, and it cannot be ruled out that it was introduced to the West via Venice itself, given the city's close links with the Byzantine empire.

The pheasant is of a full, delicate flavour, especially if caught in woodland or mountain areas. The bird has to hang, unplucked, for a good 8 to 10 days before being cooked. It was traditionally cooked in a sweet red wine from the Veneto; a full-bodied and not-too-dry red wine such as Amarone or Barolo can be now used instead.

*1 young oven-ready pheasant,
weighing about 1 kg / 2¼ lb
1 slice of* lardo *or* pancetta
*75 ml / 2½ fl oz olive oil
45 g / 2 oz butter
1 litre / 1¾ pints Marzemino
(sweet red wine) or Amarone
a small glass of brandy
salt and pepper*

Stuffing

*2 hard-boiled eggs, chopped
150 g / 5 oz* sopressa *(soft salami)
50 g / 1 oz fresh parsley and sage,
chopped
45 g / 2 oz butter*

Pass the bird rapidly over a naked flame to get rid of any traces of plumage. Wash and dry, then sprinkle with pepper and salt. Bind the bird so it does not lose its shape during cooking and wrap the breast in a slice of *lardo* or *pancetta*; the fat serves to tenderize the particularly firm meat of the bird. Now stuff the pheasant with a mixture of chopped boiled egg, soft *sopressa* (salami), parsley, sage and butter.

Put the oil and butter in a heatproof casserole over a medium heat and add the peasant. As the bird begins to cook, add the red wine. Cover the dish and cook on a low heat for at least 4 to 5 hours. Just before serving, sprinkle with a small glass of brandy.

The pheasant can also be cooked in a slow oven (150°C / 300°F / Gas Mark 2) for about the same time.

Salsa valesana per osei selvadegi
Valle-style sauce for game birds

Serves 6

*100 g / 3½ oz olive oil
100 g / 3½ oz butter
4 salted anchovies, chopped
½ onion, chopped
100 g / 3½ oz sultanas
150 g / 5 oz mostarda,
(a fruit-based mustard,
available from Italian
delicatessens)
60 g / generous 2 oz pine nuts
100 g / 3½ oz sugar
a glass of strong balsamic vinegar
half a glass dry white wine*

It is accepted wisdom that the sauce served with game birds must be of a strong enough flavour to match that of the game itself. This *salsa valesana* was developed to accompany the game birds that were hunted in the lagoon, where there are still many 'hides' used by huntsmen and also some, albeit fewer, wildfowl.

In the early centuries of the Venetian Republic there was a tradition that the Doge presented the members of the Great Council with some *osele* (wild ducks) hunted in the lagoon, every year. However, after the famous *serrata* (closure) of that Council in 1297 – when an (almost) unchanging list was drawn up of the families that had a right to a seat in the Chamber – the numbers of such dignitaries increased and it became difficult to find *osele* for all of them. Thus, from 1521 onwards, the Doge no longer presented the noblemen with *osei de Maran* – 'one thin, one plump' according to the popular saying – but with silver or gold medals bearing effigies of ducks. Called *oselle*, these coins were minted right up until the fall of the Venetian Republic.

———✷———

Sauté some salted anchovies in oil and butter with the chopped onion. When they have begun to colour, add the sultanas, the sweet mostarda, pine nuts, sugar and aromatic vinegar. Continue cooking for a few minutes, then add the dry white wine.

The wild birds that this sauce accompanies are sometimes cut into pieces and cooked in the sauce itself, with the entrails being used to enrich the sauce. Serve it with any of the poultry or game recipes in this book.

Fasan e pernici al paneto
Pheasant and partridge in bread dough

Serves 4
*2 oven-ready pheasants
or 8 partridges or 4 pigeons
75 g / 3 oz Parma ham, diced
40 g / 1½ oz pancetta, diced
½ onion, chopped
60 ml / 2 fl oz olive oil
a small glass of plum liqueur
100 g / 3½ oz mushrooms, chopped
(or a small amount of truffles if
using pigeons)
some spoonfuls of stock
1 kg / 2¼ lb plain flour
salt and pepper*

Autumn is the season for wild game and, during these months, enthusiasts can enjoy any number of delicacies prepared using hare or a wide variety of richly flavoured game birds. This local recipe for preparing pheasant and partridges in bread dough comes from the area of Treviso that borders on Friuli.

Instead of pheasants and partridges you can use pigeons, but in this case use truffles rather than mushrooms in the stuffing because they add a delicious aroma.

———⸒⸒⸒———

Preheat the oven to 220°C / 425°F / Gas Mark 7. Pass the birds over a naked flame to get rid of any remnants of plumage. Now sprinkle with salt and pepper. Make the stuffing by sautéing the ham, *pancetta* and chopped onion in the oil, then add the plum liqueur, mushrooms, the birds' livers if you have them and a little stock. Divide the stuffing among the body cavities of the birds.

For each bird (pheasant-size): Mix 500 g (1 lb 2 oz) plain flour in a bowl with 250 to 300 ml (9 to 10 fl oz) of cold water, then turn out and knead until it forms a soft but not sticky dough. Roll it out. Wrap the birds in greaseproof paper and then wrap each in dough. Press the edges together to seal the birds in. Place the loaves in the very hot oven and then bake for approximately one hour, less for smaller birds. The loaves should be very dark, almost blackened.

Bring the loaves to the table and then break them open to release the full fragrance of the roasted birds.

Pastisso di caccia
Game pie

Serves 4
800 g / 1¾ lb oven-ready hare,
partridge and/or quails
1 litre / 1¾ pints dry white wine
thyme and rosemary
a few peppercorns
2 spicy sausages
60 g / generous 2 oz butter
1 onion, chopped
100 g / 3½ oz mushrooms, sliced
100 g / 3½ oz soft bread
(without crusts)
100 ml / 3½ fl oz milk
50 g / 2 oz Parmesan, grated
2 or 3 eggs, beaten
salt and peppercorns

Pastry
350 g / 12 oz plain white flour
125 g / 4 oz unsalted butter
125 g / 4 oz lard
pinch of salt
milk or beaten egg yolk, to glaze

Good food and great wines have long been a boast of the Montello area: the Abbey of Nervesa was famous for its kitchens, and prelates and noblemen travelling northwards used to make a point of stopping off here to enjoy the monks' hospitality. One recipe that is still jealously preserved in the farmhouses and villas of this area is this 'game pie', a perfect blend of all the gastronomic riches of the area: fine wild mushrooms, strong-flavoured game and abundant quantities of great white wine. You can make this dish with hare but it is more delicate when made with quails; thrushes would have been the traditional choice but they are now protected. Partridges, snipe and woodcock would be tasty too, if available.

———— ∞∞∞ ————

Leave the birds to marinate in a mix of white wine, herbs and peppercorns. Then transfer to an ovenproof or heatproof dish, with the sausages, butter and chopped onion and mushrooms and cook on low heat on the hob or in a slow oven (150°C / 300°F / Gas Mark 2) for 1½ to 2 hours; during the cooking, gradually add the wine in which the game has soaked.

Meanwhile, make the pastry. Sift the flour and salt into a bowl, cut in the butter and lard in small pieces and rub in with your fingers until the mixture resembles breadcrumbs. Add just enough very cold water to bring the dough together and then wrap in foil or cling film and chill until required.

Put the bread to soak in the milk for a few minutes.

Once the birds are cooked and when cool enough to handle, remove the flesh from the bones and carefully strain the cooking juices, which may need to be reduced by simmering. Add the bread soaked in milk to the meat and juices, with the cheese, binding the mix with the beaten egg.

Preheat the oven to 200°C / 400°F / Gas Mark 6. Roll out the pastry into two circles of 30 cm (12 in) diameter. Put the filling in the centre of one circle and put the second one on top. Pinch the pastry together around the edges and brush with a little milk or beaten egg. Bake for 45 minutes to an hour. The pie should be served steaming hot – and the enthusiastic reception it receives is the reward for all the time you have spent making it. This is a dish that will inevitably conjure up thoughts of castle halls adorned with tapestries and armour, and of tables groaning under bounteous wines, delicacies and bunches of grapes.

Pastisso di lièvoro
Hare pie

Serves 4

1.5 kg / 3½ lb oven-ready hare,
jointed
250 g / 8 oz lean boneless pork,
diced
75 g / 3 oz lardo, *chopped finely*
1 onion, chopped
75 g / 3 oz of butter
4–5 cloves
1 cinnamon stick,
broken into pieces
1 litre / 1¾ pints dry white wine
1 litre / 1¾ pints red wine
(Merlot or Clinton)
small glass of brandy
2 rounded tsp cornflour,
slaked with a little water
a little game or beef stock,
if necessary
salt and pepper

Pastry

350 g / 12 oz plain white flour
125 g / 4 oz unsalted butter
125 g / 4 oz lard
pinch of salt
egg yolk and melted butter, to glaze

One area with a long tradition of hunting is among the ridges of the pre-Alps that stretch between Monte Grappa and Conegliano. There, the preparation of game is an almost magical ritual.

———⁂———

Brown the pieces of hare with the diced lean pork, *lardo* (cured pork fat) and chopped onion, in the butter. Add the cloves and cinnamon, tied in a piece of muslin so you can remove them easily, and some salt and pepper and leave the meat to cook on very low heat for at least 3 hours, periodically pouring in some dry white wine and red Merlot or Clinton. If possible, the source of heat should not be gas, but a wood-burning stove or electric hotplate, because these deliver heat more uniformly.

To make the pastry, sift the flour and salt into a bowl, cut in the butter and lard in small pieces and rub in with your fingers until the mixture resembles breadcrumbs. Add just enough very cold water to bring the dough together and then wrap in foil or cling film and chill for 20 minutes or until required.

Roll the pastry out to a thickness of about 5 mm (¼ in). Use a bit more than half to line a fairly deep, well-greased pie dish.

Preheat the oven to 180°C / 350°F / Gas Mark 4. Now take the pieces of meat and the bag of spices from the dish and add a small glass of brandy to the juices that are left; continue to heat and stir in the cornflour to thicken (if it becomes too thick, you can add some beef stock). Stir the boneless meat back into the liquid, then pour everything into the pie dish. Roll out the remaining pastry for the lid and place it on top, carefully nipping and sealing the edges together. Brush the pastry with a mix of melted butter and egg yolk. Bake for 25 minutes.

Conigio alla Veneta
Rabbit stew

Serves 4
*800 g / 1¾ lb oven-ready rabbit,
with liver, kidneys and heart if
possible
60 ml / 2 fl oz olive oil
60 g / generous 2 oz butter
grated zest of 1 lemon
1 garlic clove
salt and pepper*

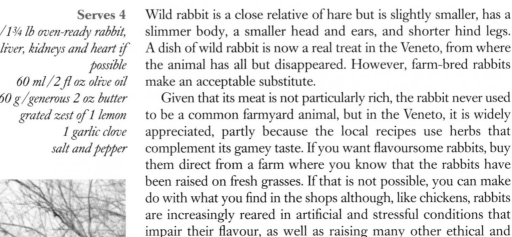

Wild rabbit is a close relative of hare but is slightly smaller, has a slimmer body, a smaller head and ears, and shorter hind legs. A dish of wild rabbit is now a real treat in the Veneto, from where the animal has all but disappeared. However, farm-bred rabbits make an acceptable substitute.

Given that its meat is not particularly rich, the rabbit never used to be a common farmyard animal, but in the Veneto, it is widely appreciated, partly because the local recipes use herbs that complement its gamey taste. If you want flavoursome rabbits, buy them direct from a farm where you know that the rabbits have been raised on fresh grasses. If that is not possible, you can make do with what you find in the shops although, like chickens, rabbits are increasingly reared in artificial and stressful conditions that impair their flavour, as well as raising many other ethical and environmental concerns.

Some complain that rabbits have too 'gamey' a taste but there is a secret here, one of those classic tips to be learned from the grandmothers and aged aunts who were renowned for their cooking: as soon as you have washed and dried the rabbit, cook it whole or in pieces at a very high temperature for 5 to 6 minutes without adding any seasoning. This draws off a lot of the liquid in the meat, which is responsible for the strong taste that can ruin the final dish. Then proceed to cook the rabbit, as you want.

One of the most popular dishes involving rabbit is *salmì*. However, I also know other traditional recipes for rabbit with lemon, roast rabbit, rabbit stew, rabbit with radicchio and rabbit stuffed with cumin. The most typical version is simply known as rabbit *alla Veneta*.

To make the sauce, finely chop the rabbit liver, kidneys and heart and then sauté them in half the oil and butter. Halfway through the cooking process, add salt, pepper and lots of grated lemon zest.

Cut the rabbit into medium-sized pieces. Cook in another pan with the remaining oil, butter and a whole garlic clove (to be removed later), until the pieces are sealed all over. Pour over the sauce and leave to simmer for 15 minutes. If the cooking juices don't suffice, add some water or white wine, little by little.

Rabbit *alla Veneta* is best served, as ever, with polenta, either freshly-prepared or sliced and grilled.

Penin co le verze
Pig's trotters with cabbage

Serves 4
2 preserved pig's trotters
1 medium-sized green cabbage,
sliced finely
½ onion, chopped
50 g / 2 oz lardo, finely chopped
fresh rosemary sprig

With its predilection for pork, Venetian cuisine has recipes for all cuts of the meat, including the trotters. Added to vegetable soups and pasta dishes it renders them so substantial that they make a meal in themselves. If you are getting on a bit and worry about your heart or consider yourself to be one or two kilos overweight, you should either avoid this dish altogether or indulge with caution.

As well as being used plain, pig's trotters can be salted and smoked, then braised or boiled and served with stewed cabbage or mashed potatoes. The most important dish in which they figure is undoubtedly the *zampone* that is an essential part of any New Year's Eve dinner, when thick slices of the boiled *zampone* are served on a bed of lentils (these not only taste good but are also said to bring good luck and fortune in the coming year).

Soak the trotters in cold water for a few hours or even overnight, if possible. Drain and put in a pot of fresh water and slowly bring to the boil. Remove the surface scum and continue to boil gently, taking care that the trotters don't break up, for 3 hours.

Cook the cabbage and onion in the *lardo*, with the rosemary sprig. Add the trotters and simmer until the flavours are evenly distributed and the cabbage is soft and forms a sort of paste similar to *Verze sofegae*.

Porseo al latte
Pork poached in milk

Serves 6
1 kg / 2¼ lb lean boneless pork
500 ml / 18 fl oz white wine
60 g / generous 2 oz butter
fresh sage leaves
fresh rosemary sprig
about 1 litre / 1¾ pints milk
salt and pepper

Pork is eaten throughout the year in Venice, a city where people appreciate its delicate flavour. This recipe for pork, one of our family favourites – and almost foolproof – brings out all the best qualities of the succulent meat. The result is delicious and the taste unusual.

———— ✦ ————

An optional first step is to put a fine cut of lean boneless pork to marinate for a couple of days in white wine and drain well before cooking begins.

Fry the meat in the butter until well browned all over. Add some salt and pepper, the sage leaves and rosemary and then enough milk to cover the pork in a casserole dish. Now simmer until the meat is nearly cooked, adding more milk if anything starts to stick; a few minutes before the end, increase the heat to reduce the liquid in which the pork has cooked. By now, the sauce has become rich-brown in colour and has an interesting lumpy texture. The tender, cooked meat should be sliced thinly and laid out on a deep plate; pour a little of the sauce over it and keep the rest for the sauceboat.

Pastizzada
Beef stew

Serves 6
1 kg / 2¼ lb lean boneless beef,
in one piece
2 garlic cloves, cut in slivers
a few cloves
1 cinnamon stick, broken into pieces
1 litre / 1¾ pints full-bodied
dry red wine
1 onion, coarsely chopped
few celery tips, coarsely chopped
1 carrot, coarsely chopped
a little chopped fresh rosemary
75 g / 3 oz lardo
salt and peppercorns

This is an extremely special type of stew, involving an elaborate preparation and lengthy marinating of the meat in wine or vinegar.

———— ✦ ————

Use a fine cut of lean boneless beef and make various incisions, into which you insert garlic, cloves and some pieces of cinnamon. Leave the beef to marinate in a tub of full-bodied red wine in which you have put the onion, celery, carrot, rosemary, salt and peppercorns. Leave for a full day, turning the meat every now and again so that all sides become equally flavoured.

Preheat the oven to 150°C / 350°F / Gas Mark 2. Having removed the meat from the marinade, wrap it in small strips of *lardo* (cured pork fat) and return to the marinade for the cooking stage; this is best done in a glass or pyrex dish. Cover the dish, place in the oven and leave the meat to simmer slowly for 2 to 3 hours. Regularly turn the beef over in the liquid. Towards the end of the cooking time, break up the vegetables in the marinade with a wooden spoon to thicken the sauce.

Serve in a deep bowl, swimming in its sauce and accompanied by white or yellow polenta.

Gran bollito alla padovana
Boiled meats

Serves 4
1.4 litres / 3 pints water
1.5 kg / 3¼ lb beef
1 onion
8 cloves
1 carrot
3 garlic cloves
3 celery sticks
bunch of fresh parsley sprigs
3 bay leaves
1 chicken
1 tongue, pickled or plain
1 musetto *pork sausage*
end of leg of Parma ham

The tradition at wedding banquets was that the roast meats be preceded by the boiled: beef, chicken, sausage, tongue as well as duck, goose and guinea fowl – if desired. These were served with cooked vegetables, horseradish sauce, 'green sauce', sweet spicy mustards and coarse-grain salt. Galileo Galilei, the legendary astronomer, physicist, philosopher and astrologer, was a great aficionado of such dishes: documents have been found recording that he purchased enormous quantities of meat from a butcher in Abano (not far from Padua, where he taught at the university).

The end of leg of Parma ham is just used for flavouring; ask your delicatessen to give you what remains of a leg of ham when no more slices can be cut from it.

———

Bring a large saucepan of water to the boil, then add the beef, onion (spiked with the cloves), carrot, garlic cloves, celery, parsley and bay leaves. Ensure the meat is covered with water, add salt and simmer for about 3 hours. Then add the chicken and simmer for a further 2 hours.

Separately, boil the tongue for 2 hours. Then change the water and boil for another 2. Boil the end of the ham leg with the tongue (having removed the rind). Peel the skin off the tongue while it is hot. The authentic version of this recipe calls for a pickled tongue but then the result is very strong; at home we use fresh tongue.

Boil the *musetto* pork sausage separately.

Arrange the various meats on a large platter and serve with coarse salt, green sauce and a sauce made of finely grated horseradish that has been pickled in vinegar for at least a month (ready-made creamed horseradish is a good substitute). The dish should be accompanied by a fresh and fruity young red wine.

The leftover meat stock is delicious and can be used for making *tortellini in brodo* – basically cook some Parma ham tortellini in boiling broth and serve in bowls. A perfect entrée to the *bollito*. These two dishes are the mainstay of our Christmas lunch.

Salsa peverada
Peppered sauce

Serves 4
*500 ml / 18 fl oz meat stock
(from the boiled meat), well reduced
200 g / 7 oz fresh breadcrumbs
half a glass of Greek white wine
(optional)
75 g / 3 oz sultanas
60 g / generous 2 oz pine nuts
1 tsp ground cinnamon
salt and freshly ground pepper
few slices sopressa (soft salami)
and a few anchovies,
or game bird livers, finely chopped*

In the late Middle Ages and the Renaissance, peppery and hot sauces were very popular in Venice. Hot sauces were even considered an aphrodisiac, as well as conveniently masking the taste of meat that was perhaps past its prime.

Ragù, a term left over from the brief French dominion in the Veneto, refers to meat sauces and has been incorporated into Italian cooking ever since. It is effective in exalting the flavours of potentially insipid cereal-based dishes such as rice and polenta. Other versions exist – known as 'fake' *ragù* – which combine multiple flavours and vegetables. *Salsa peverada* is one of the best known of these and was served at the tables of patricians and humble folk alike, in silver or ceramic sauceboats respectively. It generally accompanies richly flavoured boiled meats (for example, boar), as well as game, poultry and beef.

The sauce is made with a mixture of breadcrumbs, spices (ground cinnamon and pepper), sultanas, pine nuts, salt and abundant freshly ground pepper, all of which are added to a substantially reduced broth, left over from boiling the meats that the sauce is meant to accompany and including some of the finely chopped, tender boiled meat itself. Some strong Greek wine may also be added for extra flavour. Puréed livers of game birds are traditionally added to the *peverada,* but you can substitute finely chopped *sopressa* and anchovies.

———— ✦ ————

Start by cooking some of the broth on a low heat with the breadcrumbs. When these have taken on a deep colour, add a little more broth (with the livers or *sopressa* and anchovies) or the wine, with some salt and a lot – a lot! – of pepper, together with the sultanas, pine nuts and cinnamon. Reduce the sauce by simmering, if necessary. Some grated Parmesan is sometimes added at the end.

This is good with any boiled meats.

Serves 4
*200 g / 7 oz fresh parsley, chopped
2 anchovy fillets
1 small pickled cucumber
1 garlic clove
1 boiled potato
good extra virgin olive oil
15 ml / 1 tbsp vinegar*

Salsa verde per carni bollite
Green sauce for boiled meats

Chop all the ingredients finely and then combine, cover with oil, add the vinegar and mix thoroughly.

Castradina della Salute
Salute-style stewed smoked lamb

Serves 4
*800 g / 1¾ lb leg of castradina
(smoked leg of lamb)
1.8 litres / 4 pints
Verze sofegae (stewed cabbage),
to serve*

This dish has a decisive flavour. It is not native to Venice but was introduced from the mountain regions of Dalmatia and Albania during the terrible plague of 1630. Because the meat was dried and heavily salted, it was believed that it was less likely than fresh meat to carry contagion. Given the terror caused by the plague, the city was almost entirely cut off from the farms and vegetable gardens of the mainland, so *castradina* – brought by the ships from beyond the lagoon – was a crucial source of sustenance for the Venetians. It has remained part of Venetian cuisine ever since.

In mid-November, the butcher's shops in Rialto begin to stock large smoke-browned cuts of meat, which used to be brought specially from Dalmatia or Albania and were festively decorated with evergreens and coloured ribbons. The traditional feast of *La Salute* (21 November) involves certain rituals, some dating from longer ago than others: a visit to the votive church of the Madonna della Salute (to light a candle thanking the Virgin for her intercession in ending the plague and continuing to protect our health) and a meal of *castradina* are among the longest standing customs of the day. Helium balloons for the children and bags of sweets from Sicilian stallholders are a more recent introduction!

Cooking the dish is quite straightforward, because it basically consists of boiled meat.

———⁂———

Clean the dried lamb well by removing the skin and then the fat, which has a heavy, smoky flavour. Wash the golden-brown meat for a long time in tepid water and then cut into medium-sized pieces, leaving it on the bone. Put in a pan with plenty of cold water, bring to the boil and discard the water. Repeat. In a third lot of fresh cold water, simmer until the *castradina* is tender: about 2 hours. If produced locally, the *castradina* should cook for 2 to 3 hours, whereas that from Dalmatia or Albania will take 6 to 7 hours because it is so much tougher.

Meanwhile, make the dish of stewed cabbage, which is the standard accompaniment for *castradina*, according to the instructions in the Vegetables section of this book.

The meat – and its gravy – should be served in a big bowl with the cabbage.

Figà la veneziana
Venetian-style liver and onions

Serves 4
500 g / 1 lb calf's liver
750 g / 1½ lb white onions
60 ml / 2 fl oz olive oil
40 g / 1½ oz butter
*handful of chopped fresh
parsley (optional)*
lemon juice (optional)
salt and pepper
lemon wedges, to serve

If it was hunger that originally drove people to eat the inner organs of beasts and fowls with relish, the relish was particularly great when it came to the *figà* (liver). *Figà a la veneziana* is now an acclaimed dish worldwide.

Chopping onions is notorious for making cooks cry but, they're not real tears, of course, and there is a fitting Venetian expression, '*Dopio come le ceole*' ('as many-layered as an onion'), which refers to someone's wealth and possessions as well as their falsity and hypocrisy. A vegetable that was first cultivated thousands of years ago, the onion has been a staple of European cuisine for at least 500 years; it is particularly important in northern Europe, where it grows easily. But onions also feature largely in the cuisine of the Veneto, with those grown in Chioggia and the other areas of the river estuaries being particularly good. Sautéed onions lie at the foundations of risottos, soups and sauces – and, of course, onions are an essential ingredient of *figà a la veneziana*, as vital to the dish as the liver itself.

The finest liver is calf's liver, which is pale pink. Cut into strips, it can also be cooked on a griddle, fried in a pan or casseroled with sauces that often include lemon juice or vinegar. One can also roast the entire liver, covering it with strips of bacon and seasoning it with herbs and light spices. Lamb's liver, too, is perfect cooked this way (or diced and skewered). Beef liver is a bit leathery, and sheep's liver of very modest quality. *Figà a la veneziana* is best prepared in autumn and winter because, like all animal innards, liver can easily go off. The procedure is straightforward.

———— ∞ ————

Slice the liver and onions thinly. Cook the onions for 5 to 10 minutes in oil, adding salt and pepper. Then add the liver and turn up the heat. It is better if cooked very hot, tossing the ingredients in the pan (which, therefore, should be long-handled). Cook only for a few minutes, otherwise the liver gets too tough. If you like, sprinkle the dish with chopped parsley and a little lemon juice shortly before serving, complemented by a good slice of polenta.

Medaglioni di salame bellunese
Medallions of Belluno salami

Serves 4

150 g / 5 oz lean beef, minced
75 g / 3 oz lean pork, minced
200 g / 7 oz Belluno or other soft,
tasty salami, finely chopped
salt and pepper
ground spices, e.g. fennel

In 1162 Ulrich, Patriarch of Aquileia, occupied Grado with an army of men from Friuli. The Venetian response was immediate and Doge Vitale II Michiel led a fleet against the city, re-conquering it and bringing the patriarch and 12 of his canons to Venice as prisoners. The Republic's firm intention was to behead the rebels but the Pope intervened and the clerics were sent back to their city, having signed an agreement that, on each Thursday of Carnival, they would supply Venice with one bull and 12 pigs (mocking symbols for the patriarch and his canons). The tradition lasted a long time, with the animals publicly slaughtered in St Mark's Square. After the open-air celebration of the occasion – which included fireworks in broad daylight – the Doge and his councillors moved in procession to the Doge's palace where, with their rods of office, they solemnly demolished wooden models intended to represent the castles of Friuli.

Perhaps another reason for the popularity of pork in both the Veneto and Venice itself is that most pigs are raised on dairy farms and their feed includes leftover dairy products, which may enhance the delicate flavour of the meat. In mountain areas, salting and preserving pork are especially common, given that cooler temperatures mean there is less risk of the meat going off. This dish originates in farmhouses of the Belluno area.

―――――∞∞∞―――――

Mix the minced meats with the chopped salami. Flavour with salt, pepper and other spices as you desire. Form into four medallions that are about 1 cm (½ inch) thick. These can be grilled but are even better if cooked over an open fire; do not overcook, or they will lose the pork fat that binds them together. The medallions should be served hot with yellow polenta or mashed potatoes.

CALENDARIO ROMANO
2004

18 M...
19 M...
20 G...
21 V...
22 S...
23 D...
24 L...
25 M...
26 M...
27 G...
28 V...
29 S...
30 D...
31 L...

Shopping lists & Jupiter's moons: astronomy & gastronomy

LONGSIDE his discovery of the moons of Jupiter, thanks to his telescope and his other astronomical research, Galileo's reputation at the University of Padua was further enhanced by his depth of knowledge as a gastronome – in particular meat dishes, foremost among which was the *gran bollito*, a mixture of boiled meats.

This combination of scientific and mathematical genius with gastronomic ability was much appreciated by such learned Venetian patricians as Morosini and Dandolo, as well as by one of the Gonzagas, lords of Mantua. Galileo's skill in the kitchen was particularly useful because – as was the custom of the day – professors of international fame who attracted students from outside the city used to also house a number in their own homes, providing bed and board in return for a monthly payment. These students would certainly have enjoyed Galileo's version of the *gran bollito alla Padovano*, already a typical dish in the city.

Acclaimed by the Venetian Republic for his scientific discoveries, Galileo was also voraciously competent when it came to buying meat. A bill from one of the best butchers in Abano (a town near Padua) for the year 1604 lists 260 lbs of beef, 83 lbs of *sorenella* (top-quality veal) and 54 lbs of average-quality veal. Between 11 December 1604 and 29 January 1605, we know that his household consumed vast quantities of beef shank, boiled poultry, veal heads and pickled tongue. Then, of course, there was wine, both red and white, which the scientist purchased from a certain Bartolomeo, steward to the Contarini household, according to the records.

Amid all this cooking and eating, Galileo found time to work on the development of his telescope, an invention that was of particular interest to the Venetians – not so much for its use in astronomy but in navigation, as a way of identifying ships at a distance. Indeed, telescopes played an important role in the great victories that Francesco Morosini achieved in the 20 years of the War of Candia and in the later conquest of the Peloponnese.

Born in Pisa on 15 February 1564, Galileo Galilei was the son of a moderately wealthy burgher family. When he was 10 years old, the family moved to Florence, where he completed his first studies in logic and literature. In 1581 Galileo complied with his father's wishes and enrolled at the faculty of medicine in Pisa; however, the subject had no real appeal for him and he returned to Florence. There he pursued his study of mathematics and began to carry out experiments in physics. During this time he formulated various theorems regarding geometry and mechanics. For example, in 1586 his study of Archimedes led to the invention of a balance to determine the specific weight of bodies. Three years later he was appointed to the Chair of Mathematics in Pisa, a position he kept for a further three years and where he discovered, amongst other things, the 'law of the falling of heavy bodies', which Johannes Kepler, a German astronomer, immediately recognized as an important contribution to science. This plaudit greatly increased Galileo's fame and in 1598 he moved to teach mathematics at the University of Padua, where he remained for 18 years.

When Galileo built his first telescope in 1609, he gave Venetian officials and noblemen a demonstration from St Mark's Bell Tower – the very same tower from which the 37-year-old Goethe would later get his first glimpse of the sea. Using this instrument, Galileo then began to make the great astronomical discoveries on which his fame now rests. However, he also began making enemies: Cardinal Bellarmino warned him against the Copernican ideas that offended the beliefs of both church hierarchy and the Aristotelian establishment within academia. But Galileo continued with his studies, publishing his discussion of the Ptolemaic and Copernican theories – *Dialogue on the Two Great World Systems* – in Florence in 1632. By September of that year he had been summoned by the Pope to appear before the Holy Office of the Inquisition. The entire episode inspired Bertolt Brecht to write one of his most famous plays, the *Life of Galileo*, which includes this passage:

It is said that on Mardi Gras 1632, this ditty was being sung in the public squares of Italy:

The learned Galileo
took a look at the skies
and said: 'There's nothing true in Genesis.'
Now, there's a nerve! Not to be taken lightly.
Nowadays these heresies are spreading like diseases.
What is left if you change the Scriptures?
Everyone will say and do what suits him without fear.
If certain ideas get a foothold, my people,
what will happen?
There will be no more altar boys at mass;
servants won't want to make your bed.
A bad business! Not to be taken lightly.
Free thought catches on, like an epidemic.
Life is sweet, man is non-rational
and, for a change, it is pleasant to do what one wants!
Since long past, poor mankind has obeyed the Gospels
    and governments,
has turned the other cheek
to win eternal recompense,
to become even more obedient.
Get wise to things!
It's time for everyone to look out for himself!

When the minstrel who speaks these lines finishes, a larger-than-life-sized puppet appears: Galileo bows to the public. In front of him, a child carries a huge open bible, with some pages crossed out. The minstrel begins again: 'Here is Galileo Galilei, the Bible Slayer'.

The Church condemned the scientist for having contradicted the cosmology that underpinned Catholic dogma; the trial lasted until June 1633 and ended with a sentence of life imprisonment. However, Galileo was soon transferred to much less harsh conditions in Siena and from there he was allowed to go to his own home in Arcetri, in the hills to the south of Florence. This would be his prison for the last years of his life, during which his eyesight gradually failed. Galileo died on the morning of 8 January 1642, just a few weeks before the birth of Isaac Newton.

It is said that many of Galileo's scientific papers were lost after his condemnation by the Church. However, it would appear that a bundle of autograph documents (including original studies of catenary curves) was discovered in 1700 – at a butcher's shop, where the sheets were being used to wrap meat.

Vegetables

Vegetables

Our ancestors have long been aware of the beneficial effects of plants and herbs. Often these curative or purgative properties are still exploited in warm infusions or tisanes. To aid digestion, there is the camomile that our grandmothers used to make; known to the Romans, this also calms the nerves (as does an infusion of poppy seeds). Ivy can be used to treat coughs; sweet marjoram for insomnia; melissa (lemon balm) for dizziness, palpitations and headaches; and mint works as a stimulant. As for rosemary, it not only serves to flavour roast meats but it also aids the working of the liver. In Venice, the street of San Nicoletto della Lattuga is named after a small monastery church. It was built by one Nicolò Lion in thanksgiving for his recovery from a serious illness – a recovery that he attributed to eating *lattuga* (lettuce) grown in the garden of the monastery. In the Belluno area there is a herb that is actually called San Giovanni, which – if gathered on the evening of St John the Baptist's feast day (24 June) – can be burned to ward off storms. But along with herbs, all nature of vegetables and plants provide feasts of colour, hopes of wellbeing and culinary delights – be they from the estuary of the Venetian lagoon, the Po valley or even farther afield.

Tomatoes are ubiquitous, appearing in just about every type of kitchen that comes to mind, as is the pleasure of sharing a favourite recipe. Here is a letter my great aunt once received from a lady she met while staying at a spa near Padua.

Re: American-style tomatoes, 11 September 1905

My Dear Countess.
At Abano I promised to give you a recipe for American-style tomatoes, but then I forgot to do so before leaving. I am writing to you now to make up for that oversight.

I heard from Madame Lascaris that you had a bad fall during the last few days of your stay in Abano. I hope that you did not feel any ill effects, and that now, together with your family, you can enjoy the peace and quiet of the autumn countryside. I, too, found my family in the best of health, and we are spending these fine days most pleasantly.

My dear countess, please accept my friendly good wishes.

Affectionately yours
Beatrice Pandolfini Corsini

American-style tomatoes

Take a few well-ripe tomatoes, make a crossways incision in the skin and then drop them in boiling water; this makes it easy to peel them.

Leave them to marinate for 7 to 8 hours in a mix of vinegar, all sorts of aromatic herbs and finely chopped onion, with a little red pepper. Drain off the vinegar and then keep them on ice for a couple of hours. Serve with mayonnaise in which you have mixed a little red pepper.

N.B. The red pepper can be omitted, according to taste. But it does add a lot to the flavour.

The tomatoes are better if they are well-iced.

A nephew of the writer of this letter, Prince Giovanni Corsini, an officer in the Italian army during the Second World War, was held as a prisoner of war in Kenya, where he laid a one-pound wager with the English officer commanding the prison camp that, sooner or later, he would manage to escape. No sooner said than done. Having got hold of a British uniform, Prince Corsini carried off the part of a non-commissioned officer to perfection: he spoke English as if it were his mother tongue. In this disguise, he managed to get hold of an English lorry, onto which he loaded four fellow Italian soldiers, whom he passed off as prisoners being transferred to another camp by Corporal J. A. Dickson (himself).

In spite of the many controls and checks that he passed through, the prince made it, travelling 2,800 km in 31 days, passing through the British colonies of Kenya, Tanganyika and Nyasaland to Mozambique, which at the time was a Portuguese colony and therefore neutral. It is said that, after the war, the commander of the camp paid up the pound he had wagered.

As for Prince Corsini, he – like so many others – had caught *mal d'Afrique* and settled in Mozambique.

With its sweet peppers, courgettes and aubergines, Italian cuisine does not need American-style – or even African-style – tomatoes to be rich in colours of its own. Gleaming red or dazzling yellow peppers are often eaten raw with *pinzimonio*, a mix of olive oil and vinegar seasoned with salt and pepper. In Piedmont, raw peppers are eaten with another traditional sauce, *bagna cauda* (warm sauce), which is a mix of olive oil and butter (in equal amounts) with mashed anchovy fillets and garlic. Kept warm by a spirit lamp, the pot containing this sauce is placed in the middle of the table, so that each guest can dip into it a variety of crudités. The presentation of this very tasty dip makes it a sort of celebration of communal eating. Of course, a glass or two of full-bodied Piedmontese wine helps to overcome any initial shyness about taking part in this ritual – and those who, even then, show themselves to be timid are fittingly said to be as 'red as a pepper'.

Another boast of Italian cuisine is the artichoke, which comes in a rich variety of colours depending upon species and where it is grown. The plant seems to have originated in the rough terrain of Sicily and then gradually spread throughout the peninsula, changing colour and form as it went. There is, for example, the 'early' Palermo variety, with purplish leaves ending in a tough yellow spike. The 'Roman' artichoke is fat and round, with grey-green leaves. Then there are the violet-coloured artichokes of Tuscany, Naples and Chioggia. But from wherever it came, the artichoke was long considered to have aphrodisiacal properties and the sexist logic of the day meant that women were almost always forbidden from eating them. However, that did not stop Catherine de' Medici. She had an almost insatiable appetite for this vegetable and so it was inevitable that, when she became Queen of France, she took Italian artichoke plants with her and vehemently encouraged the local farmers to grow lots of them.

Within the Veneto, the cultivation of artichokes is a long-standing tradition because the sandy terrain of the lagoon shores, lido and islands is perfectly suited to this plant. However, the fact that artichokes ripen only towards late spring led to the emergence of a very special local delicacy: *castraure*. These are tender young heads snipped from the plant in early spring in order to give the remaining artichokes the chance to grow to full size. Usually, the growers on the islands – notably Sant'Erasmo and in the estuary area leave only three or four artichokes per plant and harvest the rest as delicious *castraure*. They are so small that they can be eaten in a single mouthful, or they can be chopped finely and eaten raw as a salad.

During the hot summer months in Venice and the Veneto, *insalatoni* are very popular. These 'large salads' not only have the advantage of being served cold but also combine a rich variety of tastes. There is, for example, a classic salad of lettuce, radicchio, rocket and hard-boiled eggs, perhaps with the addition of chopped anchovies, boiled shrimps or canned tuna; another favourite uses *nervetti* (boiled beef tendons) and a mix of leeks, sweet onions, and radishes, all dressed with salt, pepper, lots of oil and a few spoonfuls of vinegar, together with crushed garlic and parsley. The *nervetti* are left to marinate like this for two to three days and then served cold in bowls. Another type of salad that is very common among fieldworkers taking a break during the hottest hours of the day is made using rocket (often found growing wild), cucumbers and green tomatoes simply dressed with oil, vinegar and salt and pepper.

Omnipresent throughout the Veneto, red radicchio is the pride and joy of the Treviso area. Because of the plant's colourful, flower-like appearance and the fact that it is really a winter vegetable, red radicchio is known as 'the winter flower'. Just a few days before Christmas, the Loggia dei Trecento in Treviso hosts a remarkable fair, in which local farmers display baskets of their prize radicchio, which in colour and beauty rival roses and orchids. A favourite Treviso story tells of a local girl who, when she first saw a splendid display of orchids, burst out: 'but since when have people started putting vases of radicchio in their sitting rooms?'

And there is also a culinary rival for the perfume of flowers: the rich aroma of the *chiodini*, *porcini* and other wild mushrooms that make their appearance in the local markets around autumn time. Later on in the season, it is the turn of the several cabbages that are a traditional feature of Veneto cuisine, featuring in rich and tasty soups or as the perfect accompaniment to main courses of roast and boiled meats.

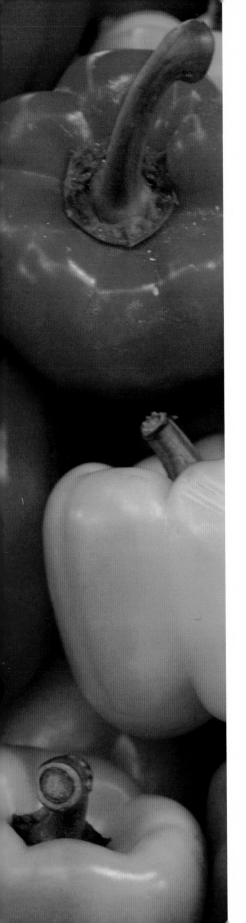

Peperonata alla veneta
Sweet peppers

Although peppers are primarily associated with the colour red in Italy, indeed the expression *rosso come un peperone* describes a furious blush, this vegetable also comes in yellow, green, yellow-green and green-red versions. The plant was first introduced into Europe from the New World and variations in colour reflected different stages of ripening, from green through yellow to red. Nowadays the colours are actually associated with different varieties of pepper. *Corno di toro* (Bull's horn) peppers are large and red or yellow in colour. Very fleshy and not over-peppery, they are perfect for cooking either over an open fire or in the oven; when ready, they are peeled and served cold with olive oil, pepper, a little of the liquid released during the cooking and a few drops of balsamic vinegar.

In summer and early autumn, the heat in Venice can be terrible so it is best to opt for a diet composed largely of fruit and vegetables – also because this is the time of the year when they taste best and are most abundant. Throughout the Mediterranean one recurrent theme is dishes with peppers playing a central role: in Spain there is chilled *gazpacho*, in Sicily *caponata*, in France *ratatouille*, in Serbia *juvesh* – and here *peperonata*. The version served in Venice is very similar to the Neapolitan dish of the same name, and comprises mild peppers (yellow, or else green), small aubergines, small nut-sized onions and the juicy small tomatoes you find in the market at the same time of year as sweet peppers, still attached to their branches.

Serves 4

1 garlic clove
60 g / generous 2 oz butter
60 ml / 2 fl oz olive oil
300 g / 10 oz button onions
or shallots, chopped or halved
(if very small)
400 g / 14 oz aubergines, diced
500 g / 1 lb yellow or green
peppers, de-seeded and sliced
into strips
300 g / 10 oz tomatoes,
skinned and roughly cut up
a little white wine
salt

Sauté the garlic clove in the oil and butter and then remove from the pan as soon as it starts to turn golden brown. Then start to fry the onions, the ingredient which takes the longest to cook; shortly after, add the diced aubergines and then the peppers. Finally, come the tomatoes. Salt the mixture, add a little white wine and simmer, taking care that it does not stick or burn, for about 40 minutes.

The *peperonata* should be served cold or tepid and accompanied by a white wine that exalts the flavour of the individual ingredients.

For those worried about indigestion, the *peperonata* can be made without the onions, and with other variations on the basic recipe, such as the addition of chopped fresh basil during cooking and using courgettes instead of onion. If the basic ingredients aren't fresh and bursting with flavour, it might help to add a stock cube and a can of chopped tomatoes. Whatever the permutation of ingredients, this dish always seems to be a hit.

Sparasi de Bassan
White Bassano asparagus

Serves 4

1 kg / 2¼ lb white Bassano asparagus
4 eggs, soft boiled and roughly chopped
60 ml / 2 fl oz good-quality olive oil
salt and pepper

In the foothills of Bassano, plump white asparagus are produced which beat any to be found elsewhere in size and flavour. The pride and significance is even reflected in a local saying: '*Quando a Bassan vien primavera, se verze la cà e la sparesera*' ('When spring arrives in Bassano, people open up their homes – and their asparagus plots'). The whole stretch of the Brenta river that tumbles down through this pleasant town and rolls smoothly and calmly across the green fields of the plain below, is renowned for its asparagus.

⸺⸺

White asparagus are fairly easy to prepare: boil in a small amount of water until just tender and then lay them on a plate with the tips pointing towards the centre. Place the soft-boiled eggs on the top. Liberally dress with olive oil, salt and pepper.

You can also cook the asparagus tied in a bundle and placed upright in a tall pot with two-thirds of their length immersed in cold water. After the water comes to a boil and the steam has begun to make the tips droop (10 to 12 minutes of cooking) remove and untie the bundle and put the asparagus to soak in a pan of cold water for at least 15 minutes, to set the colour and texture.

In the Veneto, a typical asparagus sauce consists of boiled egg yolks mashed with vinegar, olive oil, salt and pepper and then mixed with finely chopped egg whites. Capers and chopped anchovy fillets may be added to heighten the flavour – but that is not always advisable, given the delicate taste of the asparagus. Alternatively, serve the asparagus boiling hot, with a sauce of melted butter and lemon juice.

Melanzane in tecia
Stewed aubergine

Serves 4

1 kg / 2¼ lb large round aubergines
plain white flour, for coating
200 ml / 7 fl oz olive oil

Sauce

60 ml / 2 fl oz olive oil
50 g / 2 oz butter
25 g / 1 oz fresh parsley, chopped
1 garlic clove
200 g / 7 oz tomatoes, skinned
and roughly cut up
salt

As a boy, at the end of every summer, I would visit my aunt and uncle in the country and I was especially fond of their cook, Ida. To my eyes she was as ancient as she was kind. She sometimes made a dish similar to this one, coating the slices of aubergine in breadcrumbs, like veal cutlets. My brother, cousins and I would stand at the kitchen door like customs officers, so the large platter Ida was preparing for lunch was always empty: warm and freshly made; these aubergines were too good to resist!

Wash the aubergines and then remove the seeds and cut the flesh into thin slices. Sprinkle with salt and leave to sweat, preferably on a slatted-wood chopping board so the juices can drain away. When the surface of the strips has almost dried out, dip in flour and then fry in hot olive oil.

Meanwhile, prepare the sauce. Heat the oil and butter with the parsley in a pan, flavouring it with a garlic clove (to be removed when it is thoroughly golden). Add the peeled tomatoes cut into pieces. Cook on a moderate heat until the liquid is almost entirely reduced. Serve the aubergines on a large platter, covered with the dense tomato sauce.

Melanzane al fongheto
Mushroom-style aubergine

Serves 4

1 kg / 2¼ lb long, thin aubergines
1 garlic clove
75 ml / 2½ fl oz oil
25 g / 1 oz fresh parsley, chopped
salt

The long, thin aubergines should also be very deeply coloured. Wash them and remove the seeds, then cut into regular-sized chunks. Sprinkle with salt and place in a bowl to settle, while you sauté a whole garlic clove in the oil with the chopped parsley. Remove the garlic clove when it is golden. Add the aubergines and simmer in an open pan until they release most of their liquid and the skin starts to have the same kind of texture as mushrooms (hence the name of the dish).

Serve hot as a side dish with strongly flavoured meat and game. It is ideal with red wines such as Merlot, Raboso or Amarone della Valpolicella.

Melanzane scaltrie
Sautéed aubergine

Serves 4
1 kg / 2¼ lb aubergines
60 ml / 2 fl oz olive oil
40 g / 1½ oz butter
salt

Now rather a commonplace, humble vegetable, the aubergine was once a rarer delicacy. It flourishes in the market gardens of the Veneto coast, where – perhaps due to the sea air – it loses some of the bitter taste that is one of its distinctive, yet unappreciated, characteristics. One of the simplest and tastiest preparations, among many, is this recipe for sautéed aubergines.

⁂

While in other areas of Italy, aubergines are peeled and then diced (with only the very core of the 'belly' discarded), in Venice all that is used is the skin itself, peeled so that only a thin layer of the underlying flesh remains attached. Cut the peel into slices about 5mm (¼ in) wide, then wash, salt and lay out on a wooden chopping board (preferably slatted, so the juices drain away) for a few hours to sweat.

When the strips are ready, simmer them in oil and butter, while stirring frequently so that they neither stick to the pan nor dry out too much. Some people flavour the olive oil with a garlic clove, which should be removed before cooking the aubergine. Sautéed in this way, the aubergines make a fine side dish; they can also be served on their own, with a good red wine.

Patate alla veneziana
Venetian-style potatoes

The potato was already widespread in Peru when the ruthless conquistador Francisco Pizarro arrived there at the beginning of the sixteenth century. However, though the first Europeans brought back samples of the plant to the Old World, the potato was not widely cultivated here until the end of the seventeenth century. It was particularly appreciated in France and, above all, in Germany (like the onion, it grew underground so was better able to resist the freezing northern temperatures).

It may have been the botanical gardens in Padua that produced the first potatoes to be grown in Italy (in 1590) and this was probably the centre from which the plant spread to the rest of the continent. Certainly, the Botanical Gardens have played a central role in European horticulture and were recognized as a World Heritage Site in 1997 by UNESCO: 'the botanic gardens of Padua are the origin of all botanic gardens of the world and represent the cradle of science, scientific exchanges and comprehension of the relationships between nature and culture'. It was also here that a palm tree, *Chamaerops humilis*, suggested to the poet Goethe the ideas that resulted in his theory of the metamorphosis of plants.

Returning to the potato: during the Thirty Years' War in the first half of the seventeenth century, the marauding armies of Sweden and the Holy Roman Empire wreaked such havoc with German agriculture that the resulting famine is said to have killed more than a third of the population. During this period the success of potatoes was established because the peasants realized that it was easy to keep the crop hidden from soldiers, since it grew underground, and they harvested them only at night. This decisive contribution to the survival of the peasants of central Europe meant that the potato became a staple of not only diet but also of legend and myth.

With this background, it was perhaps inevitable that the potato should be 'snubbed' by the high and mighty, who considered it fit only for struggling underlings. However, thanks to Parmentier's studies of its virtues in the late eighteenth century, the potato made a triumphant entry into French cuisine. Since then, it has been used in a large number of refined and complex dishes with such high-sounding names as *patates duchesses*. The following recipe is the most common way of preparing potatoes in Venice.

Serves 4
1 onion, chopped
40 g / 1½ oz butter
60 ml / 2 fl oz olive oil
600 g / 1¼ lb potatoes
25 g / 1 oz fresh parsley, chopped
salt

Sauté the chopped onion in the butter and oil. Peel and eye the potatoes and cut each one into large bite-sized pieces. Then add to the pan, turn the potatoes and sauté at a moderate heat, being careful that they neither break up nor stick to the pan. When they are almost cooked, after 15 to 20 minutes, add salt and sprinkle with chopped parsley. Now cook for a further 5 minutes and serve hot as a side dish with meat or fish.

The humbler form of the recipe omits the parsley and a tasty variation uses sprigs of rosemary.

Verze sofegae
Stewed cabbage

Serves 4
1 winter cabbage (not too big)
60 ml / 2 fl oz olive oil
50 g / 2 oz pancetta, chopped
1 garlic clove
chopped fresh rosemary
salt

Traditional to the Veneto, *verze sofegae* is a smooth, almost creamy, dish that is served with strongly flavoured foods. The preparation requires so much time that one rarely finds this dish on menus these days.

※

Remove the largest and thickest outside leaves and then slice the cabbage thinly and sauté in the oil with the chopped *pancetta*, garlic and rosemary (removing the garlic when it is golden). Add water and salt and then simmer for a couple of hours, at least, with the lid on the pan and stirring periodically, so that the cabbage gradually becomes very soft. The old women of the Veneto will tell you that the cabbage should actually simmer on a very low heat for a good 24 hours, until it is light brown in colour and so smooth it seems like a cream.

Verze sofagae is served with dishes such as *castradina* (stewed lamb), sausages and pig's trotters.

Verze soto aseo

Pickled cabbage

Serves 4
1 winter cabbage (not too big),
cut into large wedges
600 ml / 1 pint water
aromatic red wine vinegar
salt and pepper

To serve
olive oil or lard, for frying
diced pancetta

Common throughout central Europe, sauerkraut is the classic form of conserved greens and is particularly associated with Alsace, where a special 'salting' procedure is used to preserve the cabbage for the winter months. The dish, in fact, reflects the hunger for the sun that is felt by the people of the North during the long and dark winter months, when the choice of vegetables available is limited to potatoes, onions, cabbages and little else.

There is a form of sauerkraut – pickled cabbage – that is traditional in the Veneto. Until about 50 years ago this dish was quite common in the area, and every *biavarol* (flour vendor) also kept a large barrel of pickled cabbage. Such shops meant that there was always some type of vegetable ready to hand, even for some-one with little time or inclination for cooking and preparing.

Cook the cabbage in boiling, salted water for 15 minutes. Drain well. Place in layers in a ceramic dish (traditionally, a wooden barrel). Cover each layer with a generous sprinkling of aromatic vinegar and salt and pepper (the quantities varying according to personal taste). Cover tightly.

Leave the cabbage for a month or so. To serve, fry in olive oil or lard with diced *pancetta*.

Fondi di carciofo
Artichoke bottoms

Serves 4
12 fresh globe artichokes
60 ml / 2 fl oz olive oil
25 g / 1 oz fresh parsley, chopped
1 garlic clove
salt and pepper

Early on summer mornings near the Rialto market you may well see stallholders taking advantage of the still cool air. At their feet are large buckets and in their hands sharp, pointed knives. As they chat to each other, they dexterously manicure their artichokes with a few deft swipes to remove the stems and large tops of the leaves and then trim the edge of the heart itself, leaving only a tender, celadon-coloured flat disk that is dropped into a bucket of water and lemon juice (this stops the artichokes from discolouring).

Like all garden vegetables, artichokes are low in calories; however, they are rich in potassium and iron. Part of their success in Italian cuisine is because the flowering heads were considered to have aphrodisiacal qualities. We are more certain, however, that they are good for one's kidneys and liver, and are often used in medicines for various ailments of old age.

Artichoke bottoms are a specifically Venetian delicacy. Strangely ignored by most important cookbooks, this succulent treat is greatly appreciated by locals. Up until just a few years ago, they were available only in season, from the lagoon as well as from Sicily and Lazio. Recently, French and Spanish varieties have come on the scene and there's hardly a moment in the year when artichokes aren't available.

I buy the bottoms freshly prepared at the market or by green-grocers in Venice. To prepare them yourself, you need an extremely sharp knife. First, cut off the prickly tips of the leaves so you can hold the artichoke in your hand. Then cut all around the circumference of the bottom before chopping off the top part of the flower, along with the hairy 'choke' from the centre. Finally, cut off the bottom part including the stem, and you should be left with a smooth white disk. Store in water to stop them discolouring.

Heat the oil with the garlic clove. Remove the garlic when it is golden-brown. Fry the chopped parsley in the garlic-flavoured hot oil, add the artichoke bottoms and cook on a low to moderate heat until they take on a good colour and turn soft. Overcooking makes them tough and dry. Add some water, if necessary.

Place the artichoke bottoms in a deep dish and cover with the oil from the pan. They make an ideal side dish for roast meat or braised beef – all served with a full-bodied wine such as Merlot or Raboso del Piave.

Another simple way of preparing artichoke bottoms is to simmer them until tender and then dress them with good olive oil, chopped parsley, salt and pepper.

Fonghetti conzì
Mushroom stew

Serves 4
700 g / 1½ lb mushrooms
60 ml / 2 fl oz olive oil
1 garlic clove
fresh thyme
or some other aromatic herb
125 g / 4 oz canned
chopped tomatoes
salt and pepper

Unlike the other fruits of nature, mushrooms are associated with night and darkness, with hidden secret places. Hence, our fascination with them – a fascination reinforced by the mysteriousness of their hallucinatory or even poisonous powers. Mushrooms seem to be the product of spontaneous generation; they emerge in the shadows of the dense forests and woods, which our imaginations populate with the elves, dwarves, wizards and hobbits that are such a feature of European literature.

For the true gourmet, a good plate of mushrooms is a perfect substitute for a meat dish in terms of flavour and any dietician will confirm that it is just as nourishing. There are a vast variety of mushrooms out there, but only a few of the edible sort ever reach the market because the local health authorities impose increasingly strict limitations. The most common wild mushrooms to be found in the markets of the Veneto are *chiodini, porcini, ovoli, prataioli* and *galletti.* There are those who grill them, or turn them into a type of mousse, or stew them using the same recipe as for tripe.

The following is a very popular approach to preparing any kind of mushrooms but medium-sized *porcini* or *chiodini* are the best choice.

———— ⋙ ————

Break the mushroom heads from the stalks and then wash several times, because there will be a lot of earth clinging to the mushrooms. Chop the heads and stalks into pieces. Heat the oil in a pan with the garlic clove and some herbs (wild catmint is especially good). When the oil is hot, add the mushrooms with some pepper and salt. Halfway through cooking add the tomatoes and some more oil (but not too much because mushrooms do not absorb oil).

Serve hot with yellow polenta. The mushrooms are also good when fried in large chunks.

Cotolete de fonghi
Mushroom cutlets

Serves 4

800 g / 1¾ lb large ovoli or
porcini mushrooms
8 slices Fontina
or other mild, full-fat cheese
8 slices of Parma ham
2 eggs, beaten
100 g / 3½ oz dried breadcrumbs
100 g / 3½ oz butter
100 ml / 3½ fl oz olive oil
salt and white pepper

The *ovolo* (*Amanita cesarea*) is the veritable queen of mushrooms, and has been well regarded since Roman times, as the Latin name suggests. But the *porcino* is the prince-consort. While the former is strikingly lobster-red and ivory in colour, the latter combines nuances of black and brown, russet and chestnut; while the former is delicate in taste, the latter is full and refined. Atop a plump stalk that thins upwards, the *chiodino* (*Boletus edulis*) has an almost hemispherical (and sometimes convex) head measuring 5 to 25 cm (2 to 10 in) in diameter. Its flesh is firm and full, with nuances of yellow and orange against white, and has an excellent nutty flavour. This is a prized find for mushroom hunters, though one must be aware of the ease with which it can be confused with the poisonous *Boletus satana*, which is dirty-white on top and red beneath. The *porcino* grows incredibly quickly at the base of large conifers and broadleaf trees such as chestnuts, oaks, beech and ash, both in the plains and in the mountains. It is to be found in the period that runs from summer to the beginning of autumn. Every year, it returns in clumps to the same spot, because they reproduce themselves, like brambles, by vegetative propagation. Whilst *porcini* are excellent eaten raw in a salad, they are also very good when sautéed with oil and parsley. The larger porcini and *ovoli* can be sliced and then coated in polenta to be fried as cutlets – a dish that captures all the intense flavour of this woodland delicacy.

Use the large red and yellow *ovoli* or *porcini*. After cleaning, slice the mushrooms thickly, and together with a slice of non-mature cheese, wrap each chunk of mushroom in a slice of Parma ham, to form 'cutlets'. Dip them into beaten egg mixed with salt and then coat with breadcrumbs. Season with pepper and then fry in the butter and oil. You may prefer to cook the cutlets on a griddle after smearing them with oil and melted butter and sprinkling with white pepper. These cutlets make a good second course because they are as filling as a meat dish. They should be served on a warm plate with fried potatoes, preferably accompanied by a local red wine.

Vovi con fongheto
Eggs and mushrooms

Serves 4

200 g / 7 oz dried mushrooms
60 ml / 2 fl oz olive oil
60 g / generous 2 oz butter
chopped fresh parsley
½ garlic clove, finely chopped
3 eggs
1 tbsp plain flour
30 ml / 2 tbsp milk
75 g / 3 oz Parmesan
or similar cheese, grated
salt

Below: Le Arti che vanno per Via *('Street Crafts') was a series of prints in which Gaetano Zampini, a painter and engraver active in eighteenth-century Venice, depicted not only the city's itinerant traders but also various aspects of popular life. One of the prints shows the odd and amusing game of egg-rolling, which is still played around Easter time in some of the villages of the Po delta. Entitled* La Battaglia dei Vovi *('The Battle of the Eggs'), the image shows two young men, each using an egg to try and break that of his opponent while keeping his own intact.*

The basilisk is a monstrous creature, legend of the Dolomites. Born of the egg of a three-year-old cockerel, it has the head of a serpent, the wings of a bird and the tail of a fish. The beast kills not only with its pestilential breath (capable of withering plants and trees) but also by its glance: if the basilisk sees you before you see it, you are dead. At least the peasants of Cadore and Belluno feel safe: how could the beast catch first sight of them when they are so familiar with its appearance from their city's crest, which includes a rampant basilisk in a red field. Basilisk eggs, however, play no part in this traditional recipe of the Veneto hills, where mushrooms have long been collected and dried for use in the winter.

Place the dried mushrooms to soak in hot water for a few hours. Then wash carefully and cut into small pieces. Sauté in the oil and butter, with the chopped parsley and garlic. Add salt.

Preheat the oven to 200°C / 400°F / Gas Mark 6. Whisk together the eggs, flour, milk and a pinch of salt. Heat a little oil in a small non-stick frying-pan and make thin 'omelettes' with the egg mixture, using a couple of tablespoons at a time and tilting the pan rather as if you were making pancakes. Leave these to cool and then cut into strips about as wide as your finger. Place the strips and mushrooms in a low dish with a knob of butter and sprinkle with the Parmesan. Cook in the hot oven for no longer than 5 minutes – the time it takes for the Parmesan to melt and bind with the eggs and the mushrooms. *Vovi col fongheto* is served hot straight from the oven and is eaten with home-made bread – the perfect way to bring out the full delicate flavour of the dish.

Da Pasqua un'arte nova in sta Città
Se mette fora de zogar ai vovi ;
E, chi nò rompe el vovo ha guadagnà.

Fonghi sott'olio
Mushrooms in oil

Make as many as you wish
fresh mushrooms
wine vinegar
garlic cloves
bay leaves
olive oil
peppercorns
salt

Visit almost any farmhouse kitchen in the Montello area between Verona and Vicenza and you will see large glass jars of mushrooms in oil, with perhaps a bay leaf pressed flat against the glass. The preserved mushrooms are usually the smaller *porcini*, which in autumn you can find out on the crags through which the river Piave flows towards the Adriatic Sea.

Clean the mushrooms well and wash in cold water then leave to dry without covering them. The most delicate phase is the actual cooking, which should be done in abundant strong wine vinegar flavoured with garlic cloves, bay leaves and a little salt. Use an enamelled or ovenproof dish as these do not affect the flavour of the food cooked in them. The mushrooms should boil for at least 15 minutes, totally immersed in the liquid. Leave to cool.

When stone-cold, place the mushrooms in large glass jars, a few at a time, pouring oil over each layer and adding some more bay leaves and some peppercorns. Set the mushrooms aside in sealed jars for at least 40 days. They make a perfect side dish for boiled meats, or can be served with sliced cold meats or even canned fish.

Fasioi in salsa
Beans in anchovy sauce

Serves 4
250 g / 8 oz dried lamon
or flageolet beans
1 garlic clove
60 ml / 2 oz olive oil
25 g / 1 oz fresh parsley
4 salted anchovies, filleted
a glass of aromatic wine vinegar
pepper

Leave the dried beans to soak and soften for about 15 hours – but not more, because they will begin to sprout. Then cook in simmering water (without salt, which hardens the beans) for about 2 hours.

Remove the pan from the heat but keep the beans warm. Sauté a garlic glove in a pan with the oil and parsley; remove the clove when golden and add the anchovy fillets and simmer until they break up completely. Pour the vinegar into the pan and add pepper. Simmer for 10 minutes or so.

Drain the beans and place in a dish, pouring the sauce over them. Leave for at least an hour so that they absorb the full flavour of the sauce, before serving.

Torre di Mosto

T O ILLUSTRATE Venetian economic life, I will now talk about the position of my own family around the middle of the fifteenth century – the time of the navigator Alvise da Mosto, the first European to describe West Africa and discover the islands of Cape Verde. The family properties were then to be found in Venice itself, in the Verona area and at Torre di Mosto. In Roman and pre-Roman times, this latter had been part of the system of lagoons running down the coast from Caorle to Venice. Then, in 131 BC, the Consul Annius Rufus laid down along one side of this network of lagoons the Via Annia that ran from Aquileia towards Rome, and – in the fifth century AD – other Romans constructed a *turris* (tower) at a bend in the river Livenza as part of their defences against the raiding parties of barbarians from the north.

Ca' da Mosto, the family *palazzo* in Venice, dated from the Byzantine period; overlooking the Grand Canal, it can be seen in Vittore Carpaccio's painting of the patriarch of Grado driving out demons with a reliquary of the True Cross. It would seem that the building was actually started by the Barozzi, a family that supplied Venice with patriarchs, bishops, men of arms and scholars. One member of the family – Francesco Barozzi – was, however, too learned for his own good: in 1587 he was sentenced to perpetual imprisonment by the Holy Office of the Inquisition. An astrologer and sorcerer, he was said to be able to make himself invisible, to conjure up demons within a circle traced with a knife dipped in the blood of a murdered man and to have obtained from the island of Crete a *herba felix* that would render anyone wise and knowledgeable.

By the time of the Navigator Alvise, the da Mosto family lived on the first floor of the building and the ground floor was occupied by a certain Simone, a basket weaver, who paid an annual rent of 13 ducats together with an *onoranza* (tribute payment) of 4 glass 'pumpkins' (demijohns) bound in straw and 4 small baskets worth 16 *soldi* each.

To give an idea of the value of the money of the day, I will make a short digression on economic matters. Originally, Venice had used either silver coins minted locally or gold coins minted in Byzantium. Then, in 1284, Doge Giovanni Dandolo II issued the first golden *ducato* to be minted in Venice; equivalent to the Florentine *fiorino*, it ultimately took the name of *zecchino* (sequin), which derives from the Arabic *sikka* (a fitting term for gold coins, because it derives from the Arabic verb 'to dig': *sakk*). The 1284 *zecchino* (gold ducat) bore on one side an image of the Doge kneeling before St Mark and on the other an image of Jesus Christ contained within a *mandorla*. The weight of precious metal within it – approximately 3.44 grams of 24C gold – remained unvaried for over 500 years, right up to the fall of the Republic. Hence, this very stable currency was one of the main measures of commercial wealth throughout the late middle ages and the early modern period.

In 1455 the currency value of the Venetian *zecchino* was fixed at 124 silver *soldi*. However, another conversion rate made it equal to two Venetian *lire* and eight *soldi*. By the end of the Republic, the *zecchino*, whose weight had remained unvaried, was valued at 20 *lire*, the *lira veneta* was valued at 20 *soldi* and each *soldo* in turn was worth 12 *bagattini*. As for what you could actually buy with one *zecchino*, its value amounted to a normal non-luxury item of clothing, the price of a good dinner shared with friends or the cost of visiting an average-looking courtesan.

As for rents, one might mention the two warehouses near the above-mentioned home of the basket-weaver, each of which was rented for 7 ducats. The colonnaded portico along the waterfront of the *palazzo* served as mooring for the gondolas providing a ferry service across the Grand Canal at this point; each boat paid an annual rent of 1 ducat. Furthermore, within the *palazzo* there were other apartments that yielded total rents of around 40 ducats a year.

In the Verona area the family owned a *stancia nova* (new settlement) at Bardolino valued at 1200 ducats; it was this estate that gave its name to the famous Verona wine. As for the property at Torre, it first entered the family's

possession at the beginning of the fourteenth century; eventually, it became so large that the place itself became known as Torre di Mosto.

In the seventh century, this area of lagoons had become a place of refuge for the inhabitants of Oderzo fleeing from the Longobards. The city of Heraclia was founded, and became a flourishing centre of maritime and lagoon trade. Towards the end of the seventh century, however, Heraclia was already in decline, its place being taken by the more safely located Venice. Made progressively more marshy by the continual flooding of the rivers Piave and Livenza, this territory was now settled by peasants who built a small village around an existing chapel dedicated to San Martino and a robust tower that the doges had had built as a defence for Heraclia; that structure itself was similar to those which, in the early Middle Ages, had been built as defences along the borders between the territory of Byzantium and that of the Holy Roman Empire.

The da Mosto property included woodland, meadows and a total of 460 *iugeri* of arable land. (A *iugeri* was the amount of land that could be ploughed in one day by one man driving a plough yoked to two oxen: approximately one quarter of a hectare.). The family property also included an upland area that the local peasants referred to as *Mota rasa*, due to the fact that the tower there had been razed to the ground; this was the site of a farmhouse surrounded by a vegetable garden and fruit orchards. The family also earned income from the toll fees paid by boats using the canals, from the sale of fish raised in the local fish runs and from its half-share in a farm estate known as *Villa Isolata*.

As owners of the land, the da Mosto family also held legal jurisdiction over the village of Torre. Their other privileges included certain *honorificentiae*, rights of pasture and the legal privileges known as *honor et signoria*. However, these rights gradually lapsed, as one can see from an application made to the Venetian Signoria and Council of Ten by the navigator Alvise da Mosto and his brothers in September 1467.

In the years 1411–12 war raged between Venice and the Holy Roman Emperor Sigismund. When the Hungarian forces of the empire invaded large parts of the *terra firma*, the village of Torre di Mosto was ravaged and its population took flight, with the result that the da Mosto family had to invest substantial sums of money to return it to its former state. One of the problems was that only three or four women of the original population were left, so the da Mostos paid for the immigration of 25 new families. The local mills had been destroyed by the Hungarians, so the people of Torre di Mosto had to travel more than 25 kilometres, to Oderzo, to get their corn ground. Obviously in wintertime the roads were difficult and this could lead to food shortages and hunger. Later, the da Mostos resolved these difficulties by building mills powered by the waters of the river Livenza, specially diverted by means of an underground channel lined with stone.

Towards the middle of the fifteenth century, the farmland, woodland and pasture owned by the navigator's family totalled around 500 *campi trevigiani* (Treviso fields), which were rented out to various farmers and shepherds. Rent was paid almost entirely 'in kind' with agricultural or pastoral produce. The former included wheat, vegetables, millet, fruit and firewood; the latter fresh and dried cheeses, curds and whey, ricotta and lambs. Along with the rent, the peasants also paid *onoranze* of young fowl, capons, chickens, geese, eggs and hams.

The following figures regarding one tenant give some idea of the productivity of the land at Torre di Mosto. The Guiza di Sola farm had 100 fields, together with the Merlo woodland, and paid an annual rent of 22 *stara* (bushels) of wheat, a *staro* of vegetables, 5 *passi* (paces) of wood and *onoranze* (gifts of tribute) of 2 hams, 2 geese, 2 capons, 2 chickens, 2 cockerels and 50 eggs. With a yield this low, it is to be supposed that the land itself was very poor farming land. As a result, the family suffered acute economic difficulties. Pietro, brother of the navigator, sent their father sums of money that were inadequate to live on. As a result, the father was obliged to sell one of the properties at Torre di Mosto for 135 gold ducats.

Opposite: *Villa da Mosto at Castion di Castelfranco, decades ago, when one of my old relations decided to venture off and find out what had become of the place.*

Below: *My great grandmother, Antonietta.*

Puddings, cakes & biscuits

Puddings, cakes & biscuits

Brought to Venice via the trade routes of the Adriatic, the magical flavours of the East had an enormous influence on Venetian cuisine, in which many dishes combine such ingredients as raisins, sultanas and pine nuts to produce that very special taste that the grand ladies of another era referred to as *dolce garbo* ('sweet mildness'). Further influences on cakes and puddings came from the Balkans and from Germany, Austria and other countries of central Europe, where the harsh climate meant that people needed to consume substantial quantities of calories and therefore desserts and sweets came into their own. One of the oldest traditional desserts in the Veneto, particularly associated with the Feast of Epiphany and dating back to periods of great poverty, is *pinza*. Made by moistening dry bread and then mixing it with raisins, dried figs, almonds, walnuts and hazelnuts, it has now been superseded in popularity by numerous kinds of sweet and fragrant *focacce*, which are bread-like cakes.

There is a story of a village in the Dolomites that was so wealthy that even the livestock were fed bread. But, for all their wealth, the villagers one day chased off two poor beggars, saying that they had nothing to give them. It was a bad decision: the two men were St Peter and Christ. Irritated by such hard-heartedness, Christ went into a wheat field and made almost all the ears of corn disappear; it would have been all of them, but St Peter reminded him that he should leave something for the sick, the very young and the Church. The two men then moved on to a poor hovel. There they found a widow whose children were weeping from hunger. The woman could only get them to go to sleep by telling them that a brick she had placed under the embers of the fire was really a *focaccia* that she was baking for the next morning. Despite her poverty, the widow greeted the two strangers hospitably and, in reward, Jesus transformed the brick into a *focaccia* and filled barrels with wine, which had stood empty and cracked for years. Having eaten and drunk together, Jesus then asked the woman if she would allow one of her sons to accompany him and bring a hammer. When they were out on the side of the mountain, he said to the boy: 'Strike hard!' One single blow was enough to bring the mountainside tumbling down upon the rich village, sparing nothing but the widow's poor hovel. It may not be connected to this legend, but I found out that every year, residents of the town of Este, near Padua, despatch one of their traditional Easter cakes, a golden *focaccia*, as a gift to the Holy Father in the Vatican. It doesn't hurt to keep in with the right people.

Other traditional cakes in the Veneto include the *bisso moro* of the Padua area, the *treccia* of Thiene and the *polentina* of Cittadella. This latter is a type of *focaccia* that now has a certain international reputation. It is sold in wicker baskets made by just one local family, who use twigs from the willow trees that grow alongside the river Brenta, which flows by their home. As for Verona, it is home to the world-famous *pandoro*, which nowadays challenges the supremacy of Milan's *panettone*.

The region's cooks also produce various fruit tarts – the ripe fruit was once particularly important because it required little extra sugar – together with puddings and cooked custards (for those whose teeth are not what they were). Then there are, of course, *fritelle* (Carnival doughnuts) and *galani* or *crostoli* (Carnival crackers). Mostly, these are Carnival specialities, but in Belluno *galani* are also associated with weddings.

Around Padua and in the Po delta other traditional cakes include *castagnole* and *smejassa*, whilst in Vicenza there is *putana*, in Treviso *fregolotta* and in various parts of the region (Vicenza, Rovigo, Padua and Belluno) different types of *maccafame*. As for what are called *biscotti da credenza* (sideboard biscuits), these include not only the *baicoli* typical of Venice but also *bianchetti*, *bagarini*, *pevarini*, *forti*, *bussolai* (from Burano), *zaletti*, *ossi da morti* and *pandoli* (or *consegi*). These latter are a type of round biscuit with a hole in the middle, and were very common at the time of the city communes. When the councillors of Belluno sat to discuss affairs of local administration they kept themselves awake by eating these biscuits dunked in glasses of white wine or dessert wine; the very name *consegi* reflects the fact that they were eaten at council meetings (*consigli* in Italian, *consegi* in Veneto dialect). These tasty traditional biscuits are still made in Belluno, and every housewife jealously guards the secret of her own particular recipe.

A special end-of-meal treat, deadly for both waistline and teeth, is *torroncino* (nougat) which is particularly associated with Christmas and New Year. Proudly served up on silver platters, this can come in various forms ranging from rock-hard to soft, depending on how much flour there is in the mix. The nougat tradition dates back to the Romans; very fond of dried fruit, they mixed it with honey, pepper and oil to bake round solid cakes that were called *turundae*. In the Venice of the past one particular recipe for *torroncino* involved grinding together almonds, pine nuts, pistachios, citrons and candied orange, then mixing the ingredients with clear, golden caramel; once the cake had set, it was cut into little pieces, each of which was individually wrapped in lightweight coloured paper.

Another delicious speciality in the Veneto is the *mandorlato* (again, a type of nougat) produced at Cologna Veneta, a small town near Verona. Towards Christmas, this place buzzes with activity as the local confectioners make this soft, almond-based nougat.

The recipe was created about a century ago by an esteemed local chemist and botanist, Dottor Frigo, who was also the town pharmacist. He took the usual ingredients of the local *torroncino* and carefully calibrated the quantities so as to achieve the desired texture. Anyone who is amazed by the fact that this confection should be the brainchild of an apothecary should remember that it was usually the local *spezieri* (druggists) who prepared the syrups, balsams, sweets and digestive liqueurs. In eighteenth-century Venice, apothecaries turned out more than 90 such products.

Venice also had its itinerant ice-cream vendors. Most of these came down from the hills of Belluno in the spring to 'work the season' in the city, travelling around in a *barracchino*, a boat that was a half gondola, half swan. And, on the subject of sweets brought in from outside the city, Venetian mothers often fell victim to tantrums and tears at the winter funfair on the Riva degli Schiavoni. The cause? Itinerant traders from the Belluno and Zoldo areas who set up stalls adorned with rods of *caramei* (caramelized sweets); this fiendishly cunning way of attracting attention to their merchandise was made even more effective by the fact that some traders took up a fixed position on the Riva while others strolled back and forth along it. These rods of sweets were threaded with dried figs, prunes, hazelnuts, walnuts and almonds, all skilfully caramelized with a hard golden sugar coating that was the sworn enemy of any lingering milk teeth. In recent years, with the disappearance of low-income crafts, this centuries-old tradition has almost died out. However, the candy sticks do still reappear for big feasts like the *Festa della Salute* in November, and some restaurateurs keep the tradition alive indoors by serving *caramei* at the end of a meal, along with the traditional Venetian biscuits and sweets that are known in dialect as *golosessi* (derived from the word for greedy), the last challenge to one's digestive system after an entire evening of good eating. Fortunately – or, perhaps, not so fortunately – these sweets are followed by grappa. Some drink this from their emptied coffee cup, enjoying the mixed flavours of *el resentin*; the term comes from the Venetian verb '*resentar*', once used to describe the action of rinsing out laundry, which used to be such a common sight along the banks of the rivers and streams that criss-cross the Veneto mainland.

Pasta frola alla veneziana
Venetian shortcrust pastry

Plain version

150 g / 5 oz plain white flour
150 g / 5 oz butter or lard,
chilled and cubed
125 g / 4 oz caster sugar
100 g / 3½ oz very finely ground
almonds
3 egg yolks
grated zest of 1 lemon
pinch of salt

Polenta version

100 g / 3½ oz finely ground
polenta
50 g / 2 oz semolina flour
150 g / 5 oz butter
1 tsp vanilla essence
125 g / 4 oz caster sugar
100 g / 3½ oz very finely ground
almonds
6 egg yolks
grated zest of 1 lemon
pinch of salt

There are two versions of this mainstay of Venetian baking, based either on plain or maize flour. The distinguishing feature of either version is the addition of ground almonds. It can be used as crust for an endless variety of *crostate* (tarts) and pies. The generic *crostata* simply involves pouring one's best home-made jam over the pastry base and decorating the top with strips of pastry before baking in the oven.

———— ⚬⚬⚬ ————

The quantities specified here are for a double-crust pie, baked in a 23 cm (9 in) tin; half the amount will do for a single-crust open tart in a 25.5 cm (10 in) tin.

First, knead together the flour with the butter or lard, caster sugar, ground almonds, egg yolks, salt and lemon zest. Mix the pastry using a spoon (wooden or otherwise) or a knife because, if the pastry begins to stick to your hands, it will be ruined. If the consistency is wrong, the addition of a few drops of white wine or marsala can help to soften it. Once it is ready, wrap the pastry in foil or cling film and chill for 30 minutes before using.

If using this shortcrust pastry for pies and tarts, roll it out first with a flat rolling pin, then with a ridged one, to obtain an attractive textured pattern. As the Italian expression says: 'the eye wants its part as well'.

Tiramisù
Pick-me-up

12 egg yolks
500 g / 1 lb caster sugar
16 tbsp dry marsala
1 kg / 2¼ lb very fresh mascarpone
about 60 sponge fingers,
depending on size of dish
freshly brewed, strong black coffee
good brandy, optional
cocoa powder, to decorate

Internationally renowned, this is the archetypal Italian pudding. My grandmother used to make a similar dessert with layers of sponge fingers, *crème pâtissière* and thick *zabaione*, the whole thing covered with sugar frosting. But it was in Treviso that, after the Second World War, restauranteurs hit on the brilliant idea of using mascarpone in this way – a soft, creamy, rich, white cheese that had already figured in desserts made for the Venetian nobility. Indeed, mascarpone was considered an aphrodisiac by some, not least Giacomo Casanova, who reputedly gobbled up masses of it before setting out for amorous trysts. The final touch that the Trevigiani gave to this dish was to dust it with powdered coffee and cocoa. The result was a prized delicacy that Signora Alba di Pillo of the Treviso restaurant Le Beccherie used to eat as a pick-me-up after her work in the kitchen (*tira-me-sù* means, literally, 'pick-me-up'). There are those who say the dessert was also very popular with the street ladies of Turin when they were equally in need of a 'pick-me-up'.

———❊———

Whisk the egg yolks and sugar with the marsala to make a light *zabaione*. Mix thoroughly and warm in a *bain-marie* until stiff. Add the mascarpone and mix with a wooden spoon. Moisten enough sponge fingers to cover the base of the dish with unsugared black coffee, to which you can add a little brandy. Pour over more coffee (sweetened if you prefer) to further moisten the biscuits once placed in the dish. Cover with the *zabaione* cream and repeat the process with another layer of coffee-imbued sponge fingers. Level out and place in the fridge overnight to set. Just before serving, sprinkle liberally with cocoa powder through a fine sieve.

Torta de zucca
Pumpkin pie

600 g / 1¼ lb ripe pumpkin, peeled,
de-seeded and chopped
50 g / 2 oz sultanas
30 ml / 2 tbsp grappa
150 g / 5 oz unsalted butter
150 g / 5 oz caster sugar
50 g / 2 oz ground almonds
50 g / 2 oz candied citron
grated zest of 1 lemon
75 g / 3 oz plain white flour
2 eggs, separated
salt

Venice still remembers a comment made by a nineteenth-century lawyer known for his off-the-cuff remarks. The man was a great friend of Daniele Manin, who – together with Niccolo Tommaseo – had been the leader of the 1848–9 revolt against the Austrian occupation of Venice (an uprising that a member of the da Mosto family helped to finance by selling all his silverware). When Manin was released from prison, he was borne in triumph by the Venetians, who raised him up on a wooden board so that he could address the crowd. 'Bravo, bravo!' commented the lawyer sardonically. 'Only you and pumpkins have the honour of being carried around on wooden boards!'

As well as being a key ingredient in fine soups and first courses, pumpkin was also cooked in the following manner: cut into pieces, dipped in flour and then fried before being dusted with salt or sugar. Boiled or oven-baked pumpkin was also sold in the streets, along with roasted pumpkin seeds and sweet potatoes.

This good old recipe for pumpkin pie is still used in farmhouses and was traditionally served when the local women gathered together in the stables so that they could continue with their weaving in the warmest part of the house whilst the men got on with the milking.

⸎

Cook the pumpkin in a pan with a little of the butter. Meanwhile, put the sultanas, to soak in the grappa. Preheat the oven to 190°C / 375°F / Gas Mark 5

When the pumpkin goes soft, add a pinch of salt and the sugar, ground almonds, candied citrons and sultanas soaked in grappa and lemon zest. Sift the flour and then add to the mixture. Whisk the egg whites until stiff. Gently stir in the beaten egg yolks and then fold in the whisked egg whites. Pour into a shallow greased tin and bake in a warm oven for about an hour (until a toothpick poked into the centre comes out entirely dry).

This popular dish is even better if it is baked between two layers of shortcrust pastry or as a tart, becoming a dessert fit for even the most refined table.

Zucca candita
Candied pumpkin

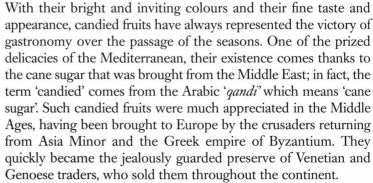

500 g / 1 lb pumpkin, peeled
and seeded
200 g / 7 oz cane sugar
500 ml / 18 fl oz water
pinch of salt

With their bright and inviting colours and their fine taste and appearance, candied fruits have always represented the victory of gastronomy over the passage of the seasons. One of the prized delicacies of the Mediterranean, their existence comes thanks to the cane sugar that was brought from the Middle East; in fact, the term 'candied' comes from the Arabic '*qandi*' which means 'cane sugar'. Such candied fruits were much appreciated in the Middle Ages, having been brought to Europe by the crusaders returning from Asia Minor and the Greek empire of Byzantium. They quickly became the jealously guarded preserve of Venetian and Genoese traders, who sold them throughout the continent.

Making these delights is not easy, because the fruit is candied by being boiled in ever more concentrated syrups, which gradually replace all the water originally contained in the fruit. For different types of fruit you need a specific type of syrup at a specific temperature if the dissolved sugar is to permeate the entire fruit gradually. The most famous candied fruits and nuts include plums, pistachios, pine nuts, apricots, hazelnuts and citrons. The procedure is particularly successful with oranges, mandarins, bergamots and, in the present recipe, pumpkin.

Boil or steam a large piece of pumpkin without letting it lose any of its firmness. Meanwhile, make a syrup by dissolving the sugar in the water. Now place the pumpkin in the syrup, leaving it to simmer gently for a long time so that it absorbs as much sugar as possible without breaking up. Eventually, the piece of pumpkin should become almost transparent. Generally, candied pumpkin is cut into cubes or coin-sized medallions and stored in sealed glass jars under a layer of icing sugar.

Pane di San Marco (marzapane)
Marzipan

2 egg whites
300 g / 10 oz ground almonds
grated zest of 1 lemon
300 g / 10 oz caster sugar

Because it kept well on long voyages, this *Pane di San Marco* – known as *marzapane* in Venetian – was exported from Venice to various countries in northern Europe. The Prussian city of Lubeck, one of the busiest ports of the Hanseatic League, appropriated the recipe some five centuries ago; however, a document dated 1530 does recognize the Venetian provenance, referring to marzipan as *Marci Panis*. The present-day confectioners in Lubeck, who export marzipan all over the world, not only use a secret ingredient (alongside almonds), but also spray their marzipan with vaporized rose water.

———✦———

Put the oven on its lowest setting (around 100°C / 210°F / Gas Mark 2). Beat the egg whites until stiff and then gradually add ground almonds, lemon zest and sugar. Model the mix into whatever shapes you fancy – small balls, half-moons, water drops – and lay out on greaseproof paper and bake for 15 minutes. Once cooled, the marzipan shapes can be lifted easily from the paper.

Pinza
Fruit cake

25 g / 1 oz raisins
25 g / 1 oz pine nuts
25 g / 1 oz dried figs
25 g / 1 oz candied pumpkin
aniseeds
60 ml / 2 fl oz grappa
a little milk
300 g / 10 oz polenta flour
200 g / 7 oz Italian 00 grade flour
150 g / 5 oz caster sugar
200 g / 7 oz unsalted butter or lard
salt

No home in the Veneto countryside is ever without polenta flour. Used to accompany so many regional dishes, it is also an important ingredient in many desserts. *Pinza* is a dense cake of candied fruits and spices that used to be eaten around New Year or at Lent, and was baked on the embers of bonfires. It started off as a sort of polenta – made of equal measures of flour and maize flour blended with pork stock – to which was added sugar or honey, as well as raisins, dried figs, walnuts, almonds, fennel seeds, candied orange peel, pieces of pumpkin and a liberal glassful of grappa. The modern-day *pinza* is rather simpler.

———✦———

Put the raisins, pine nuts, figs, candied pumpkin and aniseeds to soak in a little grappa. Preheat the oven to 190°C / 375°F / Gas Mark 5.

Heat the milk to boiling point and then mix in both types of flour. Add a pinch of salt and cook on a high heat, stirring constantly. When the mixture begins to thicken, add the sugar, the butter and the soaked ingredients. Having mixed thoroughly, pour into a cake tin and bake for about 40 minutes.

Serve tepid with dessert moscato or the popular Veneto Marzemino, which is a dense fruity and fizzy red wine.

Fugassa pasquale
Venetian Easter cake

a few tonka beans
powdered ireos (orris) root
25 g / 1 oz candied orange peel
½ tsp ground cloves
1 tsp ground cinnamon
seeds of 1 vanilla pod
small glass of kirsch

For the dough
20 g / ¾ oz brewer's yeast
or fresh yeast
450 g / scant 1 lb Italian 00 grade
white flour
20 g / ¾ oz baking powder
125 g / 4 oz caster sugar
125 g / 4 oz unsalted butter, soft
5 eggs and 3 egg yolks
salt

To decorate
coloured sugar eggs
coarse granulated sugar
40 g / 1½ oz blanched almonds,
chopped

Easter is not Easter without the *focaccia* or *colomba* (dove), which continues to be prepared in the traditional way and is served as the crowning glory of the Easter lunch, following roast baby goat or lamb. It is also a good breakfast for the sweet-toothed.

Each part of the region makes a distinctive version of the recipe; and though all are good, the most famous is the Venetian *focaccia*, moulded to form attractive dove-shaped cakes that used to be decorated with brightly coloured hens' eggs. *Pasticcerie* and bread shops also bake them and sell them wrapped in crackly cellophane. Over time, this treat has evolved from being more bread-like to the springy, rich, yellow-coloured cake that it is today. Specialist bakers use one-third Manitoba flour, derived from a hard variety of North American wheat and named after a Canadian province, which strengthens the fine flour.

Fresh eggs have always been the main ingredient of the *focaccia*. Long, complicated and onerous, its preparation remains a potentially satisfying challenge. I've never made it myself but have put together the best instructions I could find, including some ingredients that are also used in magic and alchemy!

───────

A couple of days before you want to make the dough, put all the spices and candied orange peel to soak in the kirsch.

Begin the dough by adding a few spoonfuls of warm water to the yeast. Sift the flour with the baking powder. Mix the yeast mixture with a little of the flour mixture. Leave this for a couple of hours and then repeat the operation with some more water and flour. Again wait 2 hours and then mix more flour with the egg yolks. Wait 2 more hours and then repeat with the whole beaten eggs. After another 2 hours mix in the butter with more of the flour and then, after a final 2 hours, the sugar and the last of the flour.

Now preheat the oven to 180°C / 350°F / Gas Mark 4. Then add the ingredients that give the Venetian *focaccia* its characteristic taste: the kirsch and the soaked spices and peel. The final mixture should be soft and somewhat glistening. On a greased baking sheet, form the dough into the shape of a dove, or just into a simple round, and fix some coloured sugar eggs to the top using little blobs of cake mix; Venetian bakeries use paper moulds to get the characteristic shape. Sprinkle the whole surface with sugar and chopped almonds. Bake for about 45 minutes – the cake is cooked when it sounds hollow when knocked on the base.

Panettone alla veneziana
Venetian tea cake

First dough mixture
250g / ½ lb fresh yeast
500 g / 1 lb Italian 00 grade flour
8 eggs, beaten
150 g / 5 oz caster sugar
150 g / 5 oz unsalted butter, melted

Second dough mixture
1 kg / 2¼ lb Italian 00 grade flour
150 g / 5 oz unsalted butter, melted
150 g / 5 oz caster sugar
5 eggs
15 ml / ½ fl oz grated lemon zest
100 g / 3½ oz candied citrus peel, finely chopped
100 g / 3½ oz large sultanas
salt

Topping
1 egg white, beaten
25 g / 1 oz icing sugar
1 tbsp finely ground roasted hazelnuts
2 tbsp granulated sugar
25 g / 1 oz flaked almonds

Though less famous than the Milanese *panettone*, Venice's is perhaps lighter and tastier. Some people think the name is an abbreviation of *pan de Toni* (Toni's bread) and that *panettone* was invented therefore by a baker named Toni (*Antonio* or Anthony). It isn't altogether improbable, either.

It is supposed to be eaten primarily at Christmas, just like *Pandoro di Verona* (Veronese Sponge Cake) – translated as 'golden bread', it is deliciously light and airy. Taller than *panettone*, the *pandoro* has deep grooves down the sides, which means that it bakes more easily and holds its shape while remaining light and fluffy. It is, however, so difficult to make successfully that I must advise against trying. You need patience, great experience as a baker – and knowledge of certain professional secrets. A friend who makes this every year for his family says it's like having a newborn baby each time – the periodic kneading is as demanding as the night-time feeds!

Panettone is made in two stages, with several hours' rising in between, so make sure you start in plenty of time. Again, this recipe is for the most determined cooks or those who are curious to know what happens to the long list of ingredients that food producers are obliged to put on the packaging.

———— ∞ ————

Mix the fresh yeast, flour, eggs, caster sugar and melted butter to make a rather soft dough. Place it in a just-switched-off oven or airing cupboard to rise for a few hours.

Preheat the oven to 180°C / 350°F / Gas Mark 4.

Remove the bowl from the oven and add the ingredients for the second dough mixture. Mix together well. Transfer the dough to a greased baking sheet and mould into a high, round, domed cylinder. Mix the beaten egg white, icing sugar and ground toasted hazelnuts and use to baste the top of the loaf. Sprinkle with sugar and chopped almonds. Bake the *panettone*, for an hour, then increase the oven temperature to 200°C / 400°F / Gas Mark 6 and bake for a further 20 to 30 minutes to obtain the characteristic brown crust.

Budin de ricota
Ricotta pudding

50 g / 2 oz dark chocolate
4 eggs, separated
400 g / 14 oz ricotta
250 g / 8 oz caster sugar
50 g / 2 oz amaretti biscuits, broken
1 small glass of rum
200 g / 7 oz sponge fingers
50 g / 2 oz jam
2 small glasses of brandy
50 g / 2 oz candied fruit (citrus peel), plus extra to decorate
pinch of ground cinnamon

To decorate
50 g / 2 oz raisins
50 g / 2 oz flaked almonds
granulated sugar

'*Puina*. The more you eat, the less you can walk.' This old proverb derides ricotta (*puina*) for its low nutritional value. However, there is no denying that it tastes good, especially when used in desserts. Freshly made ricotta is very easy to come by near summer pasturelands and is particularly suitable for the very young and the very old, who are taken to the mountains to build up their strength. This rustic dessert hails from the alpine foothills of the Veneto.

———

Melt the chocolate in a bowl over barely simmering water; make sure the water does not run into the bowl and the chocolate does not get too hot. Whisk the egg whites until stiff.

Take half the ricotta and mix with half the sugar and the chocolate, broken amaretti, rum and the stiff egg whites. Line a square mould with aluminium foil and fill with the mixture. Lay the sponge fingers, moistened with a mixture of jam and brandy over the top.

Beat the remaining sugar with the egg yolks until the mixture begins to thicken. Add a glass of brandy, a pinch of cinnamon, the candied fruits and the rest of the ricotta. Then pour on top of the sponge fingers and place in the fridge to set. The dessert looks good served on a silver platter, decorated with raisins, candied fruit and almonds.

Fave alla veneziana
Venetian sweet beans

300 g / 10 oz pine nuts
200 g / 7 oz caster sugar
5 egg yolks
a small glass of grappa
25 g / 1 oz chocolate, chopped
a little vanilla essence
pink food colouring
plain white flour

The founder of the Venetian branch of the Papafava family dynasty was perhaps the jurist Alessandro Papafava, who died in 1529. The original Papafava were a branch of the Carraresi family who ruled Padua. They owe their name to one Jacopo, who seems to have had two main claims to fame: in 1256 he fought against Ezzelino da Romano, at the time the dominant force in the central-eastern area of the Po valley, and he also had an apparently insatiable appetite for *fave* (beans).

Inspired by the form of beans, these Venetian sweets appear in the city's confectioner's shops around November and are identified with the *Festa dei Morti* (Feast of All Saints Day). They are easy to make and pleasant to eat.

───※───

Crush the pine nuts with the sugar and then add the egg yolks. Knead into a paste and flavour it with the grappa and chocolate, or with other flavourings and colourings, such as vanilla. Normally *fave* are made in a mixture of white, brown (chocolate) and pink (food colouring) varieties. Divide the paste into small lumps the size of coins and the shape into beans. Bake at a low temperature (around 100°C / 210°F / Gas Mark 2) on a greased tray sprinkled with flour.

Budin coi fruti de bosco
Fruits of-the-forest rice pudding

320 g / 11 oz short-grain
risotto rice
1 litre / 1¾ pints whole milk
grated zest of 1 lemon
200 g / 7 oz sweetened, dense
fruits-of-the forest purée
or strawberry, raspberry
or black cherry compote
25 g / 1 oz butter
2 eggs
50 g / 2 oz dried breadcrumbs
45 ml / 3 tbsp brandy or rum
pinch of salt

To serve
fruits of the forest purée
or strawberry, raspberry
or black cherry compote
60 ml / 2 fl oz rum or brandy
fresh fruit, for decoration

Where the wide plains of the Veneto meet the foothills of the Alps, there is a natural change in cuisine, which now becomes closer to that of the Dolomites and the Tyrol. One typical summer dessert of the Grappa area is a sort of rice pudding made with a mousse of strawberries, raspberries, blackberries or blackcurrants.

———

Preheat the oven to 190°C / 375°F / Gas Mark 5. Bring the rice to the boil in the milk and then sprinkle with a little salt and the lemon zest. After 15 minutes, stir in the dense fruit purée, with a knob of butter and two whole beaten eggs. Pour the mix into a pudding mould or soufflé dish greased with butter and lined with breadcrumbs. If the purée or compote is runny, reduce it before using by simmering until it thickens.

Bake the pudding for about 30 minutes. The dessert is ready when a toothpick stuck into it comes out clean. Serve tepid, turned out on a shallow dish with more of the thick fruit purée mixed with a little rum or brandy. Decorate with some fresh fruit.

Galani
Carnival crackers

300 g / 10 oz Italian 00 grade flour
2 eggs, beaten
50 g / 2 oz sugar
60 g / generous 2 oz butter
60 g / generous 2 oz sugar
small glass of grappa
a little milk
pinch of salt
vegetable oil, for deep-frying

To serve
icing sugar

Associated with Carnival, these sweet crackers probably originated in the Veneto, though other regions have claimed the credit for them and there are different names for the same thing throughout Italy. *Galani* – also known as *crostoli* – are very easy to make, forming a light and tasty wafer of fried pastry that contorts into the strangest shapes as it cooks.

———— ✖ ————

Mix the flour with the eggs, sugar, butter, grappa and a pinch of salt (even though it may seem odd, this latter is an essential ingredient in all types of pastries and cakes). Add enough milk to make a firm dough. Work the pastry mix intensively on a wooden board or a marble surface. Wrap in foil or cling film and chill in fridge before using.

Roll the dough out on a floured surface to the thickness of a coin. Using a knife or a cutting wheel make strips some 5 cm (2 in) wide and 20 cm (8 in) long. Make some incisions in the middle of each strip, so that it can expand during frying. Heat the oil (use plenty) for deep-frying until really hot and fry the *galani* until golden. Remove and drain on kitchen paper.

When the *galani* have cooled down, sprinkle with icing sugar and pile up in criss-cross layers on a plate. Be very careful not to break them: *galani* are very fragile. Even when eating them you are inevitably covered in crumbs and clouds of sugar.

Fritole
Carnival doughnuts

400 g / 14 oz Italian 00 grade
flour
2 eggs, beaten
60 g / generous 2 oz caster sugar
a little milk
25 g / 1 oz brewer's yeast
100 g / 3½ oz sultanas, washed
and tossed in a little flour
pinch of salt
vegetable oil, for deep-frying

To serve
50 g / 2 oz caster sugar

In the eighteenth century, the small wooden stalls of the *fritoleri* were to be found in *campi* (squares) and alleyways throughout the city, serving not only delicious and fragrant *fritole* – traditional Carnival doughnuts – but also tasty dishes of lasagne and macaroni. The stalls were passed down from father to son and when a *fritoler* died without an heir the head of the corporation of *fritoleri* proposed a substitute to the authorities, who then gave their approval (or otherwise).

Because they also served savoury dishes, *fritoleri* were often at daggers drawn with *luganegheri* (sausage makers), who also sold soups and pasta dishes. The conflict was serious because this was a very profitable business, such *minestre* forming a key part of the diet of the city's poorer classes. After several court cases, the *fritoleri*'s right to exercise their trade freely was recognized – to the great satisfaction of the ordinary consumer, who naturally enjoyed lower prices due to the competition between the two guilds.

Carnival in Venice is as synonymous with *fritole* now as it ever was. At a time when there was so much going on and you didn't want to miss anything, this simple doughnut served an important function: you could happily munch on it while looking elsewhere. Unlike many other traditional dishes described in this book, *fritole* seem to be evermore present in the *pasticcerie* of Venice; whereas they used to be served strictly during the days of Carnival, they now appear as soon as Christmas festivities are over and remain on offer until Ash Wednesday and the beginning of Lent.

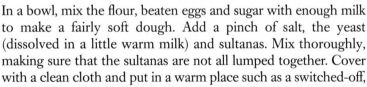

In a bowl, mix the flour, beaten eggs and sugar with enough milk to make a fairly soft dough. Add a pinch of salt, the yeast (dissolved in a little warm milk) and sultanas. Mix thoroughly, making sure that the sultanas are not all lumped together. Cover with a clean cloth and put in a warm place such as a switched-off, tepid oven to 'prove' the dough for 1 to 2 hours.

Now you are ready to fry the doughnuts in a pan with lots of boiling oil. Drop in a spoonful of dough at a time; when it becomes firm, turn it over with a skimmer until it takes on a light-brown colour all over. Remove the *fritole* from the oil and pile on a plate. Serve warm, sprinkled with sugar. If the *fritole* have been made in advance, they can be warmed up on a plate on top of the radiator.

Frittellara

Crema fritta alla veneziana
Venetian fried custard

6 egg yolks, beaten
180 g / 6 oz caster sugar
200 g / 7 oz Italian 00 grade flour,
sifted
finely grated zest of 1 lemon
800 ml / 1½ pints whole milk
2 egg whites, beaten
oil, for frying
breadcrumbs, for coating
icing sugar, to serve

Much appreciated by the Venetians, fried custard is a great dessert: light, tasty and easy to make. In Venice we can simplify our lives even further by buying the custard ready-made from confectioners who sell it by the slab. However, produced on a near-industrial scale, shop-bought custard can be rather insipid so it's best to make it yourself.

———— ∞ ————

In a medium pan, whisk together the egg yolks and sugar. Then gradually whisk in the flour and lemon zest. Slowly add the milk, beating well between each addition until the mixture is smooth and creamy with no lumps. Cook over a medium heat, stirring constantly until the mixture thickens and boils.

Remove from the heat and pour into a shallow tin or directly onto an oiled marble slab. Spread out evenly to a thickness of 2 cm (1 in), then allow to cool and set. Cut into rectangles or diamonds, dip in the lightly beaten egg whites, and then coat with dried breadcrumbs.

Deep-fry for 2 to 3 minutes until crisp and golden brown, drain well on kitchen paper and serve dusted with icing sugar.

Castagnole
'Chestnuts'

300 g / 10 oz Italian 00 grade
flour
50 g / 2 oz potato flour
2 tsp baking powder
pinch of salt
90 g / 3½ oz unsalted butter, soft
75 g / 3 oz caster sugar
2 eggs
small glass of grappa
oil, for frying
25 g / 1 oz icing sugar, to serve

These light and tasty 'chestnuts' are companions to the doughy, robust *fritole*. Their small, round form makes them easier to cook, and their flavour is considered by many to be rather more refined and much less oily. Originally, Venetian *castagnole* were made using the same ingredients as *crostoli* or *galani*, but the mix has changed, with the result that the *castagnole* are more crumbly these days.

Sift together the flour, potato flour, baking powder and a pinch of salt. Mix with the butter, sugar and eggs to form a rather firm dough, then flavour with a small glass of grappa. Leave the dough to rise for a few hours in a warm place, covered with a tea towel.

Cut the dough into small pieces and roll into balls. Heat a large pan with plenty of oil until very hot and fry the *castagnole* until deep golden-brown (2 or 3 minutes), and they look like split chestnuts. Let the excess oil drip off for a few seconds as you remove them from the pan using a slatted spoon. After arranging the *castagnole* on a plate, sprinkle with icing sugar. They are especially delicious eaten warm with a sweet white wine or liqueur; the more you eat, the more you'll want!

Torta Nicolotta
Nicolotta cake

200 g / 7 oz dry bread
300 ml / ½ pint milk
100 g / 3½ oz Italian 00 grade
flour
100 g / 3½ oz raisins
10 g / ½ oz fennel seeds
olive oil

Venice is divided in half by the serpentine Grand Canal and this is reflected in its population, who are identified with two churches that stand on either side: the *Nicolotti* take their name from San Nicolò dei Mendicoli, the *Castellani* from San Pietro di Castello, which was once the cathedral church of Venice. I am a *Nicolotto*; every time I cross the Rialto Bridge into *Castellani* territory, I feel like a *Nicolotto* going on holiday.

This dessert was very popular with the working folk of Venice; it can still be found – as authentic as ever – in some of the city's bakeries, even a couple in the *Castellano* part of town.

Preheat the oven to 200°C / 400°F / Gas Mark 6.

Cut the crusts off the bread and soak it in the milk. When the bread has softened, add the flour and raisins. Lay the mixture on a well-greased oven tray and sprinkle with fennel seeds. Bake for about 40 minutes until the cake has a firm consistency. Serve, cut in fat slices or wedges, with *vin santo* or Moscato dessert wine.

Baicoli
Venetian biscuits

400 g/14 oz plain white flour
15 g/½ oz brewer's yeast dissolved
in a little warm milk
50 g/2 oz caster sugar
25 g/1 oz unsalted butter
1 egg white, whisked
pinch of salt

These are the Venetian biscuit, *par excellence*. Created two centuries ago for the city's coffeehouses, these delicate biscuits are still ubiquitous. The name comes from their shape, like a little sea bass – which are called *baicoli* in the Venetian dialect. Though the recipe does not look difficult, it may take a few attemps before the biscuits come out perfectly. The ingredients have to be slowly and thoroughly mixed in two stages.

Baicoli are mostly factory-made these days and sold in wonderfully decorative tins, equally popular with locals and tourists to Venice. There is no comparison, however, with home-made versions; not too sweet, they are an excellent accompaniment to almost anything: tea, coffee, cheeses, ice cream and more.

———✦———

Start by making a firm mixture of one-quarter of the flour with the yeast and milk. Form this into a ball and cut an X on top with a knife. Then place in a cloth-covered bowl and leave for 30 minutes in a warm place; the dough should grow to double its original size.

Preheat the oven to 190°C/375°F/Gas Mark 5. Take the rest of the flour and mix with the sugar, butter, beaten egg white and a pinch of salt. Now add the risen dough mixture. When well combined, separate into slightly flattened oval shapes, not more than 8 cm (3 in) long. Transfer to greased oven trays. Bake for 10 mins and then turn up the temperature to 200°C/400°F/Gas Mark 6 and bake until the biscuits have turned a golden colour.

Slice each oval thinly (2 to 3 mm) and then bake again for about 20 minutes on low heat or simply place in the warm oven to dry out. This is what gives biscuits like baicoli their name – because in Italian they are '*bis-cotto*' or 'twice-cooked'.

Pevarini
Spicy biscuits

*300 g / 10 oz Italian 00 grade
flour
1 tsp baking powder
50 g / 2 oz molasses or golden syrup
25 g / 1 oz butter or lard, melted,
or oil
1 tbsp of ground cinnamon, nutmeg
and a little pepper, mixed
blanched almonds, toasted
(optional)
pinch of salt
icing sugar*

Once very common, these strongly tasting biscuits can now be found only in the Venetian *osterie* frequented by itinerant traders. In the countryside, they are sold at local fairs along with caramelized fruit on sticks and candy floss. Shaped like horses or fish and brightly decorated with silver balls and pink or blue icing, *pevarini* inevitably capture the imagination of children. And they are not complicated to make.

—⊶⊷—

Mix together the flour and baking powder with the molasses or syrup, melted butter, lard or oil (according to taste), a generous spoonful of mixed spices and a pinch of salt. Add toasted whole almonds if you want. Roll out the dense mixture to form a sheet 5 mm (¼ inch) thick.

Preheat the oven to 180°C / 350°F / Gas Mark 4. Cut the dough into shapes using a knife or cookie cutters and place on baking trays lined with greaseproof paper. Bake for 20 minutes. As soon as they come out of the oven, glaze the tops with a dense mixture of icing sugar and water.

Leave for at least a day to harden before eating. *Pevarini* will keep for some time in a sealed glass jar or tin… but they are so good, they will soon be gone.

Toto loves biscuits and they give him most of his soccer-playing sustenance.

Zaeti
Little yellow biscuits

60 g / 2½ oz raisins
small glass of grappa
300 g / 10 oz plain flour
300 g / 10 oz finely milled polenta
2 tsp baking powder
pinch of salt
150 g / 5 oz butter
2 eggs
finely grated zest of 1 lemon
150 g / 5 oz sugar
4 tbsp icing sugar

There is an amusing variety of Venetian biscuits with intriguing names: *ossi da morto* (bones of the dead); *lingua de suocera* (mother-in-law's tongue); *baci di dama* (ladies' kisses). In this case, *zaeti* in dialect means *gialletti* (yellowish), and refers to the colour of the polenta, the principal ingredient. Grandmothers make these biscuits as treats for their grandchildren, using the barest ingredients to be found in any household.

———— ❧ ————

Soak the raisins for 10 minutes in lukewarm water, then drain and squeeze to remove excess water before putting them in a bowl of grappa for a further 20 mins. Preheat the oven to 180°C / 350°F / Gas Mark 4. Meanwhile sift into a mixing bowl the flour and polenta with the baking powder and a pinch of salt. Carefully melt the butter over low heat and add the eggs. Drain the raisins from the grappa; add the raisins to the mixture with the lemon zest and sugar. Mix with a fork and ensure that the raisins are evenly distributed. If the dough is too tough, add some of the grappa used for soaking the raisins. Line a baking tray with greaseproof paper. Roll out the mixture to 1 cm (½ in) thickness and cut into lozenges 6 or 7 cm (2 to 3 in) long. Bake for 20 minutes. Serve with a dusting of icing sugar.

Delicious baci di dama *or ladies' kisses.*

Buranei
Burano biscuits

1 kg / 2¼ lb Italian 00 plain flour
250 g / ½ lb butter, soft
11 egg yolks and 1 egg
600 g / 1¼ lb caster sugar
finely grated zest of 1 lemon
2 tsp rum
pinch of salt

As characteristic of the island of Burano as the coloured houses, these biscuits are extremely nourishing or just plain rich! In the old days, the fishermen's wives would make *buranei* only in the spring, to build up everyone's energy levels after the harsh winter. Now there isn't a shop on the island, let alone throughout Venice, that doesn't permanently stock *buranei*, either shaped into '0's or the *esse* (literally, like the letter S).

———❦———

Preheat the oven to 180°C / 350°F / Gas Mark 4. Place the flour on a clean worktop and put the softened butter in a well in the centre. Beat the eggs and the sugar, pour over the butter and add the lemon, rum and salt. Mix everything together with clean, cold hands. Roll out the dough into long fingers and form into circles or S shapes.

Bake for approximately 20 minutes. Once cooled keep in an airtight tin or jar.

My friend Roberto and I sharing a large buranello *biscuit. We were in need of an energy boost – probably because we hadn't slept the night before or weren't planning to sleep the coming evening!*

Mostarda di galzignoli
Sweet pear mustard

*1 kg / 2¼ lb peretti galzignoli
(small, hard pears)
1 kg / 2¼ lb muscat grape juice
4 cloves
1 cinnamon stick
grated zest of half a lemon
300 g / 10 oz sugar or honey
mustard essence or powdered
mustard seed, to taste*

Hard little pears that ripen in autumn, these *peretti galzignoli* in all probability take their name from the town of Galzignano in the Euganean Hills, where they were once harvested in great quantities. They feature in a very old recipe for *mostarda* (sweet mustard), perhaps one of the very best in the Veneto. The *galzignoli* can also be mixed with diced, slightly underripe, quinces. This is a feisty accompaniment for boiled meats and indeed, the Christmas *panettone* or *pandoro*.

If you can't get these acclaimed pears, apples, quinces, local pears or a mixture of fresh fruits are equally suitable for making *mostarda*. Mustard essence can be difficult to find in the shops; it can be substituted by ground mustard seed. This powder should first be dissolved in a little wine and allowed to simmer for a few minutes over a low heat.

Peel and quarter the pears and boil in their own weight of muscat grape juice, with the cloves, a cinnamon stick and the lemon zest. Then add mustard, sugar or honey and, when the syrup forms threads from the spoon, remove from the heat and leave to cool.

In a jar, lay out the pear quarters and then cover with the remaining syrup, mixed with mustard (to taste).

Venditore di canditi

The coffee shop

T THE end of each meal, Uncle Franz, my mother's brother, would jokingly show off his English by ordering 'Coffee, coffee!' His own father, my grandfather, approached the issue more seriously, sipping a drink that had to be 'as black as coal, as bitter as aloes and as hot as hell'.

Vienna, 1683: the city is besieged by the Turks and an enterprising Polish soldier by the unpronounceable name of Kloschitzki disguises himself as a Turk in order to penetrate the enemy camp, where he puts his fluent Turkish to good use. After various adventures, he returns to the city to give a full and accurate account of the size and distribution of the Sultan's forces, making a key contribution to the counterattack by Austria and her allies, and thus saving the terrified Imperial capital. But what is even more important for our story is that Kloschitzki brought back with him a little bag of strange and precious beans. Curious about them, he followed the instructions he had received and toasted and ground the beans and then used them to make an infusion with boiling water. Coffee had arrived in Vienna, the heart of an empire that was a veritable melting pot of people, cultures and traditions. During the cold Austrian winters, this aromatic drink was a welcome stimulant for mind and body – and soon the city was famous for the *Kaffeehausen* (coffee houses) that would transform Viennese social life, providing a new space for public gatherings.

Venice had encountered coffee some time before, thanks to a densely woven information network fed by diplomats posted throughout Europe and the Mediterranean. The Venetian Republic was well aware that social, economic and cultural news was of essential importance to its own commercial and political standing and it was through these

My father and his brother at Caffè Florian in Piazza San Marco with their parents and friends.

sources that Venice had first heard of the existence of the valuable dark beans. Towards the end of the sixteenth century, Gianfrancesco Morosini was *bailo* of the Venetian colony in Constantinople – that is, not only ambassador to the Sultan's court but also governor of the community of Venetian traders in the city. The reports he sent back to the Republic contain the first mentions of coffee, which would be followed up by more detailed accounts from a later *bailo*, Pietro Foscarini. His letters to the Venetian government describe how, in a fit of rage, the Sultan had ordered the destruction of the places where 'the idle do nothing put sip *khave* (coffee)… play chess or other board games… and speak ill of the government, even muttering against the ministers and the Great Lord himself'.

However, coffee did not originate in Turkey. It seems to have come from the Abyssinian region of Kaffah. *Coffea arabica* is a bushy plant that stands 3 to 10 metres (10 to 32 ft) high and bears a red cherry-like fruit that yields greenish beans. Some time in the fourteenth or fifteenth centuries, these beans were taken to Moka in the Yemen (which now gives its name to our coffee machines) and from there spread to Arabia, Sudan, Egypt and Constantinople. Later, the Dutch planted the bushes in their various colonies, from Java to Suriname, and then it spread to Venezuela, Colombia, the Antilles, Central America and, of course, Brazil: nowadays the many regions of Brazil, from Santo to Bahia, from Sao Paolo to Paranà, produce half of the world's coffee.

Coffee was already being sold in Venice in 1638, probably in the same shops that sold drinking water. Presented as a medicinal product from Egypt, its price was astronomical, and 40 years later – in 1676 – the Venetian Senate imposed a tax on the beverage through its *Savi alla Mercanzia* (responsible for the collection of duty revenues on trading goods). In 1683 – the very year of the Vienna siege – there was only one coffee shop in St Mark's Square, under the colonnade of the Procuratie Nuove. However, the number soon increased and, in 1720, Floriano Francesconi opened his 'Venezia Trionfante' coffee shop. Soon famous under the simpler name of Caffè Florian, the place could list among its clients Frederick Augustus, Elector of Saxony and future King of Poland, Karl, Elector of Bavaria, and such writers as Gozzi and Rousseau.

Even the cups in which the coffee was served became

works of art – as one can see from the precious collection of Venetian and European porcelain now housed in Ca' del Duca Sforza, a building that also has another claim to fame: it was here that Titian painted some of his most famous works, revealing a remarkable eye for colour that was – almost inevitably – stimulated by the wonderful rainbows that arch across the mountains of his native Cadore after every single storm.

One of the many secret treasures of Venice, this collection of colourful and fanciful porcelain contains numerous coffee cups of the period. Amongst the most important of its kind, it was the fruit of years of passionate research by the Venetian nobleman Marino Nani Mocenigo, for whom porcelain and eighteenth-century Venetian culture were a source of endless fascination. From him, the collection passed into the hands of the Luxembourg ambassador Hugues Le Gallais, himself a collector of fine Oriental art, and thence to Le Gallais's great grandson, also Hugues. I remember discussing with him the irony of Bruce Chatwin's Utz, a porcelain collector who, as his own death approached, gradually broke every piece in his collection.

At Ca' del Duca there are swaggering, pot-bellied coffee pots decorated with stylized Chinese plants and birds in gold; elegant Venetian coffee cups and saucers (the cups typically without handles; some decorated with geometric motifs, others with Chinese motifs, and many bearing the anchor symbol of the Cozzi porcelain works); cylindrical cups dating from the 'Sorgenthal period' of Viennese porcelain; and unique pieces from Meissen, Bassano, Hewelke and Vezzi. As chance would have it, the founder of the first Venetian porcelain works, Count Vezzi, lived in the very building where I now live. The works produced some of the most elegant and desirable Venetian tableware and I continue to hope that one day, in one of the courtyard wells, I will come across a factory reject, perhaps a chipped cup or figurine.

But, to return to Venetian coffee, which – according to a local saying – should be drunk *sedendo, scotando e scrocando* (sitting, singeing and scrounging), there is no doubt that the ritual it introduced widened people's family circles. For women, in particular, it made it possible to socialize outside the family home, to exchange a few words with strangers. Even though in appearance, the coffee shop was rather austere, presenting itself as a sort of pharmacy, it enabled the often masked woman to engage in a new type of life, similar to that being enjoyed by the French and English women of the day. Dressed in clothes that ranged from the baroque to the simple – crinolines, embroidered bodices, light and airy shawls, lace kerchiefs – women could here move beyond the unchanging, traditional world in which they had been brought up; the coffee shop gave them the chance to search out the new. The rigid system of arranged family marriages now came under threat as furtive glances over steaming coffee cups revealed that women, too, were feeling the effects of that Enlightenment which had breathed new life into the ageing heart of Europe.

Wines & drinks

Wine & drinks

The origins of the da Mosto family are not clear. Traces of it in ancient chronicles or the records of the Venetian nobility date back to the thirteenth century, but not beyond. One such document records:

> These came from the Treviso area and were in origin planters of vines and tillers of the earth. Very rude men in all things but very rich and forthright, they were described as of 'coarse *provolo*' [a type of cheese; the expression is the equivalent of 'rough diamond'].They were men of good conscience and lovers of their country. Having been tribunes in Opitergio (now the town of Oderzo), they came to Venice in the year 925, on the day of June 4. They were elected to the Great Council in 1297, at the time of the Serrata (when a list was drawn up of the noble families that had a perpetual right to a place in that Council).

Used by the priests of classical antiquity to communicate with the gods, wine could be a 'divine liquid' in everyday life as well. In Campo Santa Marina, a pretty square in the heart of the Canareggio area of Venice, a church was deconsecrated in 1818 and turned into an inn. For two years after this, until it was demolished, the building was said to echo with orders such as 'a flagon for the Madonna!', 'a jug for the Most Holy!', depending upon which of the ex-chapels the customers were sitting in.

Not far away stands another church, in which wine played a more tragic role. On 9 June 1601 the Prior of the Monastery of the Misericordia, a man of great learning and devotion, died of the poison that another priest had poured into the communion wine. Before dying, however, the prior was true to the name of his monastery and had the mercy to ask that his murderer not be punished.

On other occasions, wine has proved more medicinal. In Venice, in fact, there are alleys and a bridge called 'del Rimedio' because of the fortifying virtues of the malmsey wine sold in a nearby shop. And wine shops did not only sell wine. There were those known as *magazzini*, which were also pawn shops. One curious feature of the loans they granted was that a third of it was paid in wine… of poor quality and thus the expression '*vin de pegni*' ('pawn wine') was applied to any bad-tasting wine. Another service provided by these *magazzini* is mentioned in these lines from a satirical poem: 'Others go to the *magazzini*, where there is no shortage/Of welcoming rooms for lust.'

Inevitably, therefore, one of the clients of these *magazzini* was Giacomo Casanova. One night during the Carnival of 1745, he and some friends brought to the Osteria delle Spade a humble woman to whom they had taken a fancy. They got rid of her inconvenient husband by pretending to be public functionaries and dragged the poor man off to the island of San Giorgio Maggiore, where they abandoned him. If the man spent all night in the open-air, his wife spent it in the comfort of the inn. Of course, it is just possible that they were merely playing cards.

The Venetian deck of the day already consisted of 52 cards, and the games were for two or four people. One game was known as '*gilè alla greca*' because it had been imported into the city by the soldiers and sailors who had served in Dalmatia and on the Ionian Islands, where the game went by the Greek name '*mikrò*' (little). *Gilè alla greca* was so popular in the city that the government of the Republic considered imposing stamp duty on the cards themselves. Furthermore, for 'the protection and propriety of all Venetians', it also ordered a *Procuratore di San Marco* to issue an authorized book of instructions in Greek, Slav and Venetian, so that all players would observe the same rules and fights could be avoided. The *Procuratore* subsequently ordered that a copy of the book had to be on display in every shop where wine and liqueurs were sold.

According to a Venetian saying, '*Bacco, tabacco e Venere, riducono l'uomo in cenere*' ('Bacchus, Tobacco and Venus reduce a man to ashes'). Wine and women could often become trading commodities. For example, in centuries gone by, every wedding party that passed over the river Piave had to buy a drink for the local bargemen. Unhappy was any couple who refused to comply: the bargemen could hold the bride hostage, until the ransom of a cask of wine was paid. The more cunning newly weds used to dress up an old woman as a bride and disguise the real bride in rags so the bargemen's hostage was the oldest woman in the bridal party, not the blushing bride herself!

In Venice, strong, aromatic wines used to be very popular, such as *il vin greco* (a sweet muscatel obtained from vines originally from Crete) and *malvasia* (malmsey, obtained from vines originating on Cyprus). Native wines of northern Italy and widely drunk in Venice included *Vernaccia* (a strong wine made using sun-dried grapes) from Lodi, Crema, Brescia, Como, Verona and Conegliano; *Chiarello* (d'Alba, di Saluzzo and d'Acqui) and the various *Borgnoli* wines from Friuli. When Henri III made his way back from Poland to France, where the vacant throne awaited him, he couldn't resist a stopover in Venice. He also enjoyed a triumphant reception at Conegliano. The palace where he stayed was magnificently draped in tapestries; but what most struck the illustrious visitor was the fountain of Neptune in the main square: for the two whole days and nights of his visit, it

The classic Venetian aperitif is called an ombra, *and is normally a glass of chilled Tocai or Prosecco. This expression comes from the fact that the casks were kept cool in the shadow (*ombra*) of St Mark's Bell Tower. Instead of being served with banal crisps, peanuts or salted cocktail biscuits, the authentic* ombra *'nibbles' would be hard-boiled eggs, boiled octopus (in oil, pepper and parsley), pieces of cheese and salami, shrimps, toasted bread with fried spleen (prepared with garlic and parsley) and* nervetti. *These are the tendons of young bulls or calves and can still be found in butchers' shops in the Rialto.*

gushed forth nothing but the 'finest wine of Conegliano' for the sovereign and his retinue (more than 100 carriages) as well as the merry locals. Whilst the wine was given away on this occasion, the ancient statutes of Conegliano laid down rigorous laws regarding the 'theft of grapes, olives and wheat':

> The guilty man is to be set in the stocks for a whole day with the evidence of his crime hanging around his neck. And if the theft was committed at night, the offender is to be whipped from door to door within the city of Conegliano.

Severe, it's true, but other types of theft were punished with branding. 'Let the guilty man be marked using red-hot irons bearing the crest of the commune of Conegliano: one on the forehead and one on either cheek.' And for the habitual criminal, the punishment was 'amputation of the right hand'.

Body parts could be put to the strangest uses. Much earlier in history, Albuin, the Longobard king, had overindulged in revelry one night and as a result forced his wife, Rosmunda, to drink wine from the skull of her father, Cunimund, who had been deposed and killed by Albuin himself. Deeply upset and infuriated, Rosmunda found an accomplice to get her revenge, and the body that later came to light in a circular tomb complete with Lombard weapons was possibly that of Albuin himself.

Jumping forwards in time, to the eighteenth century, the cuisine of Venetian 'high society' had become more international, and this was reflected in the contents of the wine stores of the *palazzi* that line the Grand Canal. No longer were these stocked solely from the vineyards of the adjoining *terra firma* (mainland) and Greece, as one can see from what was served at the wedding of the aristocratic couple Alvise Zorzi Contarini and Caterina Civran in 1755, for which the drinks list reads as follows:

> Tokay, Cape of Good Hope, Burgundy, Champagne, Graves, Canary Island (Sherry), Rhine, Panzaret, Tintiglia di Rota, Canary Malmsey, Spanish Malaga, Saragozza, Vermouth, Canary Island Muscadel, Peralta, Setuva, Monte Moro, True Jamaica Rum, English Beer, Palma di Majorca, Hungarian Wine, Madeira, Grenoble Ratafia, Cyprus Muscadel, Old Cyprus Wine, Contraltdolce, Medium-Sweet White, Rosé, Contraltrosso, Picolit, Monte Libando, Lunel, San Lorans, Scopolo, Rosolio, Vanilla, Canelin, Maraschino, Elizir Vita.

This was the best of the best, offered in a profusion that reflected the extent to which the Venetian patricians wanted to demonstrate that Venice was far from in decline. A delightful, slightly ironic, poem that the Venetian playwright Carlo Goldoni wrote at the time of another noble wedding – between Pietro Contarini and Marina Venier – reflects this tendency:

With a glass brimming with Burgundy,
    France rises to offer its wedding toast.
With wine grown on the Rhine,
    Germany too prepares to follow suit.
Spain does no less, providing animation with its *vin tinto*.
And England has a glass of punch in its hand, whilst Friuli
    has a glass of *picolit*, and Persia a glass of Cyprus wine.
'But bring me a glass of local wine,' says the laughing
    Venetian wit.
'We, too, have got wines of quality,
    much better than Burgundy or Alicante.
From Padua and from Vicenza come wines
    that are liked by East and West.
I know what comes from afar is held in high esteem.
But me, when it's good, I drink our local stuff.'

The true bases for ongoing traditions in Venetian wine and food are found among the humbler classes in the city, whose frugality and sobriety were much appreciated: only certain feast days during the course of the year were celebrated with copious meals and special foods. Generally, they had simple tastes and were so moderate in their drinking that they were very rarely seen drunk in the streets.

Wine was produced – and much appreciated – throughout the Veneto. 'Wine from Breganze and salt from the sea, there is no lack of either in any home' goes a local saying in a town near Vicenza, where the vineyards not only produce grapes for red Cabernet but also a very sweet grape that is ripe by August and has to be harvested quickly because it is a favourite with the wasps. So the white wine produced from these grapes is actually called *Vespaiolo*, from the Italian for 'wasp' ('*vespa* ').

The very name of the Veneto comes, according to one etymology, from the Greek word for wine ('*enos*') and the fame of the Veneti for cultivating vines and making wine (skills they had learned in Paphlagonia in Asia Minor). Local producers are now trying to revive and exploit a number of prized ancient varieties of vines and grapes, while also maintaining the many French vines that have been so skilfully cultivated over the past 80 years or so.

I still remember the stories that my father and grandfather told about the years after the First World War, when the Veneto to the south and north of the river Piave was left in ruins and all the vineyards had to be replanted. This was not the first time the area – including the lands of my forebears – had suffered the devastation of war. When the Hungarians invaded the *terra firma* in the years 1411–12, during the violent war between Venice and Emperor Sigismund, the town of Torre di Mosto was completely destroyed and its population decimated. The da

New Year's Eve, 1908, at the Circolo dell'Unione, Venice.

Mosto family took upon itself the great expense of returning it to the state it had been in before. There was almost no wine because the vineyards had been devastated by the Hungarians. A plan was drawn up by Giovanni da Mosto (father of the legendary navigator Alvise da Mosto) for their replanting. His tenants were obliged to plant a certain number of rows of vines, together with willows, according to conditions laid down in the tenancy agreement; those failing to comply incurred a fine.

A similar situation arose after the trench warfare of 1914–18, when enormous resources were needed for widespread reconstruction of the Veneto, but the Italian state did not have the means to bear the burden, so more than a million people left the region to settle (some temporarily, but most permanently) in other areas of Italy. Reconstruction work was required as much in urban as rural areas, and the economy of Venice itself was so compromised that the city could not provide the finances it had made available in similar circumstances five centuries earlier. Many local farmers were reduced to indigence and their daughters had to go into 'household service' in homes throughout Italy (the dim-witted or crafty Venetian maid is a stock figure in Italian films of the post-war period).

Replanting the vineyards was a massive task, for which farmers had neither adequate means nor moral support, at least from the State. But French winegrowers benevolently gave the farmers of the Veneto the vines they needed, hence so many Veneto wines have French names, even if the different climate and soil have inevitably influenced the grapes, giving them characteristics that are specific to the Veneto. So, while the French State, headed by 'Le Tigre' Clemenceau, denied Italy the spheres of influence in Dalmatia and elsewhere within the Mediterranean that had been promised by the Treaty of London, the winegrowers of France generously repaid Italy for its intervention in the First World War with the stocks needed at least to revive wine making.

Wines and what they go with

Thanks to some viticultural research, the Sauvignon, Merlot, Pinot Grigrio and Cabernet produced in the Veneto have developed their own special bouquets and tastes. As for native Veneto, one should mention the Raboso of the Piave area and of the Eugeanean Hills, Verduzzo (or Verdiso), the Prosecco and Cartizze of Valdobiadene and Soave. This latter is a clear, white wine which is much appreciated with fried fish, as is the deeper-coloured white from the Conegliano area. Other native wines include the white Custoza from the Colli Berici and the famous and richly bouqueted Venegazzù del Montello. Among the dessert wines those which stand out are Moscato di Arquà, Torcolato di Breganze, Gambellara Passito and the much-prized Picolit.

The Verona area produces several wines of repute: Valpolicella, Bardolino (the grapes thrive in the clay soil of the region) and its near cousin, Valpanetena. The local boast, however, is Recioto Amarone, a very prestigious, full-bodied wine that is perfect for game and roast meats. There is also a dessert Recioto made using grapes that have been left to dry in the sun for a number of days before processing.

The list of fine Veneto wines could go on and on. Also worth mentioning is a wonderful Marzemino from Treviso and Terrematte di Montegalda (a Friulan wine that the Widman, an aristocratic family of Austro-Carinthian origin, produced at their Bagnoli estate outside Padua).

Then there are several varieties of German wines (from Rhenish Riesling to Widlbaker) and the wines produced from American vines such as Baco and Clinton. I remember once when I played truant from school and ventured off to a bar in Treviso, where I enjoyed my first taste of Clinton; it left a red stain inside the cup. The taste is very similar to that of the *uva fragola* (strawberry grape) that has long been grown in Veneto vineyards and produces a strong, sweet-tasting wine, Fragolino, much appreciated by housewives and children.

At table in the Veneto spirit (although it could apply to anywhere), the food served is thought of as the basic content of a meal, whilst the accompanying wine is the poetry that harmonizes the whole. For example, an opening glass of Prosecco not only tastes good, it also stimulates the gastric juices that give us an appetite.

The general rule that fish is to be eaten with white wine and meats with red isn't totally rigid in the Veneto either. A white wine such as a Sauvignon has a warmth, freshness and mellowness that means it can also be served with polenta and radicchio sauce, and even with sausage. And I even prefer a mild-bodied red with fish. For example, the herb-scented Merlot is a perfect wine to drink when it is young; its slightly acid taste also counteracts greasy food.

Due to length of exposure to the sun and the degree of tannin in the wine, alcohol levels can increase over time. With its 13 per cent alcohol, a full-bodied red such as Raboso is said to be a 'man's wine', and goes perfectly with game, which would overwhelm wines without a certain substance.

Spritz
Apéritif

⅓ Aperol Campari or Select
⅓ white wine (best if Prosecco,
because it is sparkling)
⅓ soda water
olive on a stick and
½ slice of lemon
or orange per glass

Though its origins are uncertain, it seems likely that the *spritz* was first introduced by Austrian soldiers stationed in the territories of what had been the Venetian Republic, where the local wines were rather strong for their taste and so were diluted using seltzer water. As the tradition spread, different cities began to add a note of colour to this drink by mixing in Aperol, Cynar, Campari, Select or China Martini, together with a slice of lemon or an olive.

The more traditional form of *spritz* – sparkling mineral water (or seltz) with red or white wine – is still common in the Trieste area, whereas the cocktail varieties are now to be found throughout the Veneto and Trentino regions.

In Venice, the *spritz* is a veritable ritual involving both young and old. An embodiment of the sparkling atmosphere of the city itself, it is drunk from late morning onwards.

———— ✺ ————

Use a slice of lemon and an olive for the Campari or Select version; use orange instead of lemon in the Aperol version. A stronger spritz can be made with just Prosecco and Aperol / Campari / Select in equal amounts, without adding any fizzy water. Simply mix the liquid and add the fruit.

Vin brulé
Hot wine punch

500 ml / 18 fl oz good-quality
red wine
200 g / 7 oz of sugar
6 cloves
piece of cinnamon stick
peel of 1 lemon
pinch of nutmeg

A warm burst of energy comes with this popular version of the old English punch, which was made using rum with orange or lemon liqueur, it is best enjoyed on cold days in the mountains. Usually, it is made using strong red wine, which is then boiled with various spices, most usually just a few cloves and a lot of sugar. The old family recipe is as follows:

———— ✺ ————

Mix all the ingredients together and bring to the boil. Burn off the alcohol – it's a treat for the kids to see the blue whispy heat – and stir the pan for a good minute or so. After removing from the heat, strain the liquid through a gauze and serve immediately in thick beakers that can retain the heat.

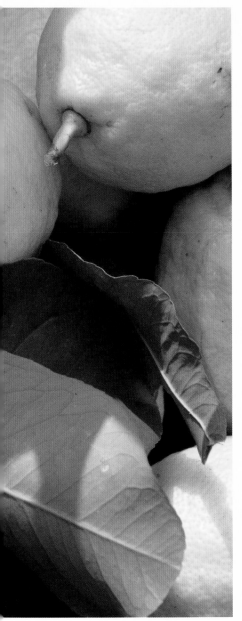

Sgroppino
'Drain cleaner'

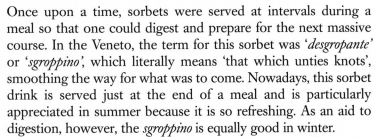

Prosecco
lemon ice cream
(or other fruit ice cream)
vodka

Once upon a time, sorbets were served at intervals during a meal so that one could digest and prepare for the next massive course. In the Veneto, the term for this sorbet was *'desgropante'* or *'sgroppino'*, which literally means 'that which unties knots', smoothing the way for what was to come. Nowadays, this sorbet drink is served just at the end of a meal and is particularly appreciated in summer because it is so refreshing. As an aid to digestion, however, the *sgroppino* is equally good in winter.

The history of the sorbet goes back a long way: we know that the Greeks and the Romans used drops of fruit juice, honey and syrup to flavour pure, crushed snow. Those who produced ice creams that are most like the ones we know now were the Turks who, in the eighteenth century, were followed by enterprizing French and Venetian cooks. The most common – and best – *sgroppino* is the classic one made with lemon ice cream, but it can also be prepared using all sorts of (often exotic) fruits with wildly varying results. This is how I make *sgroppino*.

You need a big glass bowl, a spoon and a metal whisk. Whisk together the ice cream and Prosecco, a little at a time, gradually adding more of each and making sure that the mixture does not collapse. If you let someone else take over, they should continue turning the whisk in the same direction. Towards the end, add a little vodka as you continue whisking and then pour into long-stemmed glasses. Of course, you can do the whole thing with an electric blender, as they do in most restaurants, but the performance for guests should be part of the experience of this foamy delight.

Weddings: today and from this day forth

IKE every other country in the world, the Veneto had its own curious traditions governing courtship, betrothal and marriage. Let's start with courtship. In the province of Rovigo, dancing has always been very popular; there were, in fact, a number of 'courtship' figure dances, so called because they were the only opportunities that young people had to get to know prospective spouses. The 'mirror dance' at Fratta Polesine is a fine example: young people dance around a seated girl who is holding a mirror to the music of a violin, clarinet and accordion. As the pairs of dancing youths pass behind the girl, their images are reflected in the looking-glass; if she cleans the surface – as if trying to wipe away their appearance – that means that neither of the two has met with her favour. If one of the two youths does take her fancy, she gets up and dances with him. The mirror is handed to the other young man, who sits down and holds it. Now it is the turn of the girls to dance in pairs, until one of them is chosen.

In a town a short distance away, the figure dance is actually called *Il Ballo dell'Aihmè* (Alas), because it begins with one of the male dancers sighing that lament. The leader of the dance then asks: 'What is the matter?', to which the dancer replies: 'I am wounded'. In answering the question 'Where?' he then has to have his wits about him, because the reply he gives must rhyme with the name or distinguishing characteristic of the girl he wishes to invite to dance. So, for example, if he wants to dance with Lalla, he says he is wounded in the *spalla* (shoulder), or if the dancing partner he desires is *la Regina della festa* (Queen of the feast), he is wounded in the *testa* (head).

From dancing to courtship proper it was a very short step … and in this latter phase all sorts of ritual gestures came into play. At Christmas, the young man would give his beloved a box of nougat and a small jar of sweet mustard; at All Saints, a bag of *confetti* (sugared almonds); and on the Feast of St Martin (11 November), roast chestnuts. This latter feast day is now purely a children's event, in which they go around the streets of the town (especially Venice) beating pots and pans and singing rhymes to get sweets and coins from passers-by and shopkeepers. Bakeries mark the occasion with the characteristic San Martino shortbread; modelled in the form of the saint on horseback, it is decorated with icing, chocolate and coloured balls of sugar. The most significant gift exchanged between young lovers was perhaps the red *boccolo* (budding rose) that a young man presented to his beloved on St Mark's Day (25 April). Symbolic of the return of fine weather, the gift was also tantamount to a declaration of love because it was associated with an old legend of star-crossed lovers. A young man of humble birth was said to have fallen in love with a Doge's daughter and, to prove his worth, left to fight in the East. Mortally wounded in combat, he plucked a bloom from a bush of white roses to be sent back to his beloved; but as he lay dying, the flower absorbed the colour of his blood.

At Easter, the traditional gift to one's beloved was a *focaccia* and two bottles of Cyprus wine. Then came the moment when the young man 'crossed the river' (proposed marriage). This traditionally happened on the third Sunday after Easter: the lover, on his way to ask for his sweetheart's hand in marriage, brought with him two bottles of *rosolio* (sweet wine) and a bundled napkin containing walnuts, hazelnuts, carobs and oranges. To demonstrate that his intentions were serious, the young man had to let himself be seen by the entire community leaving Vespers on his way to bear these ritual gifts to the house of his beloved. There were even ritual non-gifts – that is, things that a lover would not dream of offering or accepting. These included combs (associated with witches), images of saints and missals (said to bring pain and suffering), scissors (symbols of gossip and slander) and needles and pins (associated with stings and bites).

In the Cortina area of the Dolomites, various wedding rituals are still observed. A week before the wedding there is a lunch in the home of the prospective bride to celebrate the official engagement. The traditional menu includes

In the early 1970s, my parents were invited to a dinner which reproduced the menu of the dinner depicted in this painting by Pietro Longhi – Banquet in the House of Nani in the Giudecca quarter, Venice.

round doughnuts and *crostoli* in the holes of the doughnuts. Then the family members exchange gifts: the future bride-groom presents his mother-in-law, sisters-in-law and the maids of honour with the silk kerchiefs that form part of the traditional local dress. The bride gives the best man a tie and a shirt. The couple also exchange gifts with each other: a ring for the bride and cufflinks and a tie pin for the bride-groom. From the day that the banns are first published in the church, the couple go to visit the homes of everyone they intend to invite to the wedding, taking with them gifts and *confetti*; in return, they receive gifts of half a dozen eggs. It is very important that these visits are made in strict 'geographical' order, with immediate neighbours being the first to be invited to the wedding and the couple then moving on to homes that are farther away. It is also essential that the invitation visits be completed by 11 am on the Sunday before the wedding; beyond that time, they are no longer accepted. On the day of the wedding itself, the bridegroom collects the bride's maids of honour, the best man and a bouquet of flowers. Then he goes to the bride's house to present her with the 'apron' that is a traditional part of her wedding dress and with filigree pins for her hair. On their way to the church, the wedding procession will find the road blocked by a barrier of flowers and work tools erected by friends, neighbours and colleagues; the best man must pay a toll fee for the procession to be allowed through. And as they leave the church, the newly weds pass under an arcade of skis or ice-hockey sticks held aloft by their friends.

Now comes the reception and the colossal wedding lunch, a no-holds-barred expression of hope for future abundance. To symbolize the continuation of the marriage union through the coming years, the bride and groom make their way to church each with one half of the same bread bun in their pockets. Even after the celebration of the marriage, the two pieces of bread were not to be eaten by the happy couple but given to the first child or pauper that they encountered. The ritual had its origin in superstition and meant not only that the newly weds were now beyond the power of witches but also that their first-born would be a child of fortune. There were other pagan beliefs and symbols associated with weddings. In the countryside of Treviso, for example, the bride would not kneel before the altar without carefully arranging the end of her train on the

hassock or bare wood of the kneeler so that the groom could rest at least one of his knees on top of it. This procedure, recommended by the old women of the family, was again intended to frustrate the wiles and spells of witches, who were apparently always hovering around weddings.

Furthermore, in passing along the road from the bride's house to the church, the couple were not to accept flowers from anyone en route for any reason whatsoever – to do so guaranteed that the marriage would end in infidelity. This mix of sacrament and superstition continued after the celebration of the wedding itself. For example, in the past, young people did not have the means to go away on honeymoon, so the wedding night was spent at home. One thing they had to be very careful about was that when they retired to their chamber, they left the lamp burning. This should be put out by the bride's mother (either when she wished them goodnight or, in some cases, when she sneaked back into the bedroom later). The couple could also just let the lamp burn itself out, but neither would dare to extinguish it themselves, knowing that to do so indicated that he or she would be the first of the couple to die.

In Mirano, on the mainland near Venice, mothers-in-law were strictly excluded from all the wedding preparations because their participation was said to bring bad luck. The bride's mother was not even allowed to attend the wedding ceremony itself or the reception, but she did, however, become the undisputed centre of a number of subsequent meals that involved both close and distant family. On the Sunday after the wedding, the bride's mother would visit the newly weds in their home and lunch with them. This was the ritual *revolton*, followed eight days later by the *revoltaggia*, when the newly weds – with the parents of the groom – paid a visit to the bride's family.

The menu for the wedding banquet was also governed by tradition. Then as now, it was considered best that the meal, which could often last throughout the afternoon and into the evening, should start with the traditional chicken-liver risotto. Towards the end of the 1960s, in a farmhouse at Torre di Mosto – a town on the Venetian mainland founded by my family – more than 500 guests partook of a banquet that continued this tradition. Seated at one huge table, people ate until they could eat no more, perhaps to forget the years of hunger that were behind them and also to express hope that the future would be one of plenty. Up until very recently, the ingredients for a wedding banquet in the Veneto were, per head, calculated as follows:

half a boiled pullet,
half a roast pullet,
250 g / 8 oz beef,
abundant fruit and vegetables,
a lot of bread, wine and stock,
unlimited amounts of polenta,
various cheeses
– and no end of good will.

The meal inevitably ends with dancing. As they whirl across the floor, young and old seek just a few moments of release from the cares of everyday life. And what could be a more fitting image with which to end a story that opened with the mirror dance?

A wedding attended by my grandfather at the Hotel Excelsior on the Lido. It was a novelty with its enormous dining room that could accommodate hundreds of guests.

Acknowledgements

My mother, Jane, Delia, Vettor, Pierangelo, Victoria together
with Loredana, Barbara, Emanuela, Edwina and Fatima. For
the production: Jeremy Scott, patient translator, Pia Tryde
Sandeman, Maxine Clarke and Marco Sandeman who –
literally – transformed the recipes into a visual feast and, on the
business side, Paul Stevens of ICM, Gail Rebuck and Fiona
MacIntyre, together with the team at Random House and
Strathmore. Legatoria Polliero; Luigino the grocer and at the
Rialto market: Nino the fishmonger; Moro family and L'isola
vegetable stalls; Marino, Tiziano and Lello at the Macelleria
Ragazzo; Stefano, Piero and Davide at La Baita cheeseshop;
Franco Carlon bread shop; Elio 'il re del tramezzino' and
Drogheria Mascari. Sr Colussi the legendary baker in San
Barnaba; Piera, Franco and Francesco at Le Antiche
Carampane and the waiters at Ai Cacciatori in Mazzorbo. Our
treasured lagoon friends Emilio, Ivano, Gino, Silvano, Vanni
and Vania, Angelo, Rita and Case. Cookbook experts Natasha
and Gioia.

Picture credits

Index

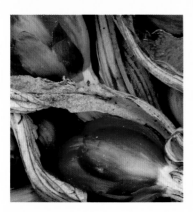

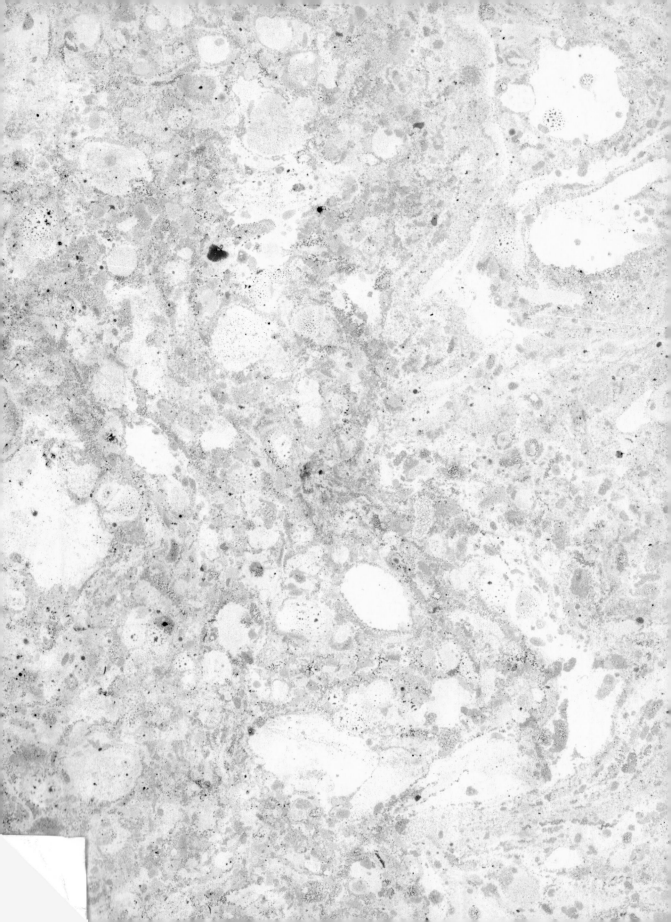